New Negro Politics in the Jim Crow South

NEW NEGRO POLITICS IN THE JIM CROW SOUTH

CLAUDRENA N. HAROLD

The University of Georgia Press *Athens*

A Sarah Mills Hodge Fund Publication

This publication is made possible, in part, through
a grant from the Hodge Foundation in memory
of its founder, Sarah Mills Hodge, who devoted
her life to the relief and education of African
Americans in Savannah, Georgia.

The Library of Congress has cataloged the
hardcover edition of this book as follows:

Names: Harold, Claudrena N., author.
Title: New Negro politics in the Jim Crow South / Claudrena N. Harold.
Description: [First edition] | Athens, GA : The University of Georgia Press, [2016] | Series: Politics and
    culture in the twentieth-century South | Includes bibliographical references and index.
Identifiers: LCCN 2016001697 | ISBN 9780820335124 (hardcover : alk. paper)
Subjects: LCSH: African Americans—Southern States—Politics and government—20th century. |
    African Americans—Race identity—Southern States—History—20th century. | Civil rights
    movements—Southern States—History—20th century. | Labor movement—Southern States—
    History—20th century. | Black nationalism—Southern States—History—20th century. | African
    Americans—Intellectual life. | Southern States—Race relations—History—20th century. |
    Southern States—Politics and government—1865–1950.
Classification: LCC E185.61 .H249 2016 | DDC 323.1196/0730750904—dc23 LC record available at http://
    lccn.loc.gov/2016001697

Paperback ISBN 978-0-8203-5476-7

TO THE BLACK STUDIES PIONEER VIVIAN VERDELL GORDON

CONTENTS

ACKNOWLEDGMENTS

Several institutions and a host of family, friends, mentors, colleagues, and students played crucial roles in this book's completion. The College of Arts and Sciences and the Corcoran Department of History at the University of Virginia (UVa) provided financial support during the most critical stages of research and writing. I am particularly grateful for the history department's administrative team of Kathleen Miller, Ella Wood, Jennifer Via, Whitney Yancey, and Kent Merritt.

This book also benefitted immensely from the expertise of archivists and librarians at Virginia Union University, Duke University, Howard University, Virginia State University, the University of North Carolina at Chapel Hill, and UVa.

A very special thanks goes to my colleague Thomas Klubock, who read the entire manuscript and provided much needed assistance. I also want to thank my colleague Grace Hale for her support of this project from its inception. She directed me to the University of Georgia Press, from which I was able to benefit from the keen insight of acquisition editor Walter Biggins, project editor John Joerschke, and freelance copyeditor Ellen Goldlust. I am also grateful to the editors of the Politics and Culture in the Twentieth-Century South series, Bryant Simon and Jane Dailey.

Davarian Baldwin's scholarly example, as well as his insightful commentary on the manuscript, strengthened this book in numerous ways. I owe him a world of gratitude. Equally important has been the work of Corey D. B. Walker, who had a profound influence on my approach to the black intellectual tradition and my chapter on Virginia Union intellectuals. To call him a colleague and a friend is a privilege I do not take for granted. I also have a great deal of appreciation and respect for my colleague and friend Marlon Ross. His work on the gender politics of the New Negro movement has influenced me greatly; in fact, it is hard to imagine even getting to this point in my career without his unwavering support. My thinking on gender and women's history has also been enriched by the scholarship of Cheryl Hicks, whose research on early twentieth-century America brilliantly captures the humanity of black working people. Long conversations about black intellectual history with Jonathan Fenderson also factored significantly in the completion of the book and helping me redefine my vocation.

Close reads and critical advice also came from scholars affiliated with the Working Group on Racial Inequality at UVa. In particular, Lawrie Balfour, Kim Forde-Mazrui, Mai-Linh Hong, Sophie Trawalter, Gordon Hylton, Derrick Alridge, Risa Goluboff, Kwame Holmes, and Andrea Simpson provided extensive commentary during my workshop on the book's sixth chapter. Their incisive critiques and encouragement boosted my confidence in this project tremendously. Thank you as well to Vesla Weaver for conceiving this working group. I would also like to thank the Miller Center and my colleague Will Hitchcock for hosting a workshop on the book's introduction. At that workshop, significant feedback came from Elizabeth Meyer, Guian McKee, Brian Balogh, Elizabeth Varon, Nicole Hemmer, Sarah Milov, Christina Mobley, Mel Leffler, Grace Hale, Lawrie Balfour, Joe Miller, and Andrew Kahrl.

On my journey toward the book's completion, Kevin Everson and Kahlil Pedizisai assisted me greatly with their intellect, humor, and deft narrative skills. In the fall of 2012, Kevin and I embarked on a journey into the complex history of African American life at UVa during the 1970s. The end result has been two films, *Sugarcoated Arsenic* and *We Demand*. Working with Kevin on those two films provided me with the unique opportunity to continue my exploration of black southern life through the interpretive power of film. Through Kevin, I also had the chance to work with Kahlil, who, like Kevin, takes seriously black working-class history and politics. Thanks also to Madeleine Molyneaux for helping me navigate this process.

Working in film has provided me with much needed balance and perspective during the writing of this book. So, too, have good friends: James Collins, Dave Crawford, Stacy Davis, Reg Jones, Greg Carr, Mario Beatty, Valethia Watkins-Beatty, Sonya Donaldson, T. Chery, Roderick Smith, Natanya Duncan, Bonnie Gordon, Ian Grandison, Solome and Justin Rose, Brandi Hughes, James T. Roane, Deirdre Cooper Owens, Nicole Ivy, Greg Tate, Gary Gallagher, Shermaine Jones, Adom Getachew, and Yolanda Willis.

Enormous thanks to my greatest source of inspiration: my current and former students. Your brilliance, your commitment, and your love never cease to amaze me. I am particularly grateful for the students in my introduction to African American and African Studies, Black Fire, Motown to Hip-Hop, Black Power, and Sounds of Blackness courses, as well as those who participated in *Sugarcoated Arsenic* and *We Demand*. It would have been impossible to complete this project without constant words of encouragement from Ardonna Hamilton, Daryl Jennings, Lauren Coleman, Henry Coley, LaRoy Reynolds, Daquan Romero, Kamille Steward, Kristen Everett, Gabrielle Long, Roxanne Campbell, Jennifer Bowles, Joshua Adams, Elysia Griffiths-Randolph, Jessica Childress, and Renee Mattox.

I also derived great encouragement from the scholarly example set by my students in the distinguished major programs in the History Department and the Carter G. Woodson Institute: Khaosara Akapolawal, Jared Brown, Danaya Hough, Ashley Lewis, Naomi Himmelstein, Gregory Schaffer, Aleshia Dunning-Benns, Krystal Commons, Loryn Crittendon, Carmel Berhanu, Wintre Foxworth, Adair Hodge, Katie Schull, Kelsey Watkins, and Japaira Williams. Critical assistance also came from Sarajanee Davis, Shannon Davis, Niya Bates, Meagan McDougall, DeAnza Cook, Luann Williams, and Magdeldin Hamid. Late night phone chats with Dana Cypress about the New Negro and Southern Renaissances proved useful during the final stretch of writing. So did her beautiful spirit. Thank you to Mr. and Mrs. Cypress for sharing her with me and always keeping me in your prayers. I also learned a great deal from my graduate students Benji Cohen and Alec Hickmott, two young scholars whose provocative ideas always put me in revisionist mode. The same can be said of Julian Hayter, who kept me sane with our talks on music and Virginia politics. With the keen insights of Julian and other scholars, I feel confident about the future of African American Studies.

New Negro Politics in the Jim Crow South

Introduction

On the morning of September 8, 1919, hundreds of African American trade unionists and left-wing activists packed the Colored YMCA in Washington, D.C., for the
first annual convention of the National Brotherhood Workers of America (NBWA).
Lauded by *New York Age* correspondent Jeannette Carter as "the largest of its kind
ever held in the city," the convention showcased the broad geographical reach of
the New Negro spirit.[1] The three-day gathering attracted labor delegates from Alabama, Mississippi, Georgia, Florida, Maryland, New York, Pennsylvania, the Caro-
linas, Illinois, and Virginia. To the nation's capital, these delegates brought not only
their political grievances but also an unwavering faith in the righteousness of the
NBWA's cause. Founded in late March by a group of labor activists based primarily
in the Hampton Roads area of Virginia, the NBWA had ambitiously set out to establish itself as the revolutionary vanguard of the black labor movement.[2] Within six
months of its founding, the Brotherhood expanded its membership to four thousand, challenged the racist structures and policies of the American Federation of
Labor (AFL), and submitted numerous complaints to the U.S. Railroad Association
on behalf of aggrieved black workers. The union's bold endeavors quickly captured
the attention of A. Philip Randolph and Chandler Owen, two New York–based
socialists who heralded the arrival of the NBWA as further evidence of a broader
shift in African American politics. "There is a new leadership for Negro workers,"
Randolph and Owen editorialized in their monthly, the *Messenger*. "It is a leadership of uncompromising manhood. It is insistent upon the Negro workers exacting
justice, both from the white labor unions and from the capitalists."[3] In their view,
the Hampton Roads trade unionists who formed the backbone of the NBWA em-
bodied the radical spirit of the times. Not just concerned with the unionization of
black workers, their political platform addressed a wide range of societal problems,
including the South's restriction of black suffrage, the federal government's persecution of left-wing radicals, and U.S. imperialist designs in Haiti and Mexico.[4]
Randolph and Owen championed the NBWA for its "sound, union principles and

militant revolutionary methods."[5] To assist the organization in its political endeavors, the enthusiastic activists not only volunteered the *Messenger* as the NBWA's publicity organ but also agreed to serve on the union's board of directors.

As Randolph and Owen institutionalized their relationship with trade unionists in Hampton Roads by supporting the NBWA, one of their chief nemeses in New York, Marcus Mosiah Garvey, also broadened his sphere of influence within the political world of coastal Virginia. By the summer of 1919, Garvey's Universal Negro Improvement Association (UNIA) claimed thousands of supporters in the cities of Norfolk, Newport News, and Portsmouth. Working-class blacks in particular heavily financed the UNIA's chief economic venture, the Black Star Line Steamship Corporation (BSL). On a fall 1919 visit to Newport News, Garvey sold more than ten thousand dollars' worth of BSL shares in a two-day span. Moved by this outpouring of support for the BSL, the UNIA leader developed a new appreciation for the revolutionary possibilities in the American South. "Away down in Virginia," Garvey proudly informed his New York supporters,

> I have discovered that the Negro of the South is a new and different man to what he was prior to the war. The bloody war has left a new spirit in the world—it has created for all mankind a new idea of liberty and democracy, and the Southern Negro now feels that he has a part to play in the affairs of the world. A new light is burning for our brothers at this end. They are determined that they too shall enjoy a portion of that democracy for which many of their sons and brothers fought for and died for in France.[6]

The political vibrancy of the Hampton Roads district in the aftermath of World War I illuminates the centrality of the South as an important incubator of black protest activity during the New Negro era. Operating in a variety of political arenas from labor conventions to college campuses, southern New Negroes fought valiantly against the structural forces that adversely affected African Americans' life chances and experiences. Their political struggles significantly informed how blacks in other parts of the country, including Harlem and Chicago, imagined, constructed, and performed in material and textual sites of political contestation. Thus, an analysis of New Negro politics and culture confined to the North obscures the complexity of a historical moment in which black southerners provided exciting organizational models of grassroots labor activism, assisted in the revitalization of black nationalist politics, engaged in robust intellectual arguments on the future of the South, and challenged the governance of historically black colleges in ways that occasioned new perspectives on the potential sites of black radical activity.

With an eye toward these and other developments, this volume narrates the story of New Negro political culture from the perspective of the black South. It details how the development and maturation of New Negro politics and thought were shaped not only by New York–based intellectuals and revolutionary transformations in Europe but also by people, ideas, and organizations rooted in the South. The aim here is not to devalue the importance of the North or Europe during this period of black political and cultural renaissance. Instead, exploring some of the critical events and developments below the Mason-Dixon Line can sharpen our understanding of how many black activists, along with particular segments of the white American Left, arrived at certain theoretical conclusions and political choices regarding the politics of race, challenges to capitalist political economy, and alternative visions of nation.

On a related note, my work illuminates the central role of black southerners in the making and remaking of New Negro modernity. Anything but tragically mute objects in the highly contested project of racial modernization, New Negro southerners possessed clear ideas on how the modern black subject should relate to its employer and existing labor unions, perform in an ever-expanding consumer culture, and negotiate its relationship to the U.S. nation-state.[7] Unlike many canonical Harlem Renaissance writers, these southerners envisioned their region and its native sons and daughters as critical to the making of a more empowering modernity for people of African descent in the United States and the world over.[8] As Lucille Hawkins of New Orleans noted in a letter to Garvey's *Negro World*, "Great things are being carried on by the New Negroes in this section. We are constantly on the firing line—the line that leads to true and lasting emancipation."[9] To better understand how Hawkins and other black southerners came to view themselves as central rather than marginal players in the unfolding political dramas of the 1920s, we must examine the political formations and movements birthed during the New Negro era. Accordingly, this book documents four important spaces in which the self-determinist spirit and modernist strivings of southern New Negroes surfaced: trade union politics, the electoral arena, the Garvey movement, and print media. The women and men attracted to these spaces had wide-ranging political perspectives and objectives. However, the common thread in all of their stories was an unwavering belief in the transformative potential of the moment. Like the literary figures discussed in Christine Stansell's *American Moderns*, they were determined to contribute to "a milieu that made democracy a palpable experience rather than a civic catchword."[10]

Nowhere was this determination more visible than in the labor arena. Throughout the New Negro era, black southerners engaged in work stoppages of varying lengths, initiated unionization drives at both the local and national levels, and pushed for substantive changes in the AFL's organizing and funding policies. These class-conscious workers constituted a visible yet enigmatic presence on the New

Negro political landscape. Less prone to the ideological rigidity that characterized certain segments of the northern black Left, they embraced strategies and visions reflective of the multidimensional nature of their oppression.[11] Though cognizant of the ways in which their lives differed from those of the white ruling elite, white workers, and the African American middle class, black working-class activists in the South were anything but isolationists. Their recognition of the specificity of their oppression did not preclude an awareness of how the profit-driven values, dictates, and relationships of the market economy dehumanized workers from various racial, ethnic, and national backgrounds. "The common people of all nations have suffered great oppression," observed John Cary, a New Orleans activist intimately involved in labor and black nationalist politics during the 1920s. "It was the common people," Cary continued, who "bore the perils of war and had their lives and property taken away in order to satisfy the wicked and selfish ambitions of men."[12] Fully aware of the ways in which economic dislocation, financial hardship, and political marginalization engulfed so many members of the world's working classes, Cary and many other black southerners recognized the need to eradicate poisonous racial divisions and chasms within the house of labor. Out of this recognition emerged significant attempts to forge alliances across racial lines with the express purpose of undermining the strength of the employer class.[13]

Frequently however, these biracial initiatives buckled under the weight of a labor movement unable to transcend the white supremacist ethos and dictates of the times.[14] Thus, the majority of southern black workers and trade unionists subscribed to a politics of pragmatic flexibility in their approach to biracial coalitions within the labor movement. The same can be said of their dealings with the black bourgeoisie and the civil rights establishment, particularly the National Association for the Advancement of Colored People (NAACP). The vitriolic attacks of "Old Crowd Negroes" so conspicuous in the writings of Randolph, Owen, and other New Negro radicals rarely appear in the public utterances of black southern workers and intellectuals intimately involved in trade union politics, in part because of the ideological shifts occurring among certain segments of the black leadership class. Across the nation, the labor provocations of black workers yielded subtle and sometimes drastic ideological changes within the larger African American community. Class struggle, as Earl Lewis and Barbara Foley note in their studies on World War I–era black politics, assumed greater importance among a select group of activists and institutions previously disposed to the idea that societal transformation depended on collaboration between the "better classes" of both races.[15] Especially noteworthy in this regard were the labor engagements of the NAACP during World War I.[16] Contrary to the myopic portraits of the NAACP found in some of the literature of the black Left, the organization was not invariably opposed to challenging the power of capital.[17] Nationally and locally, several of its leaders incorporated leftist critiques into their political analyses, mediated arguments between black workers and white organized labor, initiated grassroots struggles against discriminatory employers, and pursued numerous legal battles on behalf of aggrieved workers. In turn, many black workers and several prominent black trade unionists identified the NAACP as an important ally in their protracted struggle for social justice.

By examining these coalitional arrangements and alliances, this book sheds light on the pervasiveness of leftist ideas within the African American community. It also considers how black southerners' negotiation of those ideas laid the foundation for new nationalist articulations and enactments. Far too often, we treat leftist and nationalist formations in the black community as diametrically opposed during the New Negro era; however, the historical record abounds with cases in which working-class activists and organizations announced and articulated the existence of a national black community bound by shared material concerns. Especially as black trade unionists sought to secure a more powerful position within the world of organized labor, they increasingly identified themselves as national subjects and performed that subjectivity in ways that reflected their unique understanding of the intersectionality of race and class in their individual and collective lives. Not simply the rhetorical but the organizational strategies of blacks involved in the AFL as well as the NBWA and other independent unions assisted in the creation of what literary scholar Houston A. Baker Jr. identifies as "a vocabulary of national possibilities."[18]

Turning our analytical gaze to the South provides us with a clearer vision of how the "black nation" as both an ideological construct and a political formation frequently developed within the crucible of intense labor debates and struggles. Many (though not all) New Negro activists in the South developed a very class-inflected understanding of the political meaning and responsibilities of black nationhood, an understanding based not on essentialist notions of race but rather on their struggles with employers, their contentious encounters with white workers, and their cross-regional attempts at coalition building. This important aspect of the story of black nationality formation deserves a critical hearing not only for its challenge to knee-jerk dismissals of nationalist discourses and politics as invariably rooted in biological determinism or bourgeois reformism but also for its illumination of how nonelite women and men utilized the labor arena to challenge the cultural, economic, and political protocols of race, class, and nation in twentieth-century America.[19]

Of course, the labor arena was not the only space in which black women and men scripted new collective identities, challenged the logics and practices of white supremacy, and pressed for greater autonomy over their personal lives. If we turn to such important urban spaces as New Orleans's South Rampart Street, Jacksonville's Ashley Street and Florida Avenue, and Norfolk's Princess Anne Road, we will discover that New Negro women and men found outlets for cultural and political expression in a variety of activist organizations, social groups, churches, and entertainment dives.

With this incredible political and cultural diversity in mind, I have organized the book along chronological and thematic lines. The book's first two chapters span 1917–20, examining the many measures black workers employed to exert more influence in their communities, democratize the political economy of the South, and confront the racist ideologies, structures, and practices pervading the labor movement.[20] I demonstrate the extent to which Foley's argument about the existence of an "ecumenical radicalism" during the World War I era holds true in the South by looking at the ways in which various forms of grassroots labor activism pushed the larger black community further to the left in its response to racialized class inequalities and economic injustice.[21]

Moving from the labor world to the electoral arena, chapter 3 traces blacks' organizing efforts during the highly contested U.S. presidential and congressional campaigns of 1920. The rising militancy associated with the postwar period, in conjunction with the ratification of the Nineteenth Amendment in September 1920, influenced voter education and registration drives, reconfigured the gender politics of the black public sphere, and transformed local people's expectations of and relationship to mainstream political culture. My work builds on the insights of historians such as Paul Ortiz, whose masterful study, *Emancipation Betrayed*, reminds us that the formal political arena was not left untouched by the New Negro movement. By examining black activists who challenged the hegemony of the Republican Party, ran for office, and sought to augment the political power of newly enfranchised African American women, this chapter demonstrates how a select group of black southerners occasioned a revitalization of what political theorist Michael Dawson identifies as the radical egalitarian strain in African American political thought.[22]

Though African Americans put forth a valiant effort to increase the black electorate in 1920, the South's political arena remained impervious to change. This painful reality provided rhetorical ammunition for black activists who in the aftermath of World War I placed their faith not in the U.S. nation-state but in the Pan-African politics of Marcus Garvey's UNIA. Throughout the postwar period, the UNIA's Pan-African agenda resonated deeply among native-born blacks as well as West Indian immigrants residing in Norfolk, Mobile, Winston-Salem, New Orleans, Charleston, Miami, and other urban centers.[23] To advance the organization's agenda, they diligently read and sold the *Negro World*, raised funds to send delegates to the UNIA's annual conventions, threw their weight behind the association's nation-building initiatives in Liberia, and endured police harassment, heavy surveillance from the Bureau of Investigation, and episodic acts of violence perpetrated by angry whites. Even in the toughest of times, Garveyites' faith in the organization seemed unshakable. "I have resolved," pledged John Thurston of Miami, "to support and defend the principle of this organization, and adhere to its founder, His Excellency, Hon. Marcus Garvey."[24]

While constituting some of Garvey's most loyal supporters, southern Garveyites did not hesitate to carve out their own independent space within the movement. Their commitment to institution building at the local level was evident through their establishment of community health clinics, economic cooperatives, and adult night schools. UNIA followers also created outlets for self-expression and cultural exchange. Cognizant of the political potential of culture, southern Garveyites routinely incorporated jazz, the blues, poetry, and drama into their weekly meetings. Their cultural and political endeavors are taken up in chapter 4, which covers the period from the UNIA's arrival in the South in 1918 to its decline in the late 1920s.

On the downward slope of its popularity, the UNIA encountered another organization battling for the hearts and minds of the New Negro crowd: Randolph's Brotherhood of Sleeping Car Porters (BSCP). Founded in the summer of 1925, the Brotherhood orchestrated a remarkably courageous battle against the Pullman Company in a historic quest to secure higher wages, better working conditions, and greater respect for the porters and maids whose invaluable services contributed immensely to the company's huge profits. Much of the literature on the organization has focused primarily on its activities in New York and Chicago;[25] however, the Brotherhood's leadership placed a high priority on organizing in the South.

Several months after the union's formation, its leaders boldly declared their intention to "invade the South."[26] To do so, they rallied behind local leaders such as Oneida Brown of New Orleans and John W. Darby of Jacksonville, two dedicated activists who risked their lives to solidify the organization's base in their communities. The wife of a local porter, Brown personified the best qualities of the New Negro. Fearless in her recruitment endeavors, unafraid to challenge white authority, and willing to establish political bonds with like-minded blacks outside her immediate environment, she vowed to turn New Orleans into a BSCP stronghold. Precisely because the union attended to the labor and civil rights needs of African Americans, she anticipated tremendous success for the organization in the Crescent City. As she predicted in 1927, "The prospect of doing considerable work to promote the interests of the Brotherhood in our district is very, very bright indeed."[27]

With a focus on Brown and others who endeavored to strengthen the presence of the Brotherhood in the South, chapter 5 examines the BSCP's organizing efforts between 1925 and 1929. In addition to providing porters with an alternative to the welfare capitalism of the Pullman Company, the Brotherhood provided another layer of complexity in ongoing debates about the most effective strategies for improving African Americans' social, political, and economic position.

Like their counterparts in the North, New Negroes in the South wrestled with a series of complex questions as they sought to build meaningful political movements: What, if any, were the conceptual shortcomings and political limitations of racialist thinking? How might one reconfigure contemporary labor relations to ensure a more equitable distribution of the world's material resources? What are the connections between the oppression of blacks in the United States and that of colored people throughout the world? And which group of whites constituted African Americans' most trustworthy allies? These questions consumed trade unionists, Garveyites, and the two New Negro writers whose intellectual pursuits are the subject of chapter 6, literary critic James Waldo Ivy and labor journalist Thomas Lewis Dabney.

Coming to intellectual maturity during the unfolding of both the New Negro and southern literary renaissances, Ivy and Dabney first met each other as undergraduates at Virginia Union University in Richmond. There, they engaged in a variety of intellectual endeavors, including the formation of the Club for the Study of Socialism, an affiliate of the Intercollegiate Society, and the creation of an underground student newspaper, the *Critic*, which was styled along the lines of H. L. Mencken's *Smart Set*. Following their graduation from Virginia Union, Ivy and Dabney contributed to such respected periodicals as the *Labor Age*, *Opportunity*, the *Messenger*, and the *Southern Workman*. With great depth and thoughtfulness, they deliberated on the possibility of a postcapitalist society, the status of African Americans in leftist organizations, and the extent to which the ascendency of New South liberals could transform the region's political culture. Their broad intellectual palette endeared them to such respected thinkers as W. E. B. Du Bois, Claude McKay, and George Schuyler.

Though Ivy and Dabney never promoted themselves as experts on the South's contemporary landscape, their knowledge of the region surpassed that of most of their New Negro peers. Their essays on the South's racial politics, the shifts in its economic structure, and the intellectual renaissance developing among white liberal writers based in Chapel Hill, Nashville, New Orleans, and Richmond reflected their deep commitment to capturing the region in all of its political and cultural complexity. As Dabney noted, "The friend of the South is he who studies present-day Southern life critically and objectively."[28] The journalistic endeavors of Dabney and Ivy enable us to examine how New Negro intellectuals based in the South compared and contrasted with New Negro writers in the North as well as white southern liberals such as Howard Odum, Paul Green, and Gerald Johnson.

Ending on a blue note, the final chapter examines the decline of the New Negro movement and the ways in which black southerners responded to its collapse both locally and nationally. Conventional wisdom tells us that the Great Depression marked the death of the New Negro movement, but my analysis of the movement's decline begins in 1927, the year of the historic Mississippi flood. The sources repeatedly brought me back to this historic deluge and how it washed away the optimism that had sustained many southern New Negroes during the early postwar years.

This book captures the dynamism and the variability of the southern wing of the New Negro *movement*, offering a glimpse of the New Negro as class-conscious warrior, radical student, cosmopolitan Pan-Africanist, and civil rights agitator. The multivalent voices presented here complicate the notion of an archetypal New Negro along with the idea of a monolithic, antiquated black South. They confirm the insights of Clyde Taylor, Davarian Baldwin, and other scholars who place special emphasis on the New Negro movement's geographical breadth and ideological range.[29] "The notion of a unitary renaissance," Taylor maintains, "dissolves before any examination of the many crosscurrents and divergent shifts in interests, politics, class, gender, and regional issues that swarm across the efforts of black people to gain a foothold in modernity as it was developing in America at the time."[30]

One important way in which this book challenges the notion of a "unitary renaissance" is through its illumination of the essentiality of regional identity and perspective in shaping how black southerners not only responded to but also influenced the New Negro political terrain. Engaged in the dialectical process of building on as well as transcending the traditions and realities of their birthplace, New Negroes in Dixie wrestled with the tough question of what it meant to be both a Negro and a southerner in the context of a white supremacist culture. To better understand how they navigated this dual identity, this book relies heavily on conceptual and theoretical roadmaps provided in the writings of W. E. B. Du Bois, Sterling Brown, Horace Mann Bond, John Oliver Killens, Kalamu ya Salaam, Houston A. Baker Jr., Thadious Davis, and James Smethurst.[31] All of these writers raise fascinating questions regarding the political voice and identity of black southerners living behind the veil. Ever attuned to the variety of black life, none of them assert the existence of a monolithic black southern voice. They do, however, impart to their readers the importance of taking seriously the nuanced ways in which the political imaginations and articulations of black southerners differ in content, cadence, and rhythm from those of white southerners and black northerners.

Especially important in this regard is the work of Killens, whose novels and essays constantly affirm the existence of a distinctively southern, black political voice. Fully audible in the racial wilderness of the variegated South, he asserts, is a black voice "that is special, profound, and distinct from any other in the country. It is a voice, more often than not, that is distinguished by the quality of its anger, its righteous indignation, its reality, its truthfulness."[32] This project engages Killens's reflections, digging deeper into the meaning and special character of the southern black voice, its pregnant silences, its powerful whispers, and its eruptive rage. It also incorporates the regional perspectives of Du Bois. Not only in classic texts such as *The Souls of Black Folk* and *Black Reconstruction* but also in his essays and speeches, Du Bois routinely assigns the "black South" the task of leading the world-wide emancipatory struggle for oppressed peoples. Long before concepts such as black transnationalism and the Global South gained currency in the academy, Du Bois was situating the American South and its black laboring classes at the center of world politics. Even as African Americans moved in massive numbers to the industrial centers of the urban North, Du Bois remained attentive to developments in the South. Speaking before a group of students in 1947, he hailed the region as "the firing line not simply for the emancipation of the American Negro but for the emancipation of the African Negro and the Negroes of the West Indies, for the emancipation of the colored races, and for the emancipation of the white slaves of modern capitalistic monopoly."[33]

Occupying the center of the narrative here are women and men who shared Du Bois's views on the radical potential of the South. Opposed to the idea that the politicization of African Americans required a physical rupture from the land of Jim Crow,[34] black trade unionists, newly franchised black women, civil rights agitators, and student activists were determined to transform simultaneously themselves and the South. To borrow a phrase from Jean Toomer's *Cane*, these New Negroes embraced the opportunity to become "the face of the South."[35] This does not mean that black southerners disregarded the larger political world. On the contrary, African Americans in the South reached out to oppressed communities in other parts of the country, pushed hard to nationalize their political struggles, and rallied behind organizations seeking to forge a black transnational identity. Throughout the New Negro era, internationalist organizations such as the UNIA and the African Blood Brotherhood (ABB) found a receptive audience among black southerners who felt either connected to or inspired by the political fervor sweeping the larger African diaspora. Writing to Cyril Briggs in late 1919, one unidentified World War I veteran in Atlanta expressed his desire to help advance the ABB's revolutionary program: "Please enroll me and send me any information you care to on the subject. I am ready for any call, to the limit or beyond." Like many other New Negroes who signed up for the ABB, this man had been radicalized by his military experience: "I fought in the world war for 'democracy' and I am willing to do anything you say for the liberation of my people."[36]

The enthusiasm in which this veteran and other black southerners embraced New Negro groups such as the ABB and the UNIA deeply troubled many of the region's whites. In a letter to U.S. attorney general Harry Daugherty, George Washington of Key West, Florida, expressed disbelief at the UNIA's growing popularity among his city's black Bahamians. "These people," Washington complained, "are displaying a red, black and green flag; this they hoist on a mast at their meetings, and each of them are wearing in the lapels of their coats an emblem of their flag and going around preaching to other Negroes that it is the only flag that they honor."[37] The pride with which Garveyites waved their flag spoke not only to their confidence in the UNIA but also to their belief that meaningful political work could take place in the heart of Dixie.

On this important matter, the southern New Negroes covered here differ from those examined in Glenda Elizabeth Gilmore's *Defying Dixie*. Expanding the analytical boundaries of southern history beyond its traditional borders, Gilmore provides a fascinating account of native southerners who pursued their battles against white supremacy outside the states of the former Confederacy.[38] Such an approach, she argues, enables us to weave local, regional, national, and global history into a coherent story:

> Writing a history of the South that includes its expatriates leads one to reconsider places, ideas, and organizations generally thought of as unsouthern. I came to think of Washington, D.C., as a border post from which black Southerners kept one eye on their country. Chicago became a cache pod up the Mississippi River that harbored refugees fleeing the Deep South. So many North Carolinians settled within a few blocks of one another in New York that the Harlem Renaissance might have been the Raleigh Renaissance, North.

To muddy the waters even more, Gilmore engages the politics of expatriates in ways that complicate our understanding of the South and its scattered diaspora:

> The South could remain the South only by chasing out some of its brightest minds and most bountiful spirits, generation after generation. Many of those who left did so, directly or indirectly, because they opposed white supremacy. Counting them back into Southern history reveals an insurgent South and shows some Southerners to be a revolutionary lot that fought longer and harder than anyone else to defeat Dixie.[39]

This diasporic approach to the South definitely has its advantages, especially for those of us interested in inserting migrants back into the history of the region.

Valuable insight can be gained from embracing a more expansive notion of who represents and speaks for the South. However, our northern search for a defiant Dixie must also attend to the ways in which southern transplants' continued encounters with an ever-evolving South (and the people who inhabited that volatile region) informed their ongoing radicalization. Hence, a multidirectional conversation on the radical politics of the southern diaspora must look not only at how southern expatriates such as Randolph, James Weldon Johnson, Lovett Fort-Whiteman, and Pauli Murray lobbied critiques of the South from the North but also at how political insurgencies *within* the borders of Dixie sustained these transplants' revolutionary dreams during the most trying times.

Transregional in scope, this volume follows the lead of scholars in the field of new southern studies concerned with "understanding the U.S. South as 'thick' with border-crossings of every sort: racial, gendered, regional, transnational."[40] Emerging from this text is a politically vibrant South inhabited by black immigrants staking their claim to the fruits of U.S. citizenship; black nationalists bold in their exaltation of the principles of race pride, Pan-African unity, and black statehood; black cultural critics unafraid to speak out against white supremacy's firm grip on the region; and black laborites unrelenting in their battles against low pay, inhumane working conditions, racist white unions, and conservative black leadership. None of these activist groups lend themselves to easy characterization. Variety occurs in their political talents and aspirations, their certainties and insecurities, and their vision of how the black liberation struggle should be conceptualized and directed within the context of an increasingly heterogeneous "black nation." This story also features flawed individuals who sometimes succumbed to petty organizational jealousies, individual pride, and lapses in political integrity. If we are to create historical narratives that reclaim not only black southerners' political agency but also their humanity, we must avoid the understandable urge to sanitize their politics. Much like other activists committed to societal change and transformation, southern New Negroes had their share of navigational mishaps, theoretical shortcomings, and political miscalculations.

Nevertheless, their political activities remain both noteworthy and deserving of scholarly investigation. To uplift the race and by extension transform the world, they risked the peril of social isolation, ridicule, and even death. Their activist stories serve as important reminders that black southerners played a crucial role not only in African Americans' revolutionary quest for political empowerment, ontological clarity, and existential freedom but also in the global struggle to bring forth a more just and democratic world free from racial subjugation, dehumanizing labor practices, and colonial oppression.

ONE

The Hour Has Come

After months of scheduling speakers, wrangling over travel and lodging details, and fretting over the possibility of brutal weather conditions, Samuel Gompers and the executive council of the American Federation of Labor (AFL) could finally breathe a collective sigh of relief. Without any major glitch, the organization's thirty-seventh annual convention had opened to record attendance. On Monday morning, November 12, 1917, 440 delegates representing trade unions across the United States filed into the Broadway Auditorium in Buffalo, New York, for the convention's first session. Over the next twelve days, delegates vigorously debated labor policy, listened to inspiring speeches from members of the federation's executive council, and swapped stories of their organizing activities in their respective industries. Counted among the delegates working for the passage of resolutions specifically tailored to meet the most pressing needs of their constituencies was a group of black trade unionists from the urban South: Walter F. Green, a "general laborer" employed at the Navy Yard in Portsmouth, Virginia; Edward Thompson, a railroad helper from Jacksonville, Florida; and Sidney Burt, head of the Railroad Helpers and Laborers Union (No. 15566) in Portsmouth. On the labor movement's largest stage, Green, Burt, and Thompson not only vented their frustration at the AFL's neglect of black workers but also illuminated the federation's potential for dramatic growth below the Mason-Dixon Line, particularly in the coastal cities of the Southeast. Stating that they had "thoroughly examined the situation of organized labor," the delegates insisted that the "cause would be greatly improved if colored organizers were given a place in the working of the American Federation of Labor."[1] No small factor in their growing confidence in the AFL's ability to achieve success among black southerners was the escalating levels of proletarian insurgency in the months following Woodrow Wilson's declaration of war on Germany.

Convinced that the struggle for democracy extended beyond the bloody trenches of Europe, African Americans in the South exploited new openings for political struggle by contesting the power of their employers in the workplace, demanding full access to the labor market, and forming independent labor bodies and unions both locally and nationally.[2] As historian Eric Arnesen explains, "Not since the 1880s had black men and women organized and struck in such numbers."[3] With hopes of building on this momentum, Green, Burt, and Thompson traveled to the AFL's convention to not simply address the racist practices and policies of the federation but also to build transregional networks that would enable them to better coordinate their political endeavors. In their interactions with fellow delegates, they presented themselves as representatives of a new political vanguard determined to push both organized labor and the country in a more progressive direction.

In many respects, these delegates as well as the countless workers who inspired them performed a critical role in inaugurating the New Negro era in the South. Garveyites, newly enfranchised black women, and outspoken college students would later shape the contours of New Negro politics in very meaningful ways, but this rising class of militant black workers set the tone for a new phase in southern black activism through aggressive action against employers as well as efforts to create a more politically robust labor movement. In fact, many of the attributes we identify as defining characteristics of the New Negro—self-assertion and self-possession, a cosmopolitan outlook, race pride, and a strong modernist sensibility—were quite visible among the black workers who engaged in collective acts of resistance during the war years. These workers gave birth to activist networks and political initiatives that not only loosened racial accommodationists' stranglehold over black political discourse but also widened significantly the zones of political contact and exchange in the broader black community.

To improve their material conditions, black southern workers employed a wide range of collective and individual strategies, among them staging walkouts, switching to better-paying occupations, and migrating to larger cities. This chapter focuses on a select group of black southerners who sought to lay the foundation for a more vibrant workers' movement and carve out a larger place in the world of organized labor. Significant attention is given to trade unionists who concentrated much of their political energies on reforming the AFL, an organization many viewed as integral to their twin projects of racial uplift and economic advancement. Focusing on the AFL and particularly on black southerners' proposed resolutions at its annual conventions provides another perspective on how the exigencies of war engendered cognitive shifts in African Americans' political thinking.[4] As historian Adriane Lentz-Smith rightly notes, "The coming of the Great War both gave African Americans new weapons with which to fight and, by expanding and intensifying their struggle on fronts, foreign as well as domestic, added to their already considerable burdens."[5] The degree to which the AFL could become a formidable weapon in black southerners' democratic arsenal would be a subject of much public debate as the twists and turns of war intensified African Americans' labor activism. Between 1914 and 1918, the South experienced profound changes in its economic, political, and cultural life. A booming wartime economy, military enlistment, and massive demographic shifts altered the texture and rhythms of everyday life for millions in the region. Young servicemen departed for the battlefields of France, enthused women purchased Liberty Bonds, and aspiring laborers competed for new jobs in the South's expanding industrial sector. Of the many wartime developments, few received more public attention than the massive migration of southern blacks to the industrial North. The dramatic decline in the number of European laborers coming to the United States, along with the conscription and enlistment of millions of American workers into the armed forces, created an acute labor shortage in several industries. To maintain production levels during this period of intense demand for American goods, northern industrialists increasingly turned to southern black laborers. Swift-talking labor recruiters from Chicago, New York, Gary, Pittsburgh, and Cleveland descended on the South, promising anyone within earshot an opportunity for a new life. Their sales pitch was both consistent and persuasive: far from Jim Crow's oppressive regime, blacks could secure better employment opportunities, better housing, a quality education for their children, and a life free of the political restrictions and violent racism that marred their experiences in the South. Anything but hasty in relocating north, prospective migrants carefully considered transportation costs, the availability of employment in their particular line of work, the emotional toll relocation might exact on their children, and perceived cultural differences between themselves and black northerners. Leaving the South was a major move not to be taken lightly, leading some women and men to wait months before finally deciding whether to go North.

Taking seriously the advice of family, friends, and community leaders, a critical mass of black southerners opted for a new life in the North.[6] Lives as well as communities were permanently changed by the migratory fever sweeping the South. Young adults who remained in the region searched for new lovers, companions, and friends. Store owners struggled to adjust to the loss of regular customers, while ministers bemoaned the dwindling numbers in the church pews. A few whites even engaged in critical reflection regarding the outrages (Jim Crow legislation, lynching, political oppression) contributing to the North's attractiveness for many black southerners. "The truth might as well be faced," a white newspaper in Greenville, South Carolina, bluntly admitted; "the treatment of the Negro in the South must change or the South will lose the Negro."[7] So focused on black southerners moving north, white journalists sometimes ignored the political activities of those who remained in the land of Jim Crow.

Across the South, African Americans waged collective and individual battles against the discriminatory hiring policies of war industries, residential segregation, Jim Crow public accommodations, the unfair application of federal and local work-or-fight ordinances, and systematic exclusion from the political arena. The combined effects of international conflict in Europe and leadership shifts engendered by the declining influence and 1915 death of Booker T. Washington generated a new sense of democratic possibility among established as well as emerging political figures within the black community. As older activists recommitted themselves to the struggle for racial and economic justice, some younger women and men plunged for the first time into the turbulent waters of southern racial politics. Whites who expected African Americans to set aside their political grievances during the war were in for a major disappointment. As one New Orleans resident noted in 1918, "If Democracy is worth fighting for across the ocean, it is worth fighting for here in New Orleans."[8]

Not just in the Crescent City but throughout the South, African Americans put the nation's commitment to democracy to the ultimate test. On streetcars, in courtrooms, and in the workplace, black women and men challenged the legal edifice of white supremacy as well as those everyday practices that normalized the region's Jim Crow system. In his travels through the South as the field secretary for the National Association for the Advancement of Colored People (NAACP), James Weldon Johnson detected a noticeable shift in the political mood and energy of black southerners. Much to his delight, they responded enthusiastically to his efforts to expand the NAACP's political influence. "I am not only gratified by the campaign in the South," Johnson boasted to peers at the association's New York office, "but I have been encouraged and inspired by it." Thanks in part to Johnson's tireless recruiting, the NAACP was becoming a political player in the region 90 percent of African Americans still called home.[9] When the association released its annual report at the end of 1917, it claimed eighty branches and nearly ten thousand members in the South.[10] An eclectic group, southern supporters of the civil rights organization included social elites and common laborers, native-born blacks and West Indian immigrants, political novices and seasoned activists. Not beholden to one particular agenda, the southern wing of the NAACP pushed hard to improve African Americans' quality of life by testing the constitutionality of residential segregation ordinances, fighting for the passage of antilynching legislation, and demanding high quality state-supported education for African American children. Functioning at times as a quasi-trade union, the NAACP also rallied behind the economic struggles of black workers.[11]

Concurrent with the NAACP's expansion in the wartime South was an equally compelling development for many political observers: the escalating levels of labor organizing among black southern women and men. Within a year of Wilson's declaration of war on Germany, the list of black workers involved in labor disputes and work stoppages included sanitation workers and longshoremen in Savannah, Georgia; mill operatives and railroad helpers in Rocky Mount, North Carolina; oyster shuckers, domestics, and tobacco stemmers in Norfolk, Virginia; teamsters in New Orleans; steelworkers in Birmingham, Alabama; and laundresses in Mobile, Alabama, and St. Petersburg, Florida. In most of these disputes, low pay and discriminatory wage scales topped workers' complaints. Though Europe's increased demand for American goods had provided a much-needed boost to the South's sluggish economy, dismally low wages remained a reality for most black workers. As striking black laundry workers in Alabama explained, "We have been unable to sustain ourselves on the small wages received for our work."[12] Even when granted wage increases, black workers were frequently denied the back pay afforded to their white counterparts. Such was the case in Savannah, where on August 22, 1918, four hundred black longshoremen staged a walkout after the Ocean Steamship Company denied them the six months' back pay recently given to white waterfront workers. Adamant about receiving equal pay for equal work, the men vowed to remain off the job until their demands were met.[13] This determined group of longshoremen drew inspiration from their black counterparts in Norfolk and New Orleans, who in previous months had procured wage concessions, greater control over the labor supply, and union recognition. Their confidence in their ability to secure a victory was not misguided. A day after their walkout, the Savannah longshoremen reached an agreement with their employers and returned to work.

The impact of their actions extended beyond the workplace. In addition to disrupting normal patterns of labor relations, striking workers in Savannah and elsewhere pushed black political discourse farther to the left. Terms such as *living wage* and *industrial democracy* surfaced more frequently in the political vernacular of black spokespersons previously aligned with the interests of capital. Widely distributed newspapers such as the *Savannah Tribune* and the *Norfolk Journal and Guide* increasingly expressed solidarity with African American laborers. For example, the *Journal and Guide*'s coverage of a monthlong strike by black female tobacco stemmers recognized the critical role that these women played in supporting not only their families but central institutions within the African American community, and the paper encouraged black Norfolk to stand in solidarity with the tobacco stemmers. Nudged to the left by the rising militancy of the city's black working class, the popular weekly presented female strikers as virtuous citizens deserving the same wages and benefits granted to other members of America's laboring classes.[14] The *Savannah Tribune* took a similar stance in its coverage of a wave of labor disputes that struck the South Georgia city in the spring and summer of 1918. During this period, tranquility on the labor front was a rarity: black sanitation workers and longshoremen walked off their jobs in protest of subpar pay. Confronting the labor question with a renewed intensity, the *Tribune* condemned local employers for their greed, their unwillingness to share profits with their employees, and their racist treatment of African American workers. Contending that patriotism did not entail working for below subsistence wages, the paper phrased its critique in the cadences of nineteenth-century republicanism, pointing out how a livable wage and decent hours allowed for self-development and self-cultivation. No longer, the *Tribune* insisted, could hardworking women and men be expected to perform their jobs under dehumanizing conditions and for low pay, especially with the availability of work in the North and the rising cost of living in Savannah. "Wages, in all occupations," read one editorial, "must increase to a point consistent with changed conditions." Writers also advised all businesses to put an end to differential wage scales based on race and open up their skilled positions to qualified African Americans: "There must be no element of discrimination, either in work or wages on the grounds of color."[15]

This shifting trend toward redefining racial progress according to the goals advanced by black working people also prompted intense conversations on the relationship between black workers and organized labor. In many communities, the political transformations brought about by wartime mobilization led African American workers to revisit lingering questions regarding the viability of forming alliances with white trade unionists. Could black workers singlehandedly topple the forces of white supremacy and labor exploitation? Or did they require the assistance of white laboring women and men? And if so, what was the likelihood of black and white workers building a culture of trust, mutuality, and camaraderie under the current racial order?

For many black trade unionists in the South seeking a resolution to these and other labor-oriented questions, the AFL's annual conventions provided excellent venues to articulate pressing political concerns. In fact, during the war years, black southerners came to constitute a visible presence at the federation's annual conventions. With the goal of effecting substantive changes in the AFL's organizing policies, black trade unionists from urban centers in the Southeast and on the Gulf Coast put forth resolutions specifically designed to remind the federation that southern black migrants headed north should not be its only concern. Though frequently marginalized in historical accounts of black wartime activism, the political maneuvering of black workers at the AFL's conventions was an essential component of their effort to not only improve their material condition but also position themselves at the forefront of the black freedom struggle. Perhaps nowhere was this repositioning more apparent than at the AFL's 1917 convention in Upstate New York.

On the convention's opening day, President Wilson became the first U.S. president to address an AFL gathering when he spoke to delegates representing at least 269 unions, most of them in the urban centers of the Northeast and Midwest. The pageantry included a procession of delegates and visitors, each holding an American flag. Taking the lead in the stunning procession was a one-hundred-piece band, which appeared courtesy of the Musicians' Union of Buffalo. Wilson minced no words in laying blame for the international war and its ghastly human casualties: "Germany is determined that the political power of the world shall belong to her." Perhaps anticipating dissent from left-wing activists equally troubled by the imperialist activities of Great Britain and France, Wilson emphasized what he regarded as the distinctiveness of Germany's empire-building ambitions: though "such ambitions" had previously existed, never had they "been based upon so exact, precise and scientific plan of domination." Under these circumstances, he insisted, organized labor must stand behind the United States and the Allies: "If we are true friends of freedom of our own or anybody else's, we will see that the power of this country is raised to its absolute maximum, and that absolutely nobody is allowed to stand in the way of it."[16] Applause thundered as Wilson closed his speech and cleared the podium for Gompers, the AFL's head.

Over the next few hours, delegates heard encouraging reports on the AFL's membership drives and its financial stability. "The American trade union movement," the executive council proudly reported, "is larger and stronger than ever before." To substantiate its claims, the council detailed the federation's rising membership numbers and its growing treasury, which now claimed a balance of $141,467.[17] How the AFL's growing political power and fiscal stability might benefit African Americans was foremost on the minds of black southerners gathered at the Broadway auditorium. The five months between Wilson's declaration of war on Germany and the AFL's annual gathering had witnessed a heightened level of political consciousness among southern black workers. Moved to action by transformative developments in their communities and the larger world, black laborers had engaged in and supported various strikes, aggressively proselytized the union idea, and worked hard to elevate the "class question" to a critical position in black political discourse. To build on this momentum, several black trade unions in Jacksonville, Florida; Rocky Mount, North Carolina; and Hampton Roads dispatched their most able representatives to the Buffalo convention.

The list of black delegates from the South, which was much longer than the previous year, included not only Green, Thompson, and Burt but James E. Cousins,

Hubert Fitts, William Chavis, T. B. Henry, John L. Price, and Charles Battle.[18] All of these men were immersed in the political rhythms and elaborate social networks of their communities but largely unknown among the white delegates. Their names never graced the pages of such national periodicals as the *Chicago Defender* and the *Crisis*. Yet Green and other southern African American delegates perceived themselves as movers and shakers in this new moment of political possibility. Sixty years of age at the time of the convention, Green enjoyed his brief moment in the national spotlight during and immediately after the Great War. His involvement in the National Brotherhood Workers of America as well as his presidency of the Portsmouth chapter of Marcus Garvey's Universal Negro Improvement Association presented him with leadership opportunities that had been unavailable in his younger days. Like many of his Parker Avenue neighbors in Portsmouth, Green worked at the Navy Yard.[19] Literate, married, and a homeowner, he believed in the power of collective action and took quite seriously his responsibilities as the head of the General Helpers and Laborers Union (No. 14838). To the convention, Green brought not just a deep commitment to solving the problems affecting black working people but also a very sophisticated understanding of the political terrain in which they operated at both the local and national level.

Green's fellow African American delegates were equally impressive. More than thirty years Green's junior, Burt represented a younger generation of African American workers who sought to find a political place in the house of labor. The Portsmouth resident lived in a community of renters on Effingham Avenue, not too far from Green.[20] A native of North Carolina, Burt had migrated to Portsmouth a few years before the war with the goal of pursuing a college degree. His plan to attend Hampton Institute never reached fruition, but he soon distinguished himself as a respected civic, fraternal, and labor leader. During his distinguished public career, he served as the president of a variety of organizations, most notably the Colored Helpers and Laborers Union, the Brotherhood of Railroad Carmen, and the Jefferson Ward Civic League. Burt's confidence in his leadership skills derived in part from his work as a painter for Seaboard Airline Railroad: "If the cars I have painted were coupled into one continuous train," he once boasted, "I expect that they would reach to the end of the Seaboard Line in Key West."[21] Burt's recognition of the value of his labor and expertise propelled him into the world of organized labor, where he also displayed a great deal of confidence in himself and his fellow black trade unionists. That confidence would be on display at the AFL's 1917 convention. With the assistance of delegates Thompson and Battle, Burt directed the convention's attention to the many challenges facing African American railroad workers. This sector had an embarrassing record when it came to race relations, creating all kinds of difficulties for Burt and other black organizers. In addition to low pay and poor working conditions, African Americans faced the daunting task of promoting labor solidarity across the color line in an industry where racism among white workers was widespread. During a recent labor upheaval in Rocky Mount, North Carolina, five hundred black workers employed by the Atlantic Coast Railroad Line had walked off their jobs to protest pay discrimination. Company officials had granted a 6.5 percent pay raise to white workers but had failed to adjust the wage scales of African Americans. Facing the same rising cost of living as their white counterparts, blacks demanded nothing less than equal pay for equal work. When those demands were not met, they walked off the job. The *Norfolk Journal and Guide* lauded the striking workers for their refusal to accept a pay scale determined solely by race, declaring, "Their bold stand for better conditions is a song that must be sung by the Negro race." Siding with the company, white laborites in the American Railway Union gladly filled vacancies left by striking black workers, racist behavior that the *Journal and Guide* unrelentingly criticized: "We do not comprehend the ethics of a labor union that would permit one member to take such an unfair advantage of another." Fed up with the machinations of white organized labor, the weekly counseled black workers to "exercise care and discretion in identifying with any branch of the American Federation of Labor."[22]

The fragile relationship between black railroad workers and the AFL ranked extremely high on the agenda of African American delegates at the 1917 convention. On the convention's seventh day, Burt, Thompson, and Battle presented a resolution that urged the federation to devote more of its resources to organizing black railroad workers in the Southeast. "The colored laborers and helpers throughout the southeastern district," the resolution read, "are not familiar with the labor movement as they should be. . . . There are fifteen different railroads in the district [but] there are only four colored locals on these fifteen roads." The most immediate remedy, according to the resolution, was the appointment of an African American organizer in the district: "We feel and believe that a colored organizer because of his racial and social relations among his people could accomplish much in organizing the forces into the unions."[23] Burt and Battle then shared stories of the organizing activities among black workers in the South and the vast opportunities for widespread unionization in the region. Burt invoked the recent success of black longshoremen in Norfolk as evidence of the collective power of African American workers, focusing on his union's affiliation with one of the most powerful black labor bodies in not only Hampton Roads but the entire South: "There is a union in our city known as the Transportation Working Men's Association of Virginia, with a membership of eighteen hundred, meeting in the same hall as we [and] many of our men fall in line with them."[24] By invoking the association and highlighting its existing relationship with members of his Railroad Helpers and Laborers Union,

Burt let it be known that the preparatory work necessary for the AFL to launch a major organizing drive in the area was already under way.

During the session at which Burt and other black railroad workers presented their resolution, a group of trade unionists from Virginia issued a similar call for more black organizers. Insisting that the political fate of organized labor depended on its ability to solidify its presence in the urban South, Green, Henry, Cousins, Price, and Chavis proposed a plan whereby politically adept black trade unionists would bring the region's major industrial and commercial centers under the influence of the AFL. Instead of focusing on a single industry, as Burt, Thompson, and Battle had done in their resolution, the Virginia delegation encouraged the AFL to target cities where an African American organizer could unionize "his people" in multiple occupations. The delegates identified Roanoke, Richmond, Portsmouth, Norfolk, and Suffolk in Virginia as well as Rocky Mount, North Carolina, and Jacksonville, Florida, as cities where blacks "are working at a low rate of wages per diem and need the services and advantages of American Federation of Labor organizers." Sensing great organizing potential in the South Atlantic, black Virginians believed that the AFL could democratize the labor arena and improve the lives of millions if it placed "its benefits within the reach of all its members without regard to race or color."[25]

These delegates proposed nothing short of a dramatic recasting of the southern political landscape. Stressing the need for the labor movement to exploit the vast political possibilities in the Southeast, delegates demanded that the AFL devote financial resources to placing more black recruiters in an area that had been central to the functioning of the wartime economy and had experienced a great deal of labor upheaval. Such a move, black Virginians insisted, would reconfigure the geopolitical mapping of both labor politics and the African American freedom struggle.

To their credit, African Americans who attended the Buffalo convention also boldly challenged dominant perspectives on the black southern labor problem. Their resolutions focused on workers' empowerment rather than workers' efficiency. The necessity of such an approach becomes apparent in light of the coverage of black labor in white newspapers as well as in African American periodicals aligned with white industrialists. On the pages of Hampton Institute's *Southern Workman*, for example, conversations regarding black labor in the South invariably focused on how to make African American workers more efficient, more punctual, and more obeisant in their response to managerial authority. The monthly never mentioned the activities of black labor unions despite its proximity to two of the nation's strongest black unions. Instead, writers such as Monroe Work and Robert R. Moton insisted that racial progress hinged on black labor establishing goodwill with capital and doing all in its power to assist the South in particular and the country in general in its mobilization efforts.[26] Conversely, African American delegates at the Buffalo convention promoted the merits and benefits of collective action and unionization. Substantive, material improvements, they maintained, had come to those black workers who had unionized and utilized their strategic position in the wartime economy to combat capital's exploitative policies. Workers' empowerment, not efficiency, delegates asserted, was the issue at hand.

To the predominantly white audience at the convention, African American delegates such as Burt and Green did much more than put forth a political program. They also positioned themselves (and by extension other black trade unionists) as the true authorities on the race question and the future of labor in the American South. No other group, they seemed to suggest, had a better grasp of the complex problems facing black and white workers in the South. Nor was any other political entity more prepared to speak and act in the interests of black laborers. Therefore, if the AFL was serious about capturing the South, then African American trade unionists with a firm grasp of the region's political dynamics and history should be placed in key leadership and advising roles in the nation's largest labor body. This viewpoint constituted a major shift in thinking about the South's racial/class dilemma. Challenging the idea of the southern Negro as politically backward, black delegates presented the class-conscious black worker as a modernizing agent for the South. Not just symbolically but substantively, they sought to delegitimize the dominant model of interracial relations in which the black elite spoke on behalf of black workers. In their view, the time had passed when representative leaders affiliated with the Tuskegee machine, the National Urban League, or the NAACP could speak authoritatively about the fate of African American workers without serious consultation with organized black labor.

Seemingly persuaded by arguments on the necessity of building a new political front that would cross regional and racial lines, the AFL convention adopted the two resolutions calling for more black organizers in the South. To many outsiders, the nation's largest labor body appeared ready to begin a new chapter in its complex relationship with African Americans. Several newspapers, including the *New York Age*, predicted that the AFL would launch a massive recruitment drive in the South.[27] In the weeks to follow, however, this prediction proved nothing more than wishful thinking. According to Green, the resolution calling for more funding for black organizers "was never heard from after it was referred to the finance committee for action."[28]

The federation's executive council undoubtedly would have disagreed with Green's charge that the AFL had once again dropped the ball on the "Negro question." Though Green and the other delegates never had any direct contact with federation leaders in the months following the convention, the issues raised in their resolutions sparked a great deal of conversation and debate within and beyond the world of organized labor. Three months after the 1917 convention, the AFL's executive council sent a letter inviting "leading representatives of colored workers" to "confer with us regarding plans for the organization of colored wage-earners."[29] Conspicuously absent from the list of invitees were those African American delegates who had presented the resolutions at the convention. Instead, the AFL reached out to Moton, the principal of Tuskegee Institute; John R. Shillady, secretary of the national office of the NAACP; *New York Age* editor Emmett J. Scott; Eugene Kinckle Jones of the National Urban League; and Thomas Jesse Jones, educational director of the Phelps Stokes Fund. None of these leaders had spent any meaningful time organizing workers, but for white AFL officials deeply concerned about the federation's image in the African American community, support from these men was paramount in changing times. Especially as black migration to the North increased the likelihood that mass industries (steel, meatpacking, automobiles, and the like) would use black strikebreakers during labor disputes, the AFL's executive council deemed it imperative to elevate its status in the African American community. In some respects, the AFL's push for an image overhaul meshed perfectly with the shifting political agenda and concerns of groups such as the NAACP and the National Urban League. Though critiqued by Harlem activist Hubert Harrison as an elitist organization concerned only about the "advancement of certain people," the NAACP was hardly divorced from the concerns and struggles of black workers.[30] Throughout the war, the civil rights organization marshaled its resources to address issues of importance to black labor. In Charleston, South Carolina, for example, the local NAACP collaborated with Shillady and Archibald Grimké, a Charleston-born lawyer working in Washington, D.C., in an effort to reverse the hiring policies at a clothing factory that initially refused to hire African Americans.[31] Elsewhere, NAACP activists spoke out against law enforcement officials' discriminatory application of work-or-fight laws, the harsh working conditions and subpar pay many black workers endured, and the exclusionary practices of white trade unionists.

National Urban League officials also engaged in in-depth conversations on the condition and future of black labor. Eugene Kinckle Jones, who had been included on the AFL's select list of invitees, and several of his Urban League colleagues regarded the unionization of African American workers as an important step in their overall push to inculcate the values of thrift, frugality, punctuality, and middle-class decorum to the black masses, particularly those southerners migrating to the urban centers of the North. As historian Touré Reed explains, "Like its work in the fields of housing and job placement, the Urban League interest in organized labor was consistent with a general desire to shape the behavior and attitudes of black workers." In other words, "Leaguers . . . conceived of the union movement as a means of reorganizing the lives of Afro-American workers."[32] With this larger cultural agenda in mind, Urban League officials went on record as advising African American workers to join the AFL. At its national convention in February 1918, League officials mulled over the political and economic opportunities affiliation with the AFL provided the race. A particularly strong endorsement for greater collaboration between African Americans and the AFL came from Dr. A. A. Graham of the town of Phoebus, Virginia, near the city of Hampton. On the convention floor, Graham discussed how black trade unionists in Hampton Roads had leveraged their growing power to their advantage: "Wherever the Negro gets the chance to co-operate with the white people of this country, I say he should do it. The labor unions in Norfolk are opening their doors because they find that it is to their advantage; and I am glad to find that they are doing that thing in my community. The Negro wants a chance to be a brother to the other man in his country." For Graham and others, the adoption of a more progressive policy on the part of the AFL had positive implications that went beyond traditional bread-and-butter labor issues. Concluded Graham, "If the American Federation of Labor opens its doors to the Negro, he should walk in."[33]

Two months after the Urban League's annual convention, the AFL's top officials conferred with black leaders, who agreed to issue a statement endorsing the organization of black workers into existing or newly formed trade unions. On June 6, Gompers received a letter in which Fred Moore, Eugene Jones, and other signatories reiterated their willingness to "cooperate with the American Federation in bringing about the results of the recent conference." The committee then asked the federation's executive council to draft a statement confirming its commitment to organizing workers. When the committee gave its approval, the black leaders and the AFL would jointly issue the statement to both the black and white press. "This statement," Jones and Moore advised, "should contain a clear exposition of the reasons why certain internationals may exclude colored men as they do by constitutional provision and still be affiliated with the AFL whose declared principles are opposed to such discrimination. This we think necessary because the stated facts above alluded to will be familiar to the leaders among the colored people, particularly to editors and minsters whose cooperation it is essential to secure if the best results are to be obtained." Three other recommendations followed: the appointment of a salaried African American organizer to unionize black workers; quarterly meetings in which black leaders and the AFL's executive council assessed the progress of the federation's organizing efforts among black workers; and the release of a statement from the executive council clarifying its "advanced position in its attitude toward the organization of Negro workingmen" and the endorsement of this position by the AFL's "St. Paul convention in June."[34]

Despite the federation's symbolic gestures toward an equal partnership with black leaders, the AFL's response to this new plan of action was just as disappointing as its response to the convention delegates calling for more African American recruiters in the South. Rather than critically assessing the racism within its ranks and condemning the many unions that excluded African Americans, the federation embraced a politics of denial at its 1918 convention. "No fault," the AFL's executive council informed delegates, "is or can be found with the work done in the past." Adamant in its refusal to address the discriminatory policies of local unions, the council offered nothing more than a perfunctory statement on how its new partnership with "representative colored leaders" could better serve the needs of the labor movement in general and African American workers in particular: "We believe that with the cooperation of the leaders of that race much better results can be accomplished."[35]

Sitting in the audience of convention delegates were several black trade unionists from the South committed to testing the federation's commitment.[36] The two names that loomed the largest among the African American attendees were Thomas P. Woodland of New Orleans and George Milner of Norfolk, Virginia. Heralded as one of his city's finest and most committed labor activists, Woodland was a member of Local 237 of the International Longshoremen's Association (ILA) and served as vice president of the national ILA. With great courage and confidence, he spoke out against racial injustice, assisted in strengthening the labor movement among waterfront workers in the Gulf Coast region, and provided an exemplary model of union leadership for both his peers and subsequent generations. Like Woodland, Milner, too, found a place in the ILA hierarchy, in no small part as a consequence of his pivotal role in the growth of the Norfolk Coal Trimmers Union (Local 15277). Chartered by the AFL in 1914, the Coal Trimmers Union had secured wage concessions from employers, shorter hours, and union recognition during the war. Beyond their labor endeavors, Milner and Woodland were intimately involved in their communities' social and political institutions and thus felt immensely qualified to communicate the concerns of black workers who desperately wanted to build on the energy and momentum of the past few months. Together with J. B. Clinedinst of Newport News, F. T. Chinn of New Orleans, and B. S. Lancaster of Mobile, Milner and Woodland reiterated the need for the federation to take seriously its organizing responsibilities down south. As if to compensate for the exclusive focus on the Southeast at the previous convention, the men shifted the federation's attention to the needs of black waterfront workers along the Gulf Coast and particularly in the port city of Mobile. There, according to African American delegates, "the establishment of new shipbuilding industries by the government" had magnified the need for a stronger AFL presence. Just as their predecessors had identified the cities along the South Atlantic as an ideal recruiting ground in 1917, southern black trade unionists now identified Mobile as a strategic location in dire need of the AFL's financial and human resources. "There is quite a large number of our people in this district unorganized," the delegates noted in their resolution, "and the time and conditions make it very necessary that they be organized and educated in the labor movement." Consistent with previous requests, the men expressed their preference for an African American organizer in the area: "We believe that a colored brother, familiar with the above named facts, appointed as the organizer, to work among our people in the Mobile district, will bring satisfactory results to all concerned." Though Mobile was declared the city in most desperate need of a recruiter, delegates reminded their colleagues that aggressive recruitment drives should be undertaken in "all southern states."[37]

If delegates in the audience had been paying attention to regional developments in the months before the convention, this latest call for more organizers in the South should have hardly surprised them. On and off the job, black southern workers exhibited a growing restlessness with the status quo as the egalitarian spirit of the war rendered many of them less tolerant of racial and class inequality. During an investigation of steelworkers in Birmingham, Alabama, Raymond Swing of the National War Labor Board discerned a dramatic change in black workers' dispositions on the job, relationship with white labor (organized and unorganized), and willingness to contest employer control over working and social lives. "It is my impression," Swing reported to his colleagues in the spring of 1918, "that a new spirit has reached the colored worker."[38]

Against this backdrop of growing discontent, African American delegates at the AFL's 1918 convention pressed the federation to deepen its commitment to organizing black workers. Much like the black trade unionists in attendance at the Buffalo convention, Milner and Woodland imagined the current moment as brimming with revolutionary possibility. Now was the time for the AFL to harness the rising militancy of black workers and "the strong sentiment in favor of organized labor now prevailing among the colored people."[39] The answer to the problem of labor, they succinctly suggested, lay not just in cultivating the support of "representative colored men" but also in buttressing the efforts of laboring people already committed to the union idea. These black delegates were not alone in challenging the AFL to give "colored labor a square deal." In his passionate call for the AFL to grant an international charter to a union seeking to organize all black railroad workers, Thomas Burns, a white delegate representing the Central Labor Union in Tacoma, Washington, encouraged the federation to commit itself to a true and inclusive democracy, one in which African American workers would have all the benefits and responsibilities of their white counterparts: "The influence of world affairs on the present and future condition of the masses of laborers is such as to make necessary a closer and more kindred feeling of sympathy and purpose on the part of all who labor. . . . This spirit of oneness of purpose can and will only be most completely achieved when the benefits derived by the efforts of organized labor are not predicated on race, or creed, or sex, or color, but rather shall be the common lot and heritage of all."[40] Here, Burns repeated a refrain that had become quite common among African American workers during the war years: the future of labor's largest body was inextricably tied to its willingness to embrace African Americans as equal partners in the struggle to improve the material well-being of all workers. Even though the relationship between black workers and the AFL remained strained, many African Americans felt as if the labor movement was on the cusp of monumental change. This confidence derived not so much from the democratic commitments of white trade unionists such as Burns as from the political fervor sweeping black communities across the South. As they reflected on the challenges ahead, union stalwarts such as Milner and Woodland undoubtedly took pride in the courage and determination African American workers exhibited during the war years. Finding strength within themselves and their own communities, southern blacks had battled employers, pushed some members of the black elite to the left, and confronted the deep racism that suffocated the democratic possibilities of the labor movement. They set as their goal the creation of discursive and institutional spaces in which democratic ideas and practices could be deliberated, constructed, reformulated, and then realized. In the opinion of many observers, the world of southern black political culture was changing in ways unimaginable before the outbreak of World War I. Not only was there an explosion of local protests, but there was also a proliferation of national networks linking black southerners with activists in other parts of the country. As the editorial team of the *Savannah Tribune* enthused in 1918, "We are seeing the dawning of a new day on earth."[41]

TWO

Now Comes the Test

November 11, 1918, was a day of celebration for millions of Americans. Nearly twenty months after the United States officially entered World War I, the signing of Armistice between Germany and the Allies ended a bloody conflict responsible for an unimaginable level of human suffering. Two days after the signing, the Pan-American Labor Conference convened in Laredo, Texas, for a four-day summit featuring trade unionists from the United States, Mexico, Guatemala, Costa Rica, El Salvador, and Colombia. On the conference's closing day, Samuel Gompers showered praise on the U.S. government for its critical role in the war's triumphant close. With equal passion, Gompers reiterated his commitment to safeguarding the wage concessions and labor agreements wrung from employers during the war: "Our movement is not to destroy, but to construct, and all may just as well understand now as at any other time that the advantages which the workers of America and the allied countries have gained, and which we hope even to extend to the peoples of the conquered countries, are not going to be taken away from us." Undeterred by calls for political caution, Gompers communicated the resolve of workers to continue their fight for higher compensation, greater control over the labor supply, and more influence within the political arena: "The time has come in the world when the working people are coming into their own. They have new rights and new advantages. They have made the sacrifices, and they are going to enjoy the better times for which the whole world has been in a convulsion."[1] In the months following the convention, Gompers's commentary on the growing militancy and determination of America's laboring class proved prescient. Carefully organized strikes as well as spontaneous rebellions wreaked havoc on shop floors, destabilized production levels in mass industries, and disrupted city governance across the nation. "I really think we are facing a desperate situation," Senator Warren G. Harding bemoaned to a close friend; "It looks to me as if we are coming to a crisis in the conflict between the radical labor leaders and the capitalistic system under which we have developed the republic."[2] Trepidation over the future of the American republic was not confined to the halls of Congress. In a letter to his colleagues in the U.S. Army's Military Intelligence Division, Major J. E. Cutler expressed distress over the escalating levels of protest among members of the African American community: "There is a New Negro to be reckoned with in our political and social life. The emphasis which has been laid upon the principles of democracy and self-determination during the progress of the war has not been without its effect upon the colored people of this country."[3] Cutler drafted his letter after an extensive tour of the South, where he witnessed blacks not only challenging the existing power structure but also pushing to solidify their relationship with activists outside their communities. Much to his astonishment, a vibrant activist network anchored by the black press, trade unions, and various political groups contested the power of the ruling elite, worked determinedly to forge a nationalist consciousness within the black community, and crystallized a leftist agenda focused on improving the economic status of laboring people. Not confined to one geographical space, this expansive network extended from the shipyards of Key West to the bustling streets of Harlem.

Through an analysis of these activist networks along with the historical circumstances that contributed to them, this chapter details the postwar efforts of black southerners to build a national political culture out of regional fragments. It also considers how black political insurgency in the South fundamentally altered black northerners' perceptions of what was politically possible in the aftermath of World War I. In many respects, this regional approach represents a departure from the historiographical trend. Scholarship by Winston James, Rod Bush, Mark Solomon, Barbara Foley, Jeffrey Perry, Erik S. McDuffie, and Minkah Makalani, among others, has significantly enriched our understanding of the ways in which various New York–based activists contributed to the maturation of the black radical tradition through their erudite analyses of race, class, and international politics.[4] Shifting focus away from radical thinkers such as Cyril Briggs, Hubert Harrison, and A. Philip Randolph, my analysis centers on the black southern activists who sought to transform the political landscape through involvement with labor organizations such as the National Brotherhood Workers of America (NBWA) as well as more traditional bodies like the American Federation of Labor (AFL). This chapter does not seek a "Dixie" analogue to the New Negro radicalism in the North, particularly Harlem, but instead draws attention to how grassroots organizations and initiatives that gestated and matured in the South influenced national conversations on nation and empire building, the viability of white-black labor alliances, and whether 1919 would see the revolution's completion or a return to normalcy.

The revolutionary spirit of 1919 definitely held sway in many parts of the South. Particularly on the labor front, strikes proliferated throughout the region as working women and men pushed for a larger share of their employers' profits, union recognition, more say in the hiring and discharging of workers, and greater access to skilled jobs. The causes and effects of these labor disputes revealed the explosive nature of the political landscape, the strengths and weaknesses of many black labor bodies, and the structural forces impeding the maturation of a labor-led mass movement capable of empowering the dispossessed.

Few cities provide a better starting point for analyzing the opportunities and challenges facing black labor than Key West, Florida, the site of one of the earliest and longest labor disputes of 1919. In early January, the self-determinist spirit of black workers garnered national attention when a group of longshoremen initiated a four-month strike against one of the city's largest employers, the P&OSS Shipping Company. The incident precipitating the strike involved a white watchman, who in a fit of rage over the use of a coal chute, violently struck an African American longshoreman with a blackjack. The injured dockworker immediately notified his union, Local 1000 of the International Longshoremen's Association (ILA). The next day, members of the all-black local threatened to walk off their jobs unless the white assailant was immediately dismissed from his position. After receiving the local's demands, company officials coolly rebuked the union, refusing to address the workers' grievances. Local 1000 did not take such disregard lightly and immediately went on strike. No longer, the union proclaimed, would black workers tolerate physical and verbal abuse from their white coworkers: "It is against the laws of our union to allow our members to mistreat any of our employers or their employees while on their jobs, and the laws also state that the men are not to work on jobs where they are not given this same fair treatment."[5]

Though the vast majority of striking workers hailed from the Bahamas and had not yet been naturalized, they demanded to be afforded "the just rights of each and every American citizen." Cloaking these arguments in the language and symbols of American nationalism, the union reminded the general public of black longshoremen's centrality to the nation's war efforts: "Ammunition and food for our soldiers were necessary in winning the war, they had to be sent to the battle front, and the quicker the better; the celerity with which the colored boys in America handled all shipments is said to have excited the wonderment of all Europe; now after all the colored stevedore has done in helping bring victory to our country is he to be deprived of his livelihood simply because he asks that he be treated as an American citizen?"[6] The striking workers thus adopted a rhetorical strategy popularized by black and white laborers alike. All over the country, workers relied on the "new language of patriotism and Americanism" when fighting for improved conditions and a more expansive democracy at the workplace.[7] Despite the patriotic framing of its grievances, Local 1000 proved unable to mobilize the larger public behind its cause. Moreover, the shipping company remained steadfast in its opposition to the union and its political demands. Instead of negotiating with disgruntled workers, company officials shipped in strikebreakers from Miami.

Well aware that their geographical and political isolation hindered organizing efforts, leaders of Local 1000 sought assistance from the National Association for the Advancement of Colored People (NAACP) in New York.[8] To ensure that the outside world had knowledge of developments in Key West, L. A. Gabriel, a member of the ILA 1000 and secretary of the local NAACP, contacted its executive secretary, James Weldon Johnson.[9] Presenting the labor dispute as a civil rights issue, Gabriel lobbied hard for Johnson's assistance in raising funds for the strikers, publicizing their grievances, and garnering support from the ILA's national office. "The principle involved," he explained to Johnson, "means so much not only to these Negroes who are on strike, but to our race in general."[10]

Johnson wasted no time in responding to Local 1000's request for support. "The National Office is willing to do whatever it can to assist you in your fight," he assured Gabriel. However, Johnson expressed sympathy for the workers but stated that the NAACP, with its limited financial resources, could not provide monetary support.[11] Instead, Johnson vowed to do all in his power to persuade the ILA, particularly its president, T. V. O'Connor, and its secretary-treasurer, John J. Joyce, to intervene on the workers' behalf.[12] True to his word, Johnson immediately contacted O'Connor and Joyce. Subsequent events, however, illustrated the limits of the NAACP's power as a labor mediator. ILA officials traveled to Key West to investigate the matter, but their unwillingness to even broach the possibility of an industry-wide strike on behalf of the aggrieved black workers rendered their visit more symbolic than substantive.[13] Under these circumstances, the shipping company clearly had the upper hand. Therefore, the P&OSS Company maintained its refusal to dismiss the white longshoreman who had violently struck his black coworker.

Insufficiently supported and resourced, Local 1000's fight against racism on the job ended in bitter defeat. Nevertheless, their strike illustrated the courage and perseverance of southern black workers as well as the obstacles impeding their progress.

In many ways, the asymmetrical balance of power on the docks of Key West mirrored the labor situation in most areas. Walkouts led by African Americans erupted in one city after another in 1919, but rarely did they achieve their objectives. Three interrelated realities undermined the collective actions of black laborers: capital's drive to consolidate its power in the immediate postwar period; white workers' growing determination to circumvent blacks' employment options; and the absence of a national institution through which the black working class could mobilize against employers whose power extended beyond the local terrain.

With the goal of addressing these issues, some workers initiated discussions about forming a national labor union that would organize black workers across regional and occupational lines. Out of these conversations emerged one of the most fascinating labor federations of the New Negro era, the National Brotherhood Workers of America. Comprised primarily of black waterfront workers from the Hampton Roads area of Virginia and railroad laborers from Georgia and Florida, the NBWA was an all-black labor union organized in the nation's capital in March 1919.[14] The federation advocated the unionization of all black workers, greater federal oversight and enforcement of the government's ban on the ruthless peonage system, the abolition of Jim Crow segregation in the South, and the end of the U.S. government's imperialist activities in Haiti and Mexico. Numerous political concerns and issues drew the NBWA's attention, but most of the organization's resources were directed to forming unions among the unorganized, strengthening existing labor bodies, and empowering African Americans affiliated with the AFL. That the union prioritized addressing the AFL's racism should not be surprising given the NBWA's roots in the Norfolk–Newport News–Portsmouth corridor. Over the war years, black trade unionists from Virginia had put tremendous energy into dismantling the AFL's racist infrastructure. Time and again, they pressured the federation hierarchy to implement the policy changes necessary to equalize wages among black and white workers, increase the number of African American recruiters in the South, and improve the organization's image in the larger black community.[15] Far too often, however, these requests failed to elicit the desired response. Frustrated with the AFL's foot-dragging on key racial issues, several prominent trade unionists embraced the NBWA as a more progressive alternative. Longtime labor activist Walter Green was especially excited about the organization's potential. "Southern Negroes," Green enthused three months after the NBWA's founding, "have begun to see that they can utilize the same methods used by white men for achieving the things they desire."[16] Through organization and commitment, Green believed, black workers across the South could secure better labor contracts and agreements as well as draw more people into the labor movement.

The NBWA's prospects initially looked promising. By June 1919, the organization claimed a membership of four thousand. It also boasted an impressive leadership cadre whose political ties within and beyond the world of labor boded well for the fledging organization. Several of the labor delegates who had attended the AFL's 1917 convention were NBWA founders and officers. In addition to Green, Sidney Burt and Edward Thompson served on the union's executive council. Frontline activists in every sense of the term, Burt, Green, and Thompson initiated organizing drives, identified areas in need of immediate NBWA assistance, communicated with the U.S. Railroad Association and other federal agencies, and negotiated to ease possible tensions between the union and existing labor bodies. To help publicize and communicate their work to the general public, these men frequently turned to the NBWA's corresponding secretary, Jeannette Carter. Born in Harrisburg, Pennsylvania, in 1886, Carter lived in Washington, D.C., where she served as the local correspondent for the *New York Age*. Embracing the roles of journalist, civil rights advocate, and suffragist, Carter encouraged African American women to participate in local and national politics: "We live in a 'Grand and moving time,' when we must by our thought and activity show that we are a part of the drama or ultimately be counted in the discard."[17] Heeding her own advice, Carter ramped up her activism during the war years, becoming more engaged in the problems confronting black working women and men. She drew great inspiration from her older brother, William Justin Carter, a founding member of the Niagara movement who had gained national recognition for his work in the legal field. A Pennsylvania attorney, he used his legal expertise to advance the cause of racial and economic justice. Jeannette Carter shared many of her brother's political commitments and worked closely with the Woman Wage Earners Association, founded in 1917 to improve the earnings and working conditions of domestic laborers through negotiation and collective action.[18] On the recruiting trail for the Woman Wage Earners Association, Carter made several trips to the Hampton Roads area in her effort to mobilize black domestic workers. In the process of building the association's membership base, she befriended and worked alongside labor stalwarts in the area who would later join her in support of the fledging NBWA.

In Carter, the NBWA had a leader who possessed not just an intimate knowledge of the day-to-day struggles involved in organizing skilled and unskilled workers but also a deep understanding of political economy. As an active member of black Washington's vibrant intellectual community, she regularly participated in community forums on the leading political issues of the day. Fluent in domestic and international politics, Carter engaged in heated debates with such respected figures as George Frazier Miller and T. Thomas Fortune.[19] The NBWA profited immensely from Carter's political standing and her connections, most notably her journalistic endeavors. Her correspondence page in the *New York Age* functioned as a key venue through which the NBWA could report its activities. On numerous occasions, Carter alerted her readers to the NBWA's organizing efforts, the recruitment activities of its leaders, and the success of its public forums and conventions.

Another well-connected member of the NBWA's leadership cadre was Thomas J. Pree, a respected labor activist intimately involved in the social world of black fraternalism. A high-ranking official with the Virginia Knights of Pythias, Pree served at various times as the fraternal order's grand vice chancellor, deputy grand chancellor, and grand lecturer.[20] Though based in Newport News, Pree's leadership responsibilities for the Knights of Pythias required extended visits to Danville, Petersburg, Alexandria, Richmond, and Charlottesville, giving him an intimate knowledge of black Virginians' diverse political needs and tendencies as well as extensive political contacts that proved invaluable in strengthening the NBWA.

With respected leaders such as Pree and Carter, the NBWA embraced the challenge of winning the support of blacks in Dixie. Though the union welcomed skilled and unskilled workers from all labor sectors, its first organizing drive targeted the railroad industry.[21] The low rate of unionization among blacks employed on the South's major rail lines had been a major topic of discussion during the war years. At the 1917 AFL convention, Burt, who later served as the NBWA's vice president, had complained about the unorganized state of black workers employed by the Atlantic Seaboard, Atlantic Coast, and Norfolk Southern lines.[22] He frequently condemned these companies for assigning African Americans the duties of brakemen, switchmen, and mechanics but paying them the much lower wages given to railroad helpers. These practices, the Brotherhood noted, violated the terms of William G. McAdoo's General Order No. 27, which mandated equal pay for equal work. McAdoo, the director general of railroads, had issued the order in September 1918 to ensure fairness and minimize conflict.[23] With assistance from Burt and other union leaders, NBWA locals in both Tampa and Jacksonville filed grievances with the U.S. Railroad Association detailing how the unfair classification of African American workers robbed black families and communities of thousands of dollars. One particular case in Jacksonville involved a group of oilers who not only performed the duties that fell under their job description but also assisted white mechanics. The NBWA's president, Lewis Brown, along with Edward Thompson, the organization's fourth vice president and the head of the Colored Helpers and Laborers Union in Jacksonville, demanded an investigation from W. S. Carter, the director of labor at the Interstate Commerce Commission. Thompson and Brown declared the practice of assigning mechanic duties to African Americans oilers not only unacceptable but also a clear violation of governmental policy: "In accordance with Section 6 of Supplement #4 to General Order 27," they argued, the oilers "should be classified as mechanics and receive mechanics rates."[24] NBWA leaders also directed the federal government's attention to cases in which blacks and whites with the same job title received different pay rates. Taking advantage of the federal government's expanded role in the transportation industry, the Brotherhood worked hard to ensure that southern blacks understood their rights as both workers and citizens.

Impressed by these developments, several New Negro radicals in the North began to take notice of the NBWA's work. A. Philip Randolph and Chandler Owen ranked the NBWA among the most promising organizations established in the postwar era. Not content with simply lobbing radical critiques at the capitalist class, the NBWA engaged in the important work of educating and organizing black workers, challenging the employers' discriminatory policies, and pushing governmental agencies to address the issue of racial discrimination in employment.[25] To further advance the organization's agenda, Randolph and Owen volunteered to serve on its board of directors as well as publicize its activities in their monthly, the *Messenger*.

Though friendly with black leftists in the North, the NBWA never fully detached itself from the mainstream labor movement. Throughout the summer of 1919, black trade unionists affiliated with the NBWA partnered with other black activists in a collective effort to democratize the AFL's institutional structure, in part by participating in the organization's state and national conventions. Once again, Virginia and its black labor activists stood at the political center.

On June 4, 1919, black labor leaders turned out in impressive numbers for the annual convention of the Virginia State Federation of Labor. Held in Alexandria, the convention featured lively debates over the most effective ways to respond to postwar demobilization, maintain the steady growth of the group's membership base, and withstand capital's retrenchment. Wielding more influence than ever before, black delegates secured the appointment of the first African American to the Virginia Federation of Labor's executive council, W. H. Page of Newport News.[26]

Shortly after Page's appointment, two thousand white unionists from Richmond bolted the federation. In response, the *Virginia Pilot* praised the defectors for defending the state's white supremacist tradition.[27] Though race certainly played an important role in their departure, the noticeable shift in regional influence within the Virginia State Federation of Labor was another determining factor in their actions. In the preceding four years, the balance of power in Virginia's labor movement had shifted from Richmond to Hampton Roads, an area whose economy expanded greatly during World War I. The federation's newly elected president, vice president, and secretary-treasurer all hailed from the Norfolk–Newport News–Portsmouth area.[28] Concerned about the racial implications of this regional swing, many white labor activists from Richmond fretted over how these newly elected officials would relate to black trade unionists.

The Richmond controversy and its implications for the larger labor movement attracted attention from political observers beyond the world of the AFL. Enthused about Page's position on the Virginia Federation's executive board, the *New York Call* was confident that radical possibilities now existed in the American South. "The fact that the Virginia organization seated a Negro indicates considerable progress. . . . Those who voted in favor of seating him certainly knew that in doing so it would offend large numbers of white union members who know nothing of solidarity. The latter are union members, but not union men. They labor under a psychology that belongs to the old slave regime that was the peculiar product of slave owners."[29] Likewise, John Mitchell's *Richmond Planet* chastised white unionists (particularly those affiliated with the Central Labor Union) for failing to recognize the importance of black workers to organized labor's success: "It is impossible for labor to make a successful fight in the Southland in particular and in the Northland in general without the active aid and co-operation of the laboring colored men of the country."[30]

Uplifted by developments at the Alexandria convention, black trade unionists from Norfolk, Portsmouth, and Newport News carried their political energy and vision to the AFL's national convention, held in Atlantic City, New Jersey, from June 9 to June 31.[31] The annual gathering attracted black Virginians affiliated with the AFL and the NBWA as well as black labor leaders from New Orleans, Mobile, Tampa, Memphis, and Savannah. One would be hard-pressed to find better examples of New Negro political assertion. Working in unison rather than separately, black delegates from the South ripped white trade unionists for their racism, chastised the executive council for its halfhearted approach to organizing black workers, and reiterated their desire to have greater input in shaping the postwar economic landscape. Taking up many of the issues addressed at the AFL's national conventions in 1917 and 1918, the black delegates introduced five resolutions concerning the AFL's presence in the South, the organization of black workers, and the discriminatory policies of white trade unions. All five resolutions were presented on June 11, the day the convention set aside to address matters relating to the "Negro question." The first resolution (No. 76) highlighted the ineffectiveness of white organizers in the region and called for the AFL to appoint a "colored organizer in every state where one is needed." It also demanded the appointment of a black labor representative in the nation's capital whose chief responsibility would be lobbying Congress on behalf of the black working class. Seeing how Gompers's close relationship with President Woodrow Wilson had strengthened labor's hand during the war, southern black delegates understood that their battle for economic justice extended far beyond the workplace and the union hall.[32] Over the preceding few years, the AFL had become integrated into the federal government's bureaucracy, and black labor leaders wanted to ensure that their interests were represented and protected in the nation's capital.

Throughout the proceedings, black delegates from Virginia spoke and behaved in ways that belied the stereotypical image of African American southerners. The delegates demanded that Gompers and other high-ranking officials ensure that the AFL live up to its democratic rhetoric. "We don't ask any favors," John H. Lacey of the Norfolk Colored Labor Union informed his audience; instead, they simply wanted "a chance to live like men, with equal rights and democratic rule."[33] Defining "democratic rule" not only in political but economic terms, Lacey called for equal pay for equal work. The opportunity to "earn bread for our families at the same salary our white brothers are getting," he insisted, was the principal desire of black workers.[34] More than forty white trade unionists responded by publicly declaring their locals' unequivocal commitment to black inclusion and advancement in the economic arena. The convention also adopted a resolution (No. 12) instructing the AFL to "give a square deal to colored skilled and unskilled laborers, favorably consider an application for an International Charter of organized colored labor, or use its power or influence to have them chartered from the International Organization having jurisdiction over them."[35]

The passage of Resolution No. 12 sparked considerable discussion in both the black and white press. Praising the AFL as an organizational vehicle through which black working women and men could improve their political and economic standing, the *New York Times* envisioned better and more expansive economic opportunities for African American labor. "All over the country," the *Times* predicted, "the negro worker will have, as he has not had hitherto, a chance to enter all of the skilled, and therefore better-paid trades, and in them to be judged on his merits." Echoing those sentiments, Gompers celebrated the convention's resolution as a "milestone in the history of the Negroes' struggles for equal rights, as well as in the history of the political and economic liberty of America."[36] Others joined Gompers in presenting the Atlantic City convention as the most important civil rights development since the Emancipation Proclamation. The federation's public support of black workers, raved the *Boston Guardian*, "opens the gateway to real American life for the first time within the last half century."[37]

Randolph and Owen, however, remained much more skeptical. On the pages of the *Messenger*, the two socialists downplayed the significance of Resolution No. 12: "No real change of heart has yet affected the Federation of Labor. It is a center of reaction in the United States. We are not sure that it has undergone a real regeneration. Beware of the Greeks bearing gifts."[38] Equally distrustful of the AFL's commitment to racial and economic justice, Green confessed his readiness to part ways with the federation: "I admire the spirit of Mr. Lac[e]y very much, also that of the convention; but I fail to see how the black man can ever get justice so long denied him in that organization. I have been with the A.F. of L. for five years and have visited their National Convention, also the Virginia State Conventions, and have made request after request through resolutions for justice to my race."[39] Lacking faith in the AFL, Green put his organizational skills and energy behind the work of the NBWA.

Like his Portsmouth colleague, Burt definitely envisioned the NBWA as having an important role in advancing the larger labor movement. In a letter to AFL officials in late 1919, Burt encouraged the federation's white leaders to see the National Brotherhood as an ally rather an enemy. "Capital is trying to destroy Organized Labor," he explained, but "the National Brotherhood expect to make every effort to see that they don't use the colored man to do it." As he noted so often at AFL conventions, African American trade unionists were uniquely positioned to convert black workers to the cause of labor. "It is a known fact that the colored man understands colored men better than anybody else and knows how to deal with him better."[40]

Thanks to strong backing from Burt, Green, and other black workers along the South Atlantic coast, the NBWA's membership grew steadily.[41] Successful in bringing together disparate strands of the black Left, the NBWA pushed hard to become a major force in working-class politics. Toward this goal, the organization held its first convention in Washington, D.C., on September 8–11, 1919. Delegates from Alabama, North Carolina, Florida, Georgia, Mississippi, South Carolina, Virginia, Illinois, New York, Maryland, and West Virginia eagerly convened to discuss issues of importance to the African American community, particularly its working-class members. The resolutions passed by the convention were far more radical and expansive than anything introduced at the AFL gathering in Atlantic City.[42]

Over the course of the four-day proceedings, convention delegates fiercely condemned U.S. domestic and foreign policies, expressed their solidarity with oppressed groups throughout the world, and went on record as favoring the nationalization of railroads, mines, oil wells, and packing industries. The convention also passed a resolution promoting the right of African Americans to engage in armed self-defense. Fresh on the minds of many delegates was the slate of race riots that had marked the preceding summer.[43] Though the surge in violence was nationwide, delegates focused much of their attention on the South. As they explained in their convention notes, "The Southern states today are in such a disgraceful anarchy, that the need of the hour is federal intervention." Until that hour, black southerners must protect themselves by any means necessary. As delegates advised, "Be extremely careful not to violate the law but equally resolute in seeing to it that others shall not trample the law in the dust."[44]

Trade unionists in the NBWA also assumed a radical posture with respect to foreign policy matters. They called for the Wilson administration to lift its blockade on Russia as well as recognize that country's ruling Bolshevik Party. This bold pronouncement was a major departure from the timid posturing of the mainstream labor movement. To avoid the persecution faced by the Industrial Workers of the World during the war years, most labor bodies distanced themselves from Russia. At the AFL's convention, Gompers soundly condemned two resolutions calling for the U.S. government to withdraw from Russia and recognize that country's ruling party.[45] By contrast, the NBWA vehemently rejected the politics of anti-Red hysteria not only by celebrating the regime change in Russia but also by declaring its willingness to develop relationships with communist-affiliated groups in the United States: "We desire to court friendship with any group of people, whether white, brown, red, yellow, or black who are just and fair to Negroes."[46]

The NBWA's stance on international politics, political economy, and labor organizing was as forward-thinking as any existing black political group.[47] However, the organization also had major shortcomings with respect to its attentiveness to African American women. All the male delegates at the NBWA convention came from areas in which women had mounted campaigns against low wages, discriminatory hiring practices, and the unfair application of work-or-fight laws. Yet the gender-specific concerns of black women went unnoticed at the NBWA convention. Not once did delegates address how the combined forces of racial oppression, gender discrimination, and class exploitation imperiled black working women. Nor did they give attention to the unionization drives of their female counterparts, including those led by the sole female delegate, Jeannette Carter. By marginalizing the voices and concerns of African American women, NBWA leaders followed a troubling pattern established by black delegates at the 1917–19 AFL conventions, which also neglected the political concerns and struggles of African American female wage earners.

A stark contrast existed between the strong cooperation between black women and men at the local level and the glaring omission of women's concerns in the political engagements of black men in more national settings. Once southern trade unionists such as Burt and Green stepped on the national stage, their public representations of African Americans' struggles for economic justice transformed into exclusively male affairs. In many ways, this pattern followed the cultural politics and gender logics of the New Negro era.[48] As Marlon Ross notes in his study, *Manning the Race*, "Deciding how to stage the race always hinged on either explicit or implicit notions of the race's sexual identification and gender-role performance."[49] In light of Ross's comments, the actions of NBWA delegates make perfect sense. These trade unionists' desire to put forth a new model of black working-class manhood directly influenced their omission of black women, whose mere mention might disrupt their race-staging efforts.[50] On the gender front, the NBWA was unimaginative in crafting a political strategy responsive to the needs of black workers of both sexes. Like delegates at the wartime AFL conventions, the National Brotherhood's key leaders squandered the opportunity to put forth a more inclusive vision of economic democracy.

The NBWA was quite progressive on other fronts, however. For example, the brokerage style of racial politics in which members of the black elite and the employer class represented themselves as the arbiters of the black majority found a formidable adversary in the National Brotherhood. In an era in which most members of the black elite promoted themselves as the ideal public representatives for the race, the NBWA offered an institutional space through which black workers could articulate their opinions on a wide range of political issues affecting them. Equally important to the organization's appeal—and its distinctiveness—was its balance of theory and practice. The NBWA stood out as one of the few organizations grounded in leftist theory yet institutionally rooted in local black communities. Fusing class consciousness, a strong racial awareness, and a strident anti-imperialist position, the federation developed a political praxis responsive to the concerns of black workers and the radical black intelligentsia. On the one hand, the NBWA's equal wage appeals, combined with its unionization work, struck a responsive chord among those primarily concerned with traditional bread-and-butter issues. On the other hand, its strong anti-imperialist thrust and socialist principles appealed to self-identified radicals drawn to more internationalist and anticapitalist solutions.

Finally, the NBWA was also significant because its political engagements contributed to an important shift in how a select group of northerners viewed the South's radical potential. Randolph, Briggs, and other leftists increasingly treated southern workers as political allies rather than helpless victims perpetually in need of assistance.[51] Moving away from the elitist positions that had informed the political agenda of white and black reformers during the Progressive era, many leftists increasingly placed the burden of southern redemption on the shoulders of the South's working-class majority. "Only class-conscious, militant labor," Randolph asserted in early 1920, could "change the South from a place of autocracy and lynching to a place of democracy and freedom."[52] This line of reasoning marked a significant shift in Randolph's thought. His earlier writings had granted revolutionary potential to black southerners on the move—economically and physically. "As the Negro migrates North and West," Randolph editorialized during the height of the Great Migration, "he secures political power to help himself in his new abode and at the same time to strike a blow for his less favored brothers in wicked 'old Dixie.'"[53] In this passage, the southern transplant—transformed by the revolutionary processes of urbanization and proletarianization—possesses the greatest potential to produce real social change. Conversely, sedentary blacks, bound in Dixie, function as objects of charity in an unfolding racial drama driven primarily by activists in the North.

Several national and global realities, most notably Europe's high demand for American cotton and the Russian Revolution, occasioned a dramatic shift in how Randolph and other activists assessed the potential power of black southerners, including field hands working and living in the Delta region. Noting the significance of rural workers' strategic position in the vortex of global capitalism, Randolph used the *Messenger* to provoke a reimaging of the rural South's political possibilities. "If the Negro cotton workers were to strike," he mused, "the great cotton mills of England that rely upon the cotton exported from the South would be forced to close down. . . . Since these cotton mills are owned by the capitalists of England, who, in turn control Parliament, representations would be made immediately to America with a view to influencing the action of the government with respect to the cotton strike."[54]

A month after Randolph shared his revolutionary vision with his readers, the violent suppression of African American laborers in Phillips County, Arkansas, confirmed the growing suspicion of many black leftists that the rural South could not be omitted from their political agenda.[55] Located in the heart of the Mississippi Delta, Phillips County was the site of a three-day pogrom that left dozens of African Americans dead.[56] In addition to eliciting protest and outrage from black America, the Phillips County massacre occasioned critical reflection among political theorists and social activists seeking to situate these developments within the larger context of the various political upheavals of 1919. Especially for black leftists seeking to gauge the nation's ripeness for revolutionary change, Phillips County emerged as an intriguing case study. News of blacks' organizing efforts in the weeks before the race riot served as an important reminder that the spirit of resistance was alive and well in many rural communities in the black South. Indeed, deep in the heart of the Delta resided women and men who refused to give in to the dictates of white power. Standing up to their employers, an assertive group of field hands had summoned the courage to organize a union and use the legal system for economic redress. Moreover, by continuing to assert their collective power during the two days of mob violence, Phillips County blacks defended their lives with valor and dignity. Their courageous actions awakened many American progressives and radicals to the pivotal role that rural blacks might play in transforming American society.

In the aftermath of the Arkansas riot, Briggs encouraged African Americans to embrace new political configurations and possibilities: "Our next step must be in the direction of forming alliances with the liberal and radical forces of the country—of the world!" Seeming to suggest the dawn of a new political order, Briggs urged African Americans to unite with whites on the far left: "The radical forces in every country have opened their organizations to the Negro comrade and are showing increasing concern in the status and treatment of the darker millions as they begin to recognize that economic exploitation at home is based upon and supported by economic exploitation abroad. . . . In an alliance with the liberal and radical forces of the world the negro has 'nothing to lose but his chains' and everything—including the rights and privileges of free men—to gain." Separatist political approaches, Briggs insisted, would lead only to defeat. "To fight alone would be futile, since he is hopelessly outnumbered in this country."[57] If African American workers had any hope of escaping material deprivation and political powerlessness, the formation of biracial labor coalitions committed to the socialist restructuring of the world economy was mandatory. To those who doubted the viability of such a program, Briggs pointed to the sacrifices of two white union activists in the lumber town of Bogalusa, Louisiana. Only one month after the Phillips County massacre, Stanley O'Rourke and J. P. Bouchillon, two white trade unionists on a recruiting assignment in Bogalusa, were murdered while protecting Sol Dacus, an African American labor organizer. In the ensuing weeks, several activists in the North presented events in Bogalusa as a decisive moment in the history of the American Left.[58] An editorial in the *Messenger* trumpeted the sacrifices of the two white unionists as a "hopeful sign" for labor organizers and radicals: "White workers in the South are beginning to recognize that their interests are identified with the interests of the black workers."[59]

The Bogalusa murders stoked conversations among white and black leftists about the possibility of a "new southern alignment" between progressive white labor and southern African Americans. Social commentators and political activists such as Herbert Seligmann, the NAACP publicity director who coined the term *new southern alignment*, prophesized the formation of a revolutionary army of white and black southern workers equipped with the necessary power to overthrow the southern oligarchy. But the radical South envisioned by many of these writers never came to fruition, as the labor movement remained fractured along racial lines.

A small minority of strategically positioned black workers, particularly longshoremen, formed working relationships with their white counterparts, but for the most part, antagonism rather than cooperation defined relations between black and white workers. Furthermore, the AFL, the most powerful labor body in America, hardly qualified as a model of interracial harmony and cooperation. Save for a progressive few, AFL affiliates openly embraced a racist agenda by barring African Americans from membership, confining blacks to powerless segregated unions, and cooperating with capital to protect the interests of white workers.

Working within this very constricted political environment, African American southerners had to make the best of an extremely difficult situation. Even the most idealistic proponents of working-class solidarity had to deal realistically with workers' divisions and differences along racial, residential, and occupational lines. Left with the option of forsaking class struggle altogether or embracing all-black unions, many African American workers chose the second option.

However, as the short lifetime of the NBWA makes clear, the independent union route presented its own set of problems. In the revolutionary context of 1919, the NBWA gained the support of thousands, hosted its first convention, and planned for the production of a periodical, *The National Brotherhood*. By early 1921, however, the Brotherhood's fortunes had reversed dramatically as the postwar recession fastened its grip on the union's epicenter, Hampton Roads. Moreover, the Brotherhood faced opposition from powerful AFL affiliates. As Sterling D. Spero and Abram Harris explain, "Wherever the Brotherhood Workers succeeded in winning the adherence of successful locals, American Federation of Labor pressure became heavy upon workers concerned to change their affiliation."[60] Shipyard workers in the Tidewater area had comprised the backbone of the NBWA, but as the International Longshoremen's Association increased its power on the nation's docks and postwar conditions decreased black workers' disposable income, the vast majority of them found it difficult to remain with the NBWA. Losing members to the more powerful longshoremen's union and unable to make significant inroads in areas and industries ignored by the AFL, the organization that had once held so much promise for black southern trade unionists dissolved in 1921.

Even after the collapse of the NBWA, the labor arena remained a key battleground for black southerners committed to achieving racial and economic justice. It provided class-conscious New Negroes with a space to address not just bread-and-butter concerns but larger political issues affecting African Americans and the African diaspora. Two of the most glaring issues for many black trade unionists were African Americans' lack of political power and their negligible presence in the electoral arena. As long as the vast majority of black southerners remained disfranchised, elected officials had no reason to fret about the political consequences of their attacks on black labor. Thus, expanding African Americans' political rights became an increasingly important theme among black trade unionists. Especially after the ratification of the Nineteenth Amendment in 1920, conversations on the importance of blacks exercising the franchise, reevaluating their relationship to the Republican Party, and building independent bases of electoral power abounded in southern black political circles.

THREE

Making Way for Democracy

Eleven days after Republican Warren G. Harding won the 1920 presidential election, officials with the National Association for the Advancement of Colored People (NAACP) in New York received a detailed note from Charles McPherson, a resident of Birmingham, Alabama. Like much of the correspondence coming from the South, McPherson's letter recounted the many injustices inflicted on African Americans in the six weeks before the election. With his characteristic penchant for detail, the disgruntled activist who served as the general secretary of the Birmingham NAACP described how local registrars routinely changed office hours without notice, verbally abused civil rights organizers, and threw out voter registration applications filed by African Americans. "It seems to be the policy of those in authority," McPherson raged, "to discourage registration and voting among our people." Of the many humiliations African Americans endured during the election season, nothing angered him more than the discriminatory treatment of newly franchised African American women. Forty-five hundred black women in Birmingham had applied for voter registration cards, but only one hundred had their applications approved. Infuriated by local officials' blatant disregard for the Fourteenth, Fifteenth, and Nineteenth Amendments, McPherson vowed to "present a protest to Congress demanding a congressional investigation of the election laws of Alabama."[1]

The postelection letters McPherson and other black southerners dispatched to the NAACP's national office revealed two important realities: whites' determination to maintain political supremacy at all costs and African Americans' resolve to finally enjoy the full benefits and privileges of citizenship. Not lost on many black southerners coming to political maturity during the World War I era was how their negligible presence in the electoral arena severely hampered their individual and collective fights against economic exploitation, lynching, and legal injustice. Through violence, poll taxes, literacy tests, and various state-level constitutional amendments, the South's ruling elite effectively disfranchised much of the region's black electorate.[2] By the end of the first decade of the twentieth century, nowhere in the South did African Americans possess the political power to meaningfully improve their lives. Thus, many black southerners viewed the expansion of their electoral power as critical to the race's articulation of a more modern, cosmopolitan, and independent self. "The Southern Negro want[s] the ballot," the Reverend G. W. Williams of Dublin, Georgia, assured NAACP officials. "He want[s] the privilege to participate in government affairs."[3] The fate of the black community, Williams and many of his comrades believed, depended on its ability to forge a mass social movement equipped with the necessary resources to reconfigure the balance of political power in the United States.

Not just in the South but in the North as well, African Americans called for a change in their relationship to electoral politics. "The New Negro," A. Philip Randolph asserted in 1920, "cannot be lulled into a false sense of security with political spoils and patronage.... The New Negro demands political equality. He recognizes the necessity of selective as well as elective representation. He realizes that so long as the Negro votes for the Republican or Democratic Party, he will have only the right and privilege to elect but not to select his representatives."[4] If, as Randolph suggests, a willingness to demand political equality, embrace selective and elective representation, and forcefully critique both the Democratic and Republican Parties distinguished the New Negro from the Old Crowd Negro, then quite a few southerners warrant inclusion in the former group.

To reassert themselves as state actors, black southerners coordinated extensive voter registration drives, buttressed movements designed to reapportion southern representation in Congress, educated the populace on citizenship rights, and ran candidates for local and state offices. This renewed commitment to electoral politics surfaced in the actions of not just individuals but also institutions. Churches, fraternal orders, social clubs, and labor bodies drove home the necessity of political activism, electoral participation, and wiping out one-party rule in the South. Likewise, progressive elements of the African American press promoted the broadening of the black public sphere through the revitalization of civic and political engagement. The *Savannah Tribune*, the *Dallas Express*, Pensacola's *Colored Citizen*, New Orleans's *Vindicator*, the *Norfolk Journal and Guide*, and other newspapers repeatedly impressed on their readers the importance of preparing for and assuming the responsibilities of citizenship. Even while acknowledging that fighting for racial and social justice in the United States carried great risks, these newspapers encouraged blacks to be resilient in their struggle for the franchise. As the *Savannah Tribune* noted in 1918, "We have got to keep on fighting for this deserved and logical attribute of citizenship, unceasingly, until we have won out."[5]

This emphasis on augmenting the black electorate must be understood in the larger context of black southerners' drive not only to expand the boundaries of black political discourse but also to challenge the custodial pretensions that had characterized African American politics in the age of Booker T. Washington (1895–1915). As political scientist Adolph Reed Jr. astutely observes, state-legitimated forms of civic exclusion instituted at the turn of the century "raised the cost of popular participation by eliminating the most accessible forms of political speech—voting and other aspects of electoral action. The effect, as in any polity, was to inflect black political discourse toward the perspectives and programs of those elements of the population with access to resources that could enable other kinds of expression—for example, newspaper publishing, business or other property ownership, and affiliation with institutions that provided visibility."[6]

Increasingly during World War I, African Americans redirected their attention to voting and electoral politics. Speaking before a group of community activists in 1918, Dr. E. W. White of the New Orleans NAACP railed against those who expected blacks to fulfill the more burdensome duties of citizenship without enjoying its benefits: "To be regarded as a citizen in the payment of taxes, to be regarded as a citizen in fighting for your country, in bearing the burdens of your country, and then to be denied the rights and privileges of that government cannot have the sanction of a just and an awakened conscience."[7] Unwilling to accept second-class citizenship, White pressed African Americans to assert their presence in the political arena by registering to vote, paying their poll taxes, and forming a massive voting bloc on Election Day. The degree to which African Americans regarded the democratization of the South's electoral arena as an important part of their postwar political agenda was on full display in the months following the armistice. Concurrent with the upsurge in labor activism in many African American communities was an increased focus on expanding the number of black voters. Across the South, African Americans swarmed county registration offices. Cognizant of the challenges before them, many prepared intensely for the registration process. Family, friends, and community leaders quizzed prospective registrants on the inner workings of state and local governments, election rules, voting procedures, and constitutional law. Nevertheless, the vast majority of white registrars used race rather than performance to determine an applicant's success.

The NAACP's national office received dozens of letters from black southerners recounting obstacles to registration. Lieutenant Talmage C. Henderson, a World War I officer who had recently returned to his hometown of Greenwood, South Carolina, after fighting in France, wasted no time in testing whether the war had really made America safe for democracy. He attempted to register to vote in the spring of 1919, but the registrar angrily rejected his application without explanation.[8]

Later in the day, Greenwood blacks received another reminder of whites' determination to maintain political power at all costs. A few steps away from the registration office, a white mob viciously attacked two black ministers, R. H. Marshall and C. W. Webb.[9] Moved by a deadly combination of hate and fear, the mob delivered an unequivocal message to black Greenwood: stay away from politics or suffer the brutal consequences of disturbing the town's racial order.

Undeterred by the threats to their lives, Greenwood's blacks (and those elsewhere) pressed ahead in their efforts to secure the ballot. Such perseverance was hugely important in a racially repressive society: even when turned away by election officials, registration applicants emboldened other members of their communities. Fear of white retribution never vanished completely from the black community, but as African Americans launched voter registration drives, organized political clubs, and convened mass meetings, this intense civic engagement generated positive feelings that shifted, if only slightly, the community's sense of what was politically possible in the current social order.

The recent enfranchisement of thousands of black women also altered African Americans' political sensibilities. The ratification of the Nineteenth Amendment on August 14, 1920, sent shock waves across the nation, eliciting great debate on how women might affect the political landscape. Skepticism about female participation in electoral politics was significantly lower among blacks than whites. On the premise that the entrance of African American women into the political sphere elevated the race as a whole, many prominent black male activists focused on getting as many women as possible qualified to vote. More often than not, these men worked alongside courageous African American women. As the work of Rosalyn Terborg-Penn, Susan Lebsock, Nikki Brown, and Paul Ortiz ably demonstrates, numerous African American women leaders demanded the right to exercise the franchise.[10] "Government by man alone," activist and journalist Jeannette Carter declared in a public address, "is only half government. It is like a bird with only one wing, one-sided, imperfect; its progress impeded; a half failure." Noting that women were already immersed in public life as workers, labor activists, and religious leaders, Carter repudiated the idea that political engagement debased women's character: "To invest woman with political rights, to consult her as to the kind and quality of the men who are to make the laws to govern the country, is not to degrade her, but to elevate her."[11] Identifying with both the New Woman and New Negro movements, Carter and countless other African American women plunged into political work, creating associations and movements designed to empower themselves and their communities. "For black suffragists," Brown explains, "the right to vote appeared to be the sword with which black women might cut through the Gordian knot of racism and sexism constraining their political voices."[12] In many ways, black women's struggle for self-determination in the political arena marked a continuation of battles launched during the war years. Far from politically acquiescent, African American women had actively participated in many of their communities' campaigns for social justice. On the labor front, they squared off against their employers in the public arena, demanding greater wage compensation, reduced hours, and the right to bargain collectively.[13] The labor struggles of black women not only provided them with valuable organizing experience but also brought them into direct confrontation with the repressive power of the state.

New forms of disciplinary power sanctioned by the state circumscribed black women's rights as citizens, limited their options as workers, and restricted their choices as wives and mothers. Under the work-or-fight laws, for example, African American women were routinely arrested, imprisoned, and fined for refusing domestic service work, laboring exclusively for their families, or engaging in labor protests. Well aware of their political vulnerability, these women regarded the acquisition of the vote as a necessary step in undermining state repression. Thus, thousands of African American women stepped forward to secure political power through the franchise.

The two-month period before the 1920 presidential election saw intense organizing in rural areas, small towns, and large cities, with thousands of black women attempting to register in many cities. Community leaders and political observers marveled at the seriousness with which black women approached the process of qualifying for the vote. One woman in Hampton, Virginia, told activist Addie Hunton that "she slept with her application form, as given by her husband, for a week—studying it the last thing in the night and the first thing in the morning."[14] The white press, too, marveled at black women's electoral activism and commitment to making their political voices heard. On September 20, 1920, the *New York Times* announced, "Negro Women in the South Rushing to Register."[15]

Fearing a loss of their racial power, many white men impressed on each other the need for a temporary suspension of their opposition to white female participation in electoral politics. "In view of the excessive registration of negroes in some wards," noted one Jacksonville newspaper, "all prejudices against the ballot must be laid aside, and the white women must assume the responsibilities which have been thrust upon them and register."[16] Troubled by the large turnout of African American women on the first day of registration in Richmond, Virginia, John Purceli, chair of the local Democratic Party, pressured white women to perform their civic and racial duties: "Developments today indicate an approaching crisis in the matter of feminine registration. In view of the situation confronting us it is the duty of every woman who regards the dominion of the white race as essential to the welfare of the Southland to qualify for the ballot by paying her poll tax and registering as a voter."[17] Earlier in the year, opponents of female suffrage would have looked disapprovingly on Purceli's comments, but the activities of African American women momentarily shook up relations between white women and white men.[18] Precisely because of their desire to preserve their supremacy, white men pushed their wives, daughters, and sisters to the polls with the same urgency with which they worked to close the doors of political opportunity to African Americans.[19]

Local newspapers provided the white elite with a venue not simply for mobilizing white women but also for projecting an image of black women as social deviants lacking the qualifications for political participation. Crucial to this process was creating the idea that voter registration fraud ran rampant in the African American community. False reports circulated that voter registration books contained the names of thousands of black women who had not paid their poll taxes, who lacked the literacy requirements to vote, and who had falsified information regarding age and residency. A new specter haunted the South's electoral system: the inherently corrupt Negro woman who strove to secure Republican domination and by extension black male supremacy. Feeding a series of lies to a hate-filled populace starving for the most sensationalized news, Jacksonville's *Florida Times-Union* falsely reported that "thousands of negro women have given fictitious names and addresses. Many negro girls who gave their ages as 16 and 17 years when attending public schools last year, have since last August sworn to be 21 years old."[20]

While white journalists routinely fictionalized stories of black criminality, they conveniently ignored actual illegalities and injustices committed by white men during the campaign season. Consistent with their historically racist reporting, both the *Florida Metropolis* and the *Florida Times-Union* turned a blind eye to whites' violations of African Americans' constitutional rights, never mentioning the illegal tactics employed by the white power structure. As historian Kali Gross astutely observes, white press coverage of black criminality, whether based in truth or fiction, not only maligned black womanhood but also "muted the victimization of black women."[21]

Many African Americans refused to ignore the reality of white political corruption and intimidation, however. Complaints outlining the denial of African Americans' citizenship rights flooded the offices of the National Republican Committee and the New York NAACP. Fiery letters of protest came from urban centers and small towns, the Deep South and the Upper South. After interviewing twenty African American women in Phoebus and Hampton, Virginia, Hunton shared her findings with NAACP colleagues in New York. Foremost on Hunton's list of complaints were the glaring discrepancies in the treatment of white and black women.

Whereas white women rarely spent more than ten minutes at the registration office, the application process for black women was long and drawn out. Unlike their white counterparts, African American women were bombarded with such questions as

1. How is the Superintendent of Public Instruction elected?
2. How are vacancies filled and what is his term of office?
3. What is the maximum and minimum number of section districts in the State of Virginia?
4. What are the exceptions of compulsion education?
5. Who are exempted from paying poll tax and yet eligible to vote?
6. When can the Habeas Corpus Act be suspended?
7. What persons are not eligible to vote?
8. Under what condition can a person who commits a civil offense be free from arrest?
9. Who if they committed a civil crime, could be arrested?[22]

That white registrars asked black applicants such tough and ambiguous questions was a well-known fact in the African American community. Nonetheless, many women still rushed to qualify as voters, eager to lay the foundations for a new political reality. Martha A. Johnson, a public school teacher working in Hampton, could hardly contain herself after hearing that women could finally exercise the vote. "I was most enthusiastic about registering for the first time," the twenty-four-year-old confided to Hunton.[23] Johnson was confident in her abilities, studied hard for the literacy test, and felt as if she performed remarkably well. But the election manager declared that Johnson had failed the exam portion of the application. Stunned by the results, Johnson left the registration office devastated, discouraged, and emotionally depleted. Her experience was hardly exceptional. Sallie Fields, too, was denied a voter registration card after her answers to the registration questions were deemed insufficient. Fields scoffed at the suggestion that she was not qualified to vote: "I had studied my application from which my husband had made a typewritten copy until I could not have failed if I desired. I was actually complimented by the registrar on its perfection."[24]

The emotional toll rejection exacted on African American women did not escape the notice of black men. Interpreting the registrar's rejection of his wife's application as an affront on his manhood, attorney George Washington Fields was overcome by feelings of anger. "The morning my wife was mistreated," Fields complained bitterly, "it was she who saved me from trouble by forcibly leading me home. . . . I was ready to die for the way she was treated." The political system's blatant racism surely fueled Fields's anger, but he also despised what he viewed as his community's passive acceptance of its political condition. "We are too weak," he sighed; "some of us must just die."[25]

Such anger, Hunton noted, signaled an important shift in the black community: "One of the strongest proofs of the enormity of the humiliation and injustices to which the women were subjected is the vehement freedom with which they recite their grievances and the desire not for redress but in many cases vengeance." Much to her shock, the most extreme expressions of anger emanated not from the "radical crowd" but from individuals who had previously been "extremely conservative" in their ideas and disposition.[26]

Not content with simply verbalizing their dissatisfaction with the denial of their civil rights, several Hampton Roads leaders sprung into action. Outraged by the registrars' discriminatory treatment of African American women, George Washington Fields filed a complaint with the state's attorney general, hoping the legal system would correct the evils of the registration office. His move toward legal action proved somewhat effective. Fearing federal intervention, the registration office granted his wife and several other women their voter registration cards.[27]

Fields was not the only southern activist taking his political grievances to the courts. A group of black women in Columbia, South Carolina, also filed suit against the county registration board for its unfair administration of the state's literacy requirement. South Carolina law required that prospective voters be able to read and write any section of the state's constitution, but when attempting to register, black women were routinely asked to read and interpret the state's civil and criminal codes. And even when black women prepared for this portion of the application, their answers were deemed unsatisfactory. On September 16, 1920, thirty-two black female applicants responded to the denial of voter registration cards by taking their grievances to the state's attorney general. Eager to avoid federal intervention, the attorney general immediately put the names of the aggrieved women on the voter rolls.[28]

Such small victories were important, though many leaders regarded the acquisition of voter registration cards as only one step in the protracted struggle for political empowerment. Transforming the core of American politics entailed much more than qualifying African American women for the vote, increasing the black electorate, and voting for Republican candidates. More focus had to be given to the creation of a movement infrastructure capable of providing people with much-needed training in mass organizing tactics, gauging the varied needs within the African American community, and changing the ways in which people imagined their relationship to the political arm of the state.

No national organization understood these broader goals more than the NAACP.

On both the local and national levels, the civil rights organization invested considerable resources not simply to increase the number of black voters for the 1920 election but also to create an even more politically informed citizenry. To this end, the NAACP's *Crisis* ran detailed stories on the Republican, Democratic, and American Labor Parties; published stinging criticisms of black leaders who trivialized African Americans' involvement in politics; and kept readers informed of significant developments during the election season. To complement the important work of the *Crisis*, local branches sponsored citizenship classes in which black women and men received detailed instructions on the intricacies of voter registration, the platforms of various candidates, and important Election Day rules. These classes provided a democratic space in which people could exchange political ideas, learn more about important societal issues, and gain a better understanding of how they could improve their lives by voting.[29] Updating his New York comrades on the success of the Birmingham branch's political endeavors, McPherson rejoiced over the community's response to the twenty citizenship classes held during the registration season: "Large numbers attended eager to learn how to assume their new duties."[30]

Beyond the focus on registration and Election Day procedures, these citizenship classes were also designed to encourage greater dialogue about how black women and men might exert more independence in their political endeavors, leading to serious deliberation regarding African Americans' historic relationship with the Republican Party. Some leaders argued that if blacks were truly committed to expanding their political power, a serious reassessment of the GOP was in order. This stance developed in response to the egalitarian rhetoric associated with World War I, the Lily-Whites' growing power and influence among Republicans, and blacks' mounting frustration with the party's unwillingness to implement substantive legal, legislative, and economic reform.

Numerous African Americans affiliated with the GOP demanded an immediate change in the party's agenda and infrastructure, but their pleas fell on deaf ears. Salivating at the chance to exploit the chaotic state of the Democratic Party, the National Republican Committee saw an opportunity to gain a stronghold in the South. On board with the committee's plan for regional realignment, Lily-Whites within the GOP enticed chair Will H. Hayes and other committee members with promises of political riches in the former Confederacy. Triumphant victory over the Southern Democrats, Lily-Whites boldly predicted, would come as soon as the Republicans dispensed with their most dangerous baggage: African Americans.

To expedite the process of "Negro removal," Lily-Whites in Virginia, North Carolina, and Arkansas barred blacks from participating in Republican state conventions. Claiming to be pragmatic rather than racist, white party strategists defended these moves as necessary to improve the GOP's standing in the South. Joseph P.

Brady, a devout Virginia Republican who served as the clerk of the U.S. District Court, insisted that "no powerful Republican organization could be built up unless the dominance of the white race in the party is unquestioned."[31]

Others viewed the matter differently. Condemning Brady and his colleagues as narrow-minded opportunists, several African Americans warned the National Republican Committee that its southern strategy could create a backlash of epic proportions. Quick to remind party leaders of the growing importance of the black electorate in the North, Edward Johnson, a New York activist who attended the Republican National Convention in Chicago, counseled against conceding too much control to Lily-White Republicans: "The Negroes of the North have always been opposed to the 'Lily White' policy of the Republican Party." Noting black New Yorkers' willingness to "turn to the Democratic or Socialist Party," Johnson reminded white Republicans of the political repercussions of alienating their African American base, particularly in the North. "Unless this matter is remedied it will have a bad effect on New York Negroes."[32]

Shrugging off warnings that their exclusionary policies could hurt the party's standing among black voters in the North, Lily-White Republicans in Virginia and elsewhere continued to transform the GOP's demographic profile. When the Virginia Republican Convention opened in Roanoke in the spring of 1920, white representatives refused to seat African American delegates. One month later, the Arkansas Republican Convention closed its doors to African Americans.[33] The same scenario repeated itself in Georgia and North Carolina, where political arrogance and ineptitude temporarily blinded white Republicans to the power of southern Democrats, the strong influence of the media on white popular opinion, and the reluctance of some whites to see the GOP as anything other than a party that promoted "social equality" and "Negro Rule."[34]

All of these developments put the National Republican Committee in a precarious situation.[35] On the one hand, the committee fretted about the potential loss of the expanding black electorate in New York, Pennsylvania, Ohio, Illinois, and other states.[36] On the other hand, the chance of building a new Republican base among southern whites was quite appealing for such leading party figures as Hayes, Massachusetts senator Henry Cabot Lodge, and presidential candidate Warren G. Harding. On the campaign trail, Harding asserted that the time had come for the "Solid South" to stop adhering "blindly" to the Democratic Party.[37] To promote sectional healing and party expansion, Harding urged the National Republican Committee to "give every encouragement to a program of party promotion in a number of Southern states which are showing a tendency to make new party alignments," and he avowed, "If I can be of any assistance during the coming national campaign, I shall be more than delighted to do so."[38]

The difficulty of cracking the Solid South was greatly compounded by the ubiqui-tous race question. Convincing southern whites to join a party that continued to offer patronage positions to African Americans and openly court the northern black vote was no easy task. It was also unlikely that white southerners would over-look Harding's recent condemnation of lynching. During his formal acceptance of the Republican Party nomination, Harding embraced as part of his platform the implementation of federal laws against lynching.[39] Wary of Harding's intentions and appalled by the thought of federal intervention in their region's racial affairs, many white southerners admonished prospective voters that a ballot cast for the Republican nominee represented a devastating blow against white supremacy. All things considered, a meaningful shift in regional loyalty seemed highly unlikely in the current political environment. "The Republicans may pick up a Represen-tative or two in Southern districts," the *New York Times* observed, "but the chief argument which has held the South solid against them will almost certainly keep it so this year."[40] In other words, the "Negro question" prevented the type of re-gional unity envisioned by the ambitious Republican Party. So despite Harding's pronouncements and the Lily-Whites' efforts to strengthen the GOP's status in the South, the Party of Jackson would continue to reign supreme in Dixie.

African Americans in both the North and the South observed recent develop-ments with a keen focus on their own interests and pondered a series of tough questions: Should they continue to support the national Republican Party despite the ascendancy of the Lily-White faction in the South? Or did current conditions call for an embrace of third-party alternatives? And if the GOP was to be aban-doned, did the existing political alternatives truly possess the power or even the potential to transform the American polity?

Variability rather than consensus characterized African Americans' opinions on their relationship to the Republican Party. Some counseled leaving the GOP, while others remained staunchly loyal to the Party of Lincoln. Counted among the most steadfast GOP supporters were those who held patronage positions. Takeover attempts by the Lily-White faction of the GOP angered them but never seriously threatened their party loyalties. Quite firm in the convictions that the GOP was the ship and all else the sea, functionaries such as Henry Lincoln Johnson of Atlanta and Walter F. Cohen of New Orleans strongly objected to attempts to find alternate routes to political empowerment, opting instead to change the party by working within its institutional structures. Leaving the GOP, they repeatedly argued, bor-dered on political suicide.[41]

On the other side of the debate stood political independents open to new alli-ances and strategies. Furious at those who allowed the Republican Party to hold their votes hostage, independents encouraged political flexibility rather than dogmatic party loyalty. *Crisis* contributor and future Trotskyist Ernest McKinney detested those positing the idea that African Americans had a special obligation to the Republican Party: "The Negro today faces not the party of the Abolitionists but bidders for votes, and men lusting for power and anxious for office because the office brings with it prestige and leadership." Far too often, McKinney complained, blacks treated the party as "a kind of mass Messiah who has delivered us from the southern Romans. . . . We feel that we owe them something that can never be paid as long as the earth stands, so great is the debt."[42] Such devotion, McKinney fumed, was dangerous, unnecessary, and politically unwise.

Nannie Burroughs, a respected black educator and activist, agreed with McKinney. In an article published in the *Afro-American*, Burroughs warned against placing too much hope in the Republican Party and its election rhetoric: "Every four years we are fed on campaign dope for a few months only to starve from failure on the part of that party to stand by the measures designed to give political and economic opportunity to all. We have lived on promises without performances." Frustrated by the two major political parties, Burroughs flirted with the idea of backing the electoral campaigns of the Socialist Party.[43]

Socialist alternatives in the electoral arena never gained much traction in the black South. However, independent offshoots of the Republican Party did emerge in Arkansas, Georgia, and Virginia. Taking their self-determinist ideas into the political arena, African Americans in these states nominated separate delegations to the party's national convention as well as ran candidates for local and state offices.[44] Their message to their communities was simple: if African Americans were to save both themselves and the American democratic project, they must accept the responsibility of pursuing their own political path.

Nowhere was this independent spirit more strikingly manifest than in Richmond, Virginia. The city's black community had a rich political legacy and flourished as an epicenter of independent black Republicanism.[45] On the eve of Lily-Whites' takeover of the Virginia Republican Convention, a group of black activists led by dentist D. A. Ferguson and attorney Joseph Robert Pollard convened a mass meeting at Richmond's True Reformers Hall to discuss the most effective response to the current crisis.[46] Speakers situated the latest slight within a much larger historical context, enumerating their political grievances with great clarity and passion. "During my residence in this city for twenty years," Ferguson remarked, "the political rights and ambitions of the Virginia Negro have been crushed." Having run out of patience with Richmond politics, Ferguson vowed that he would not passively absorb the latest round of blows from the Lily-White Republicans.[47]

Ferguson launched the Independent Republican Party (IRP), which nominated Pollard for the U.S. Senate and H. H. Price for representative of the Third Congressional District. Enormously popular among blacks in Richmond, Pollard was primarily known for his litigation work against the city's housing segregation ordinance. Vehement in his opposition to all forms of racism, Pollard garnered widespread respect in the black community for his willingness to challenge white power and privilege. The chances that Pollard and Price would secure an election victory were slim, but many Richmond blacks were excited about their nominations. No longer faced with the unappealing prospect of voting for the lesser of two evils, IRP supporters looked at their choices with great pride. Though Pollard and Price lacked experience in the electoral arena, many blacks genuinely appreciated their independent character and bold stance against the Lily-White Republicans.[48]

Some African Americans, however, evinced less enthusiasm for Pollard and Price. The *Richmond Planet* suggested that the IRP's slate of candidates had not been fully vetted by the African American political community. "The men leading the movement mean well," John Mitchell wrote condescendingly, "but they have not submitted to leadership themselves in order to demand leadership at the hands of others. For many months certain patriotic, far seeing colored men have been urging the colored people to pay their poll-taxes and register. They have been endeavoring to get them to organize under the name of the Civic League and other similar organizations but there was but little interest shown. Now that the 'blow has fell,' they run to a mass-meeting to air themselves and to vent their feelings in tones of indignation."[49] Mitchell clearly took issue with the IRP, but his commentary had little influence among Richmond's African Americans. Over the seven-month period between its founding in March and the fall election, the IRP built a loyal following despite its limited resources. On October 4, the party held a mass meeting that drew more than five thousand people, signaling the community's serious commitment to self-determination in the political sphere.[50] Well aware of the obstacles in their way, the IRP's leaders had no illusions about the likelihood of victory but instead focused on building a social movement that would accomplish more than simply bringing people to the polls on Election Day. As suggested by the slogan "In defense of the children unborn," the IRP anticipated its greatest impact lay far ahead.[51]

Fifty-five years after Robert E. Lee's surrender at Appomattox, the children, grandchildren, and great-grandchildren of slaves were optimistic about their political future. In Richmond and throughout the South, African Americans' skepticism and apathy had in many cases given way to optimism and intense organizing.

Election Day proved quite memorable for thousands of southern black women and men. To minimize conflict with whites, they headed for the polls very early in the morning, sharing feelings of pride, fear, and hope and swapping tales of enduring trials and tribulations. At their polling stations, they proceeded to lines specifically designated for African Americans, which in most cities moved at a frustratingly slow pace. Election officials hoped the long wait would induce blacks to depart without casting their ballots but severely underestimated African Americans' patience and determination. Of the opinion that far too many bridges had been crossed to surrender now, the vast majority of African Americans waited for the opportunity to vote. More than five thousand Virginia blacks cast ballots for Pollard and Price. In most parts of the South, however, African Americans primarily concerned themselves with putting Harding into the White House.

Harding trounced the Democratic candidate, James Cox, but the Republican's victory was not a major conversation topic in black America. Instead, most African Americans focused on the news of widespread election fraud in the South. Continuing many of the tactics employed in previous elections, white officials worked hard to maintain the political status quo. On Election Day, they turned away large numbers of African Americans from the polls, subjected black women and men to verbal assault, and openly threw out ballots cast by Republican voters.[52]

Strong critiques of the "avalanche of lawlessness" in the South erupted in various corners of black America. Six days after the election, the NAACP's board of directors voted that "a telegram be sent to Representative Isaac Siegel, Chairman of the House Committee on the Census, urging that his colleagues abide by the laws of the Fourteenth Amendment by reducing congressional representation in Southern States in which colored voters are disfranchised."[53] Sympathetic to the NAACP's concerns, Representative George Tinkham of Massachusetts agreed on the need for a congressional hearing on black voting and reapportionment in the South. His decision was based on careful study of the regional differences in election statistics, which he believed clearly indicated that something was terribly wrong in the South. According to Tinkham,

> The total vote for Representatives in Alabama, which has ten Representatives, was 62,345, whereas the total vote for Representatives in Congress in Minnesota, which has ten representatives, was 299,127, and the total vote in Iowa, which has ten Representatives, was 316,377. The total vote for Representatives in Congress in Georgia, which has twelve Representatives, was 59,196, whereas the total vote for Representatives in Congress in New Jersey, which has twelve Representatives, was 338,461.[54]

But these statistics were not enough to overcome white southerners' claim that the differences resulted from voter apathy rather than racial repression. To provide Tinkham with further evidence, the NAACP began collecting affidavits from southern blacks who had either witnessed or been victims of racial discrimination during the election season. One of many civil rights activists who provided such information was Mrs. S. S. Humbert of Americus, Georgia, who described in detail the obstacles blacks endured during the registration period. Whenever African Americans attempted to sign up, the registrar "would hide the book or himself. He would tell the person that the registration book was in another precinct or he'd leave his office and put a lady in there who would know nothing about registration, all this would happen to 9/10 of the colored people." Persistent individuals might eventually secure registration cards, but further roadblocks stood in their way: according to Humbert, "More than 250 colored women went to the polls to vote but were turned down or their ballots refused to be taken by the election manager."[55]

Similar testimonies turned up in election reports from the National Republican Committee. North Carolinian Clara Mann offered a particularly extensive account of the constitutional violations committed by white election officials in her community:

> During the month of Oct. when the books were opened for registration I presented myself at the place for registration in my ward in this city, and was required to read the entire constitution of North Carolina. This I did, then I was requested to write it, but when I started writing, the Registrar, Frank W. Shriner, told me it mattered not if I wrote it, as he would not register me. I took the matter up with [U.S.] Attorney General [A. Mitchell] Palmer by furnishing him an affidavit stating that I had applied for registration and had been refused on grounds set out above. I am writing you this information in order that you may be properly informed as to the methods used in this section of the country to disqualify legal voters. I trust you will give this matter your earnest consideration and may I suggest that you take up this matter with the N.A.A.C.P. Office in New York City.[56]

Understanding that the stakes were extremely high and that their political duties did not end on Election Day, civil rights activists in the South put tremendous effort into the NAACP's reapportionment efforts. Their commitment testified to black southerners' thirst for freedom as well as the deepening of the civil rights movement's national networks. A strong partnership had been forged between black southerners and the NAACP's national office in New York during the war years, and both parties greatly valued that bond. Writing from Shaw University in Raleigh, North Carolina, approximately six weeks after the election, Professor William S. Turner thanked the national office for its direction and guidance: "I want to congratulate you on the great fight that you are making for our people and the efforts that you are putting forth to move Congress to action against Negro disfranchisement in the South."[57]

But the NAACP's reapportionment initiative yielded disappointing results. Nearly six months after the election, the House defeated Tinkham's resolution for a probe into election fraud in the South. Congressional leaders had mountains of evidence of constitutional violations but lacked the courage and will to take on the southern racial establishment.

Nominally free yet locked in a position of social and political marginality, African Americans faced an uphill battle in their fight for freedom, justice, and equality. Much of the white world had no desire to create a multiracial democracy in which political and social justice were granted to all. Late in the spring of 1921, the National Republican Committee (with approval from President Harding) began aggressively implementing its Georgia Plan, which prioritized the appointment of white men of prominence to positions of power in state parties.[58] African Americans clearly lacked any real ability to transform public policy in meaningful ways.

Moreover, the violence and intimidation that had marred election activities remained a part of the South's political landscape. Even as the NAACP launched an aggressive campaign against white terrorism and pushed for passage of a federal antilynching law, many in the South still relied on the most brutal forms of racial punishment when dealing with "unruly" blacks. The lynching of two hundred African Americans between 1921 and 1923, combined with nightmarish accounts of racial pogroms in Tulsa, Oklahoma, and Rosewood, Florida, caused some African American leaders to dismiss the United States as morally and politically bankrupt.[59] In an editorial for the *Negro World*, black socialist Hubert Harrison delivered a searing critique of American race relations:

> We Negroes have no faith in American democracy and can have none so long as lynching, economic and social serfdom lie in the dark alleys of its mental reservations. When a President of this country can become famous abroad for his preachments on "The New Freedom," while pregnant Negro women are roasted by white savages in his section of the South with not one word of protest coming from his lips; when "the aims of labor" on its march to justice exclude all reference to the masses of black workers whom conservative labor leaders would condemn in America to the sharks . . . when such things represent what happens every day in a "sweet land of liberty" where "democracy" is the great watchword, then we Negroes must be excused for feeling neither love nor respect for the rotten hypocrisy which masquerades as democracy in America.[60]

Harrison's blistering denunciation of American society resonated deeply with many readers, particularly those living below the Mason-Dixon Line. Over the years, black women and men had struggled mightily to bring political democracy to the South, yet the region remained racist to its core. Basic rights remained out of the grasp of most black southerners.

Despite the bleak situation, African Americans continued their fight for rights and dignity, pursuing those goals through a variety of means. Social justice advocates oriented toward liberal integrationist strategies tended to concentrate on ensuring that blacks received equitable and just treatment in the political arena, the capitalist marketplace, the world of labor, and the arts. Through organizations such as the NAACP, they worked to destroy the legal and cultural underpinnings of the Jim Crow regime so that African Americans could take their rightful place in U.S. society. Others, however, doubted that a multiracial democracy was possible in America and resurrected the Pan-African ideas espoused beginning in the mid-nineteenth century by Martin Delany and Henry McNeal Turner. In Greensboro, New Orleans, Norfolk, Savannah, Miami, and other southern cities, a critical mass of black women and men pledged their allegiance to the largest and most controversial organization of the New Negro era, Marcus Garvey's Universal Negro Improvement Association. A movement unlike anything before or since, Garveyism captured the imagination of thousands of black southerners.

FOUR

On the Firing Line

On the heels of the 1920 congressional elections, a group of sixty black women and men, mostly working-class immigrants from the Bahamas, assembled at the English Wesleyan Church in Miami, Florida, to announce the official chartering of a local division of Marcus Garvey's Universal Negro Improvement Association (UNIA). Within a matter of weeks, the fledging division expanded its membership to four hundred people as well as elected its first slate of officers. Though an African American minister, John A. Davis, initiated the division's formation and served as its first president, Afro-Bahamians formed the heart and soul of the Garvey movement in Miami. Thanks to their contributions, the local UNIA quickly emerged as an important center of both black immigrant life and New Negro expression. On Sunday afternoons, hundreds flocked to the UNIA's weekly meetings at the Airdrome building in Colored Town, where speakers mesmerized crowds with discussions on the Garvey movement and other contemporary struggles for racial justice.[1] Along with offering provocative political conversations and debates, the Miami UNIA provided lively entertainment for women and men in search of a good time, fellowship, and a much-needed respite from a hard day's work. At weekly gatherings, UNIA members and their guests frequently swayed to the sounds of live jazz, blues, and gospel. The cultural vibrancy of the local movement left a lasting impression on many visitors, including those who came from thriving UNIA branches up north.

Counted among the hundreds of local blacks who derived great pleasure and affirmation from the sociopolitical world of Miami Garveyism was Albert Gibson, a native of Eleuthera in the Bahamas who had arrived in Florida in 1910. Finding steady work as a farmer in Coconut Grove, Gibson eventually settled down and married another Bahamian immigrant, Ida Caroline. The Gibsons' home on Percival Avenue was a welcoming space in which they reared their children, entertained their dreams of economic mobility, and found happiness in each other's love. On the surface, Gibson's life appeared to be progressing remarkably well, but he struggled with feelings of social alienation. Every year, he "filled out an alien card," convinced that his time in the land of Jim Crow was only temporary. The country's white supremacist ethos and practices, he later admitted, prevented him from developing any sort of patriotic feeling toward the United States. His disconnect was particularly visible during World War I, when he informed the local draft board of his refusal to fight for the army. "I said I wasn't going. . . . [T]hose people had never done nothing to me. I can't go over and kill them." Gibson's seven years in the United States had engendered feelings of contempt rather than loyalty toward the federal government. "I ain't got no country," he allegedly shot back when draft officials threatened to deport him to the Bahamas: "This is your country and I won't get killed for it."[2] As far as the twenty-three-year-old old Gibson was concerned, his daily encounters with white supremacy and his immigrant status had rendered him nationless. Though he remained in Miami and his wife eventually became a citizen, Gibson never embraced the idea of the United States as his home.[3]

Such was the context in which Gibson found himself increasingly enamored with the nationalist symbols and language of the UNIA. Joining the association during the early 1920s, Gibson welcomed the opportunity to participate in a transnational movement with organizational roots in the United States, the Caribbean, Latin America, and Africa.[4] Self-consciously cast as a race man with a cosmopolitan outlook, he viewed the UNIA as perfectly suited to his political sensibilities.

Gibson was not alone in his devotion to the UNIA. More than any other organization of the New Negro era, the UNIA achieved remarkable success among black southerners who embraced the principles of self-determination, race pride, and Pan-African unity. Across the region, black women and men proselytized the nationalist messages of the UNIA to family and friends, reached deep into their pockets to finance the organization's various economic ventures, and adopted the *Negro World* as their political Bible. Though frequently maligned as misguided dupes or brainwashed zealots, southern Garveyites were complex political beings whose thoughts and actions defy simplistic characterization. While valiant in defending the movement against its most vocal critics, many UNIA supporters refused to censor their own commentary when the organization moved in what they believed to be the wrong direction. To be sure, southern Garveyites exhibited a deep love and appreciation for Marcus Garvey and the work of the Parent Body in New York, but within the institutional matrixes of their local divisions and chapters, they sought to shape the movement culture in their own image.

The Garvey movement and its cycle of growth, decline, and revitalization offer another glimpse into the variety and complexity of southern black political culture during the New Negro era. Moreover, an analysis of the movement's ebb and flow in the South sheds additional light on the struggles of black women and men to secure what they defined as the essential attributes of modernity: economic autonomy, self-determination in the political sphere, and cultural influence.

Southern Garveyism was born in Hampton Roads, Virginia, where working women and men flocked to the UNIA by the thousands as the organization reaped the benefits of the political unrest gripping the area during and immediately after World War I. Labor upheavals involving longshoremen, domestic workers, and tobacco stemmers combined with local activists' scathing critiques of the racial hierarchies in the American Federation of Labor (AFL) to create heated debates over African Americans' role in the political economy, the viability of biracial unionism, and the most effective response to a labor market highly stratified along the lines of race. Increasingly pushed toward transregional political strategies, black labor activists in the area endeavored to nationalize the larger African American freedom struggle by forming alliances with black trade unionists in other parts of the country. Consequently, on the eve of Garveyism's arrival in coastal Virginia, many African Americans already possessed what might be called a nationalist disposition.

Garvey surveyed the area's political climate and identified Hampton Roads as a fertile recruiting ground for the UNIA. Visiting Newport News in the fall of 1918, the Jamaican-born nationalist befriended a group of local activists who arranged for him to conduct a series of talks at First Baptist Church. Garvey lectured on the need for African Americans to develop independent bases of political and economic power, connect with oppressed blacks in other parts of the world, and commit themselves to the decolonization of Africa.[5]

On the night of Garvey's first address, one hundred women and men signed on with the UNIA's newly formed Newport News Division. "Continuously thereafter," one local later recalled, "members were enrolled to the extent of three or four thousand in less than six months." The Newport News Division also established a paramilitary group, the Universal African Legions; organized a Black Cross Nurses auxiliary; and gained a reputation for hosting some of the most riveting political meetings in the area.[6]

In nearby Norfolk, African Americans also organized a UNIA division. Lively political debates, entertaining music from the division's jazz band, and occasional appearances from Garvey, socialist Hubert Harrison, Henrietta Vinton Davis, and other leaders brought large audiences to gatherings. Strolling down Norfolk's Princess Anne Road on Sunday afternoons, casual observers routinely marveled at the long lines of black bodies proudly flowing into the Negro Longshoreman Hall for the UNIA's weekly gathering.[7]

Though the UNIA welcomed anyone of African descent into its ranks, black laborers constituted a visible majority within the movement. In fact, one of the area's most respected trade unionists, Walter F. Green, served as the president of the Portsmouth UNIA. In Green, the UNIA had a seasoned organizer whose connections and commitment to black working people were nothing short of stellar. On the front lines of a national struggle to improve black workers' position in organized labor, Green participated in local trade union politics, worked earnestly to address the AFL's many racial problems, and played a central role in the formation and growth of the National Brotherhood Workers of America (NBWA). In his capacity as vice president of the NBWA, Green organized railroad workers in various parts of Virginia, contested the discriminatory wage scales of the South's major railways, and forged political relationships with trade unionists and revolutionary socialists in other parts of the country. Though A. Philip Randolph, Cyril Briggs, and other black leftists came to view the Garvey movement as detrimental to black laborers' interests, Green envisioned the UNIA as complementing rather than hindering his activist work.

Particularly intriguing for Green and other blacks in the Hampton Roads area was the UNIA's Black Star Line Steamship Corporation (BSL). Officially launched in the summer of 1919, the BSL anchored Garvey's ambitious plans to create an integrated community of investors, managers, workers, and consumers who would advance the organization's economic agenda. Garvey envisioned BSL ships conducting commercial trade and passenger service between the Americas, the Caribbean, Europe, and West Africa. If adequately supported, Garvey promised, the line would provide employment opportunities for skilled and unskilled black workers along with hefty investment returns for stockholders. Garvey's pleas for financial assistance would not go unanswered in Hampton Roads. Garvey reported approvingly on Afro-Virginians' interest in the BSL and willingness to purchase shares in the fledging enterprise:

> I have been lecturing through the state of Virginia for fourteen days, and I must say that the people all through have been the most responsive to the new doctrine being taught, that of preparation and action in this, the age of unceasing activity. The great enterprise of the Black Star Line is receiving great support in Virginia, and I feel sure that by the splendid start by the people in [this section] that our steamship line will become one of the most prosperous ones afloat.[8]

Contributions from supporters in Norfolk, Portsmouth, and Newport News factored significantly in the BSL's initial success. In fact, as the line moved closer to its maiden voyage, scheduled for October 31, 1919, Garvey became even more dependent on the disposable income of his Virginia followers. On October 25, Garvey made an emergency trip to Newport News to conduct a massive fund-raising drive at First Baptist Church. Speaking to an audience of longshoremen, washerwomen, tobacco stemmers, riveters, and common laborers, Garvey promoted investment in the line as a fiscally responsible decision. He also championed the BSL and the UNIA as vehicles through which Virginia blacks could not only improve their material condition but also reconfigure the geopolitical mapping of the modern world:

> I want you to understand that you have an association that is one of the greatest movements in the world. The New Negro, backed by the Universal Negro Improvement Association, is determined to restore Africa to the world, and you scattered children of Africa in Newport News, you children of Ethiopia; I want you to understand that the call is now made to you. What are you going to do? Are you going to remain to yourselves in Newport News and die? Or are you going to link up your strength, morally, and financially, with the other Negroes of the world and let us all fight one battle unto victory?[9]

Inspired by Garvey's challenge, local blacks purchased nearly ten thousand dollars' worth of BSL shares during his two-day visit to the area. A week or so after his departure, the line's first ship, the *Yarmouth*, embarked on its maiden voyage to the Caribbean.[10] Over the next year, Afro-Virginians continued to purchase shares in the BSL, which procured two additional vessels, the *Kanawha* and the *Shadyside*, in 1920. Allen Hobbs, president of the Norfolk UNIA, prodded his comrades to do all in their power to make the BSL a major success: "Let us take out shares in the Black Star Line in order that we may buy more ships, better ships, and bigger ships. . . . There should be no trouble in making up your minds to help your race rise to a position in the maritime world that you and every other Negro could point to with pride."[11] In many respects, the local fervor for the BSL was part and parcel of the labor capitalist enthusiasm sweeping the nation. "Dozens of enterprises," historian Dana Frank notes in her study of postwar Seattle, "called for workers' dollars in 1919 and 1920, each advertising itself as the best economic niche into which workers' surplus money should ideally flow." These worker-enrichment schemes represented voices on the left that "advocated not a revolutionary transformation but, rather, a creative approach to successfully using capitalism to serve the working class."[12]

The UNIA's central office cultivated this perspective through its marketing schemes. Most BSL advertisements published in the *Negro World* feature an image of Garvey seated behind a desk and dressed in business attire. Standing adjacent to him is an African American man dressed in overalls and a worker's cap with the words "American Negro Labor" printed above him, suggesting the UNIA's targeted demographic. Here and in other BSL advertisements and circulars, Garvey presented the BSL shareholder as the quintessential modern. When an investor purchased shares in the line, he insisted, they accepted the responsibility of protecting themselves, their families, and the race against the vicissitudes of the postwar economic market. Inundated with these powerful images and messages, Garveyites in the Hampton Roads area rallied behind the BSL as an important enterprise and symbol. With great interest and excitement, they monitored closely the line's ventures in the United States and the Caribbean.

UNIA followers also attended to the movement's other activities. Late in the summer of 1920, for example, Virginia's Garveyites sent seven representatives to New York City for the organization's first annual convention, which included an opening ceremony at Madison Square Garden attended by a record crowd of twenty-five thousand, a festive parade down the main streets of Harlem, and the writing of one of the most important documents in Pan-African history, the *Declaration of the Rights of the Negro Peoples of the World*. Especially exciting for the Virginia delegates were the plenary sessions, during which organizers allotted time for division representatives to familiarize each other and the larger black community with the racial dynamics of their particular environment. Taking advantage of the unique opportunity to address black people from as far away as Jamaica, Liberia, and Costa Rica, the Virginians spoke openly and honestly about race and labor relations in Hampton Roads. Moving addresses came not only from Green but from Nellie Whiting of Newport News and Allen Hobbs of Norfolk. All told stories that vividly related the ubiquity of racism in Virginia. "Colored people," Hobbs raged, "are Jim-crowed, segregated, ostracized and given everything but a square deal." Echoing Hobbs, Whiting portrayed African Americans in Newport News as hardworking and morally upright people unfairly subjected to the most insidious forms of racial, economic, and sexual exploitation. Trapped in circumstances not of their choosing, black Virginians faced hardships at every turn. Despite these obstacles, Whiting and her comrades felt confident that a brighter future lay ahead. Not content with simply telling stories about their difficulties, they hoped to leave the convention with a more expansive understanding of the Pan-African world and the UNIA's political project. "I have come here to learn," delegate W. H. Johnson of Norfolk explained, and to "get everything I can to help this organization along."[13]

The 1920 convention underscored the UNIA's remarkable progress in a relatively short period. The demographic profile of its delegates also underscored the need for a more aggressive recruitment strategy down south. Seven of the nine southern delegates at the historic gathering came from Virginia, with one each from North Carolina and Georgia.[14] But by 1919, thousands of black southerners had access to the UNIA's publication, the *Negro World*, at churches, stores, train depots, and poolrooms and considered it a respected news source. The paper's success in the South, particularly its cultivation of a diasporic sensibility among its readers, became a frequent topic of conversation among federal intelligence agents and their informants. Writing to J. Edgar Hoover in December 1919, Bureau agent W. W. Bailey expressed his dismay over the weekly's presence in Nashville, Tennessee, where he found copies available at the "colored" YMCA. Believing that the continued distribution of the *Negro World* would "cause riots, revolutions, rebellions and finally chaos," Bailey urged postmaster general Albert Burleson to ban its sale and distribution.[15] A similar request came from Cocoa Beach, Florida, where one resident complained, "Such literature as this is causing a great deal of unrest among the Negroes in this section and particularly those Negroes who are trying to find some grievance against the white people."[16] Though the *Negro World* targeted no specific age group, many of its opponents expressed special concern about its influence among black youth: warned R. J. Watkins of Fort Smith, Arkansas, "There is no danger immediate or otherwise from our old time darkey but from the present younger crowd."[17]

Convinced that the UNIA had not fully exploited the recruiting opportunities opened up by the *Negro World*, Garvey dispatched several of his top recruiters to the South in early 1921. Several of these organizers were quite familiar with the region's political terrain. Garvey's lead recruiter, the Reverend James Walker Hood Eason, had received his academic and ministerial training from Livingstone College and Hood Theological Seminary in Salisbury, North Carolina. After moving to Philadelphia during World War I, Eason distinguished himself as a socially conscious minister with a deep commitment to racial justice. He joined forces with the UNIA in 1919 and accepted the position of "Leader of the American Negroes" the following year. Eason's travels for the UNIA occasionally brought him into contact with Jacob Slappy, who lacked Eason's credentials in terms of formal education but had been born and raised in Georgia. A railroad laborer who had moved to Pittsburgh in 1917, Slappy possessed a familiarity with the social mores and political rhythms of the South that made him perfectly suited for the UNIA's southern recruitment drive.[18]

Excited to fulfill Garvey's lofty expectations, Slappy, Eason, and other recruiters worked hard to ensure that local divisions were properly organized and adequately equipped to advance the work of the UNIA's central office in New York. Their responsibilities ranged from organizing mass meetings at sympathetic churches to mediating conflict between local members. By the beginning of February 1921, the UNIA's effort was well under way, with Eason leading the charge. The first stop on his southern tour was the small coastal town of Brunswick, Georgia. A brilliant orator, he held a series of mass meetings at Payne Chapel, Mt. Olive Baptist Church, and Shiloh Baptist Church.[19] His visit to Shiloh drew a crowd of 1,000, an impressive showing in a city with a black population of only 7,120.[20] By the end of the month, Eason had raised the local division's membership to seven hundred, sold more than two hundred dollars' worth of stock in the Black Star Line, and generated great interest in the organization's Liberian colonization program. Soon, one local Garveyite predicted, "there will be a thousand in our division wearing the red, black, and green."[21]

Much to the delight of the Parent Body in New York, encouraging recruiting news also came from UNIA organizers in Raleigh, North Carolina; Louisville, Kentucky; Waycross and Savannah, Georgia; and Nashville, Tennessee. Nowhere, however, was the UNIA's expansion more successful than New Orleans. Long regarded as a center of black labor organizing, the Crescent City soon emerged as one of the most dynamic UNIA strongholds. Organized on October 12, 1920, the New Orleans Division (NOD) blended perfectly into the political and cultural world of the city's Uptown district.[22] Uptown, the residential and commercial area located on the downriver side of Canal Street, supplied the movement with some of its most loyal supporters and talented organizers. Sylvester Robertson, a porter who served as the NOD's first president, resided on Philip Street, close to the Negro Longshoremen's Hall on Jackson Avenue, where the division regularly held its meetings. Not too far from Robertson, on the 900 block of 7th Street, lived Mamie Reason, a domestic worker and seamstress who served as the division's first treasurer.[23]

The spatial dynamics and demographic profile of Uptown proved advantageous for UNIA organizers such as Adrian Johnson. After arriving in New Orleans in January 1921, Johnson put tremendous effort into familiarizing himself with the city's residential patterns and cultural complexity. Navigating the political world of Uptown New Orleans was no easy task for newcomers to the area, but Johnson was confident in his ability to strengthen the UNIA's presence in the South's largest city. Of Jamaican descent, Johnson had lived in the Caribbean, Panama, and England and had served in World War I. Arguably the most important stop in his Pan-African journey was the United States, a major destination spot for thousands of West Indians. On May 10, 1920, Johnson traveled from Plymouth, England, to New York City aboard the *Philadelphia*.[24] Not long after his arrival, he gained the attention of Garvey and established himself as one of the movement's brightest organizers. Johnson possessed the rare combination of political passion and diplomatic grace, attributes needed to succeed in New Orleans. His assertion of authority as the representative of the Parent Body in New York never came across as infringing on local division leaders' rights. Though Garvey identified the NOD as underperforming, Johnson treated the division's leaders as coworkers rather than subordinates. Equally impressive was the diplomatic manner in which Johnson interacted with black New Orleans. On his visits to various churches, lodges, and benevolent societies, he effectively championed the work of the Garvey movement without alienating local activists who might have seen the UNIA's expansion as a threat to their own political work. His speeches routinely condemned the "us versus them" mentality that far too often undermined coalition-building efforts in the city. "All Negro organizations," Johnson advised a group of longshoremen in the West Indian Seaman's Social, Benevolent, and Literary Association, "should take up the fight for a better day for the race by uniting their efforts, without losing their specific identity." The UNIA sought not to replace established institutions but to enhance and broaden the struggle for racial justice within and beyond the United States. As Johnson explained, "The motto of 'One God, one aim, one destiny' should appeal to every well-thinking Negro, and they should indeed rally to join the UNIA regardless of the fact that they may be members of [an]other institution."[25]

The combination of Johnson's recruitment style and the UNIA's expansive program struck a responsive chord among many Uptown blacks. The NOD swelled from seventy members in February 1921 to nearly three thousand by the following summer.[26] When Garvey arrived in New Orleans, he reported finding "hundreds of loyal men—good men and true men—who were waiting to receive me through the great work that Johnson had done preparatory to my getting there."[27] Indeed, Johnson's recruiting style netted immediate results in terms of membership and morale. On the eve of the division's first anniversary, leaders claimed a membership of more than four thousand.[28]

Such explosive growth raises the question of why, given the plethora of social, political, and labor organizations in New Orleans, thousands of local blacks rallied behind a New York–based organization whose leader had been subjected to constant public ridicule. In what ways, if any, did the ideological tenets of Garveyism complement the racial and class consciousness of black New Orleanians? Longtime New Orleans resident Millie Charles, the granddaughter of a domestic worker who proudly "donated her dollar to the Garvey movement," attributed the UNIA's success to its articulation of a racial philosophy that had long been a part of the cultural worldview of many local blacks, including her grandmother: "The whole movement back to Africa was what intrigued her, and that kind of philosophy caught her fancy because she always had a sense of curiosity about where she came from and that sort of thing. Even though she worked for whites, she was a proud black woman." In the larger context of New Orleans's spatial and cultural dynamics, according to Charles, "It was kind of easy that a movement such as that would take hold, especially uptown. I am *not* talking about downtown."[29] Uptown blacks had already developed a race consciousness in response to their complex relationship with both Downtown creoles of color and local whites, and that consciousness pointed many Uptown blacks in the direction of the UNIA. Thus, when Garvey arrived in New Orleans with his eloquent statements on the physical, spiritual, and cultural beauty of blackness, he encountered women and men well versed in such rhetoric.

Garvey also encountered women and men with deep concerns about their economic marginality. The postwar recession hit black New Orleans extremely hard as massive layoffs and pay cuts plagued both the service and industrial sectors. The elections of John M. Parker to the Louisiana governorship and Andrew McShane as mayor of New Orleans gave the city's commercial elite even more ammunition in their war with labor over hiring practices, control of the work process, and union recognition.[30] Under these circumstances, thousands of New Orleans blacks invested tremendous hope in the UNIA, particularly its Black Star Line. Between January and June 1921, New Orleans Garveyites acquired nearly eight thousand dollars' worth of BSL shares.[31]

Visiting New Orleans in July, Garvey promoted investment in the BSL as a way not only to elevate the race's economic status but also to advance the political phase of the UNIA's Pan-African agenda. Garvey urged more than fifteen hundred supporters at National Park in Uptown New Orleans to "do for yourselves what others have done for themselves." Though the past few months had been difficult for Garvey and the Parent Body in New York, he still looked optimistically toward the future: "We are going to put up in Africa a Negro government—the greatest government on earth—to protect the Negroes from the world."[32] Garvey's speech contained no specific details about his redemption plans, but his most ardent supporters were more than familiar with his nation-building ideas. In the spring of 1920, Garvey had opened diplomatic discussions with the Liberian government, which had previously begun encouraging African American immigration. Garvey's purpose was twofold: negotiate a land deal in which the UNIA could establish a settlement in Liberia comprised of enterprising black women and men from the West, primarily the United States and the Caribbean, and assist Liberia in augmenting its political and economic power.[33]

New Orleans Garveyites welcomed the opportunity to engage in the politics of statecraft, which many perceived as integral to their status as New Negro moderns. At UNIA conventions, on the pages of the *Negro World*, and at weekly meetings, New Orleanians stated their desire to transform Liberia into a political and economic force in global politics. "The time has come," Elenore Brown insisted in the fall of 1921, "for every nation to look to his own country for a place of safety. We are looking forward to our home, 'Africa for the Africans.' We are proud of the Messiah that God has sent us, and the message of the Great Marcus Garvey is come home; where we shall no longer possess the name nigger, but we shall be a nation respected by the world." T. A. Robinson, too, envisioned great success in the UNIA's future: "This movement will grow commercially and financially in such an extent that the day may not be far distant that we may return to Africa, our home and we will be able to exclaim, we came, we see, and we are satisfied."[34]

This optimistic outlook would be severely tested in the coming months. A series of developments, most notably Garvey's arrest on mail fraud charges in January 1922 and the BSL's official suspension three months later, created great uncertainty among movement supporters. Moreover, accusations of fiscal mismanagement and political disloyalty swirled around movement headquarters in New York. Undeterred by the setbacks, Garvey refused to alter his political course and continued to campaign for his vision on trips to the West Coast, the Midwest, and the South. "Garvey," complained one Bureau of Investigation informant, "seems to have lost sight of the fact that he has ever been indicted, or that he will ever be tried. To talk with him you would think that he has never been in court."[35] After spending two weeks in June in Los Angeles and San Francisco, Garvey returned east via Baton Rouge, New Orleans, Atlanta, Newport News, and Richmond. On June 21, about three thousand of Baton Rouge's eight thousand African Americans, including decorated members of the Universal African Legions and the Black Cross Nurses, marched in a UNIA parade before adjourning to Progressive Baptist Church, where Garvey lectured for nearly an hour and a half. Louisianans clearly still held the group and its leader in very high regard.[36]

Fifty miles to the east, in New Orleans, Jackson Avenue and adjacent streets vibrated with excitement as thousands of women and men flocked to the Negro Longshoremen's Hall to hear Garvey lecture. However, city officials forced the cancellation of the speech because the NOD had failed to secure the proper permit for such a large gathering.[37] A determined Garvey vowed to remain in New Orleans until he could address his loyal following. "The next morning," he later explained, "I took the president and secretary to one of the best firms of lawyers in the city and got an injunction granted to us by Judge Parker, a brother of the Governor of the state, restraining the mayor of the city and the acting Police Commissioner from interfering with the meeting and that night we had one of the biggest meetings ever held by Negroes in the South."[38]

Satisfied with the outcome in New Orleans, Garvey then headed for Atlanta, where he met with Edward Clarke, the assistant grand imperial wizard of the Ku Klux Klan. The two men spent two hours, discussing their organizations and their mutual agreements. Clarke's request for a meeting came at an opportune time for Garvey, who later painted his dalliance with the KKK as diplomacy rather than compromise. Identifying the KKK as the "invisible government of the United States," Garvey sought to solidify his image as a skilled diplomat who possessed the political aptitude to work in the race's best interests.[39]

Continuing to move at a feverish pace, Garvey arrived in Newport News on

June 29. The postwar recession had exacted a heavy toll on the UNIA's membership there, but the turnout for Garvey's speech was impressive. "Long before the scheduled time," wrote journalist Samuel Haynes, "the crowd besieged the Evelyn Theatre, which was beautifully decorated." The mass meeting featured speeches from local division leaders, moving musical selections from the local UNIA band and choir, and crowd-pleasing oratory. If there were any doubts about Garvey's continued popularity in Hampton Roads, the thunderous applause accompanying his arrival at the podium erased them in dramatic fashion. Twice, according to the local UNIA reporter, "he attempted to make a start" but was interrupted as "the building rocked to and fro with the vociferous noise of liberty-loving souls." Once the crowd settled down, Garvey reiterated his commitment to the UNIA's empire-building efforts: "I did not come to Newport News to ask your support in building a church around the corner, to organize a social club or a colored YMCA, but I came here to ask your cooperation to build an empire, a nation." Garvey did not directly refer to his recent meeting with Clarke but assured his audience that a "definite understanding" existed "between the American white man and the UNIA." This was clearly a public relations move in which Garvey aimed to repackage the UNIA as a respectable, law-abiding organization that understood and adhered to the protocols of the Jim Crow South. Here, he benefited from the cooperation of several local UNIA leaders, who strategically portrayed his encounters with authorities as harmonious rather than contentious. The Newport News Division's synopsis of Garvey's visit not only noted the attendance of key city officials but also pointed out their agreement with his message:

> The entire staff of the city's Detective Bureau, the judges of the courts, the Commissioner of Revenue and other city officials heard the address of the President-General and cheered in unison with others. The white press the next morning hailed Garvey as an able advocate of racial progress. The *Daily Press* said that if the Negroes could fully grasp the importance of his program there would be no cause for lynching and burning in the South.[40]

Left unaddressed in this report and others was the extent to which Garvey's conservative rhetoric compromised the political integrity of the movement. His lectures in Louisiana and Virginia criticized African Americans rather than white supremacists even though his targets had made vital contributions to his political relevancy.

This trend continued in Richmond, where Garvey lectured before a packed audience at True Reformers Hall on June 30. Much of his lecture centered on the UNIA's Pan-African agenda and his plans for reorganizing the BSL; however, when a visibly exhausted Garvey turned his attention to his recent travel experiences, his commentary struck some listeners as far too accommodating to the Jim Crow regime: "I have been traveling in the South, and I have no reason to complain about the white man denying me Pullman accommodations. We Negroes do not own the Pullman cars. How many of us own a share of stock in the railroads? As long as the white man owns the railroads and he pays the expenses he will control the railroads and put the Negroes where he pleases. What we need is a railroad of our own. We need government of our own." Fixated on pushing the UNIA's particular brand of black capitalism, Garvey all but waived his right to equal accommodations, a strategy that the *Richmond Planet* described as grating "harshly upon the ears of the colored folks of the Dr. W. E. B. Du Bois type."[41]

The degree to which Garvey's transparent accommodation to the white power structure displeased his black southern followers is difficult to gauge, especially given the absence of detailed UNIA membership records and the *Negro World*'s tendency to publish only positive letters from its readers. Some UNIA supporters may have excused Garvey's conservative utterances as politically necessary in a racially repressive environment. Though he tended to focus on his legal struggles and persecution, his southern followers had also endured surveillance by federal agents, harassment by law enforcement officials, and violent attacks by members of the general public. In Miami, for example, many Garveyites retained painful memories of the brutal beating of the Reverend Ritchie Higgs, a minister at St. James Baptist Church in Coconut Grove who also served as the president of the local chapter of the UNIA. A native of the Bahamas, Higgs promoted armed self-defense, encouraged African Americans to exercise their rights as citizens, and stressed the importance of education to black youth. Infuriated by Higgs's teachings, eight Klansmen kidnapped Higgs outside his home on July 1, 1921, and then mercilessly whipped him for more than two hours. "They beat him up good," recalled Albert Gibson, a fellow Garveyite, "and gave him 48 hours to leave town."[42]

Under these circumstances, many UNIA followers may well have accepted Garvey's conservative rhetoric or his meeting with the Klan as the best way to avoid greater persecution by state authorities, federal agents, and white civilians. They may have viewed Garvey's accommodationist rhetoric as a way to keep others from suffering the same fate as Higgs or Robert B. Moseley, a UNIA organizer brutally beaten in Dallas during the summer of 1922. Whatever their reasoning, many black southerners continued to support the UNIA after Garvey's tour. Even as the "Garvey Must Go Campaign" ramped up in the North, UNIA divisions still flourished in Miami, New Orleans, Hampton Roads, and other locales. In addition to defending Garvey, a significant number of African Americans in the South continued to attend meetings, pay dues, and support their local units.

Understanding the movement's durability in light of its many challenges requires moving beyond Garvey's charismatic personality to consider the power and appeal of local Garveyism. Along with supporting the Parent Body's various projects, black women and men had built vibrant divisions that functioned as important sites for socializing, cultural affirmation, and leadership development. These divisions provided an institutional and discursive space in which laboring people could forge a movement culture, hone their leadership skills, and speak honestly about their political frustrations without fear of reprisal. Such spaces, according to John B. Cary, a dedicated member of the New Orleans UNIA, carried great value for African Americans who desired greater political autonomy within the black public sphere. Working-class blacks, he argued,

> are thinking as they never thought before. They are beginning to realize that they must think and act for themselves. The Negroes have been so often deceived by their supposed leaders that they have reached a conclusion not to be fooled any longer. During the World War they were told by those who represented selfish interests that the war would make the world safe for Democracy. Have such promises benefited the Negro? With the ending of war practically all the liberties of the Negro people have been taken away. Big business and professional politicians, supported by faithless clergy, have fastened the shackles upon the Negro people, and we continue to suffer under the terms of our deceptors.[43]

Impatient with the black leadership class, Cary and other workers yearned for institutions in which their concerns could be articulated, their voices and opinions heard, and their leadership skills cultivated to ensure a better future for themselves and their children. In many ways, the UNIA provided these and other opportunities to its members. As a group of Garveyite women reflected, "The Universal Negro Improvement Association is our church, our clubhouse, our theatre, our fraternal order and our school, and we will never forsake it while we live; neither will our men forsake it."[44]

A strong sense of what the UNIA meant to working-class families can be gleaned from the reflections of Sylvia Woods, a prominent labor activist who grew up in a Garveyite household in New Orleans. Later known for her activities in the Congress of Industrial Organizations and the Communist Party, Woods politically matured within the UNIA's institutional spaces. Though only eleven at the time of the division's founding, Woods vividly remembered the leadership lessons the movement provided:

> There was a little woman there and she used to speak every Sunday. When that woman got up to talk, my father would just sit thrilled and then he'd look at me: "Are you listening?" I'd say, "I'm listening." "I want you to hear every word she says

because I want you to be able to speak like that woman. We have to have speakers in order to get free." And when we got home he would say, "Now what did she say?" I could say it just like her, with her same voice, all of her movements, and everything. This would please him to no end.[45]

Woods's father conceived of the Garvey movement as a space in which he could not only acquire positions of leadership for himself but also prepare his daughter for her future endeavors in politics. For this activist family, the UNIA's significance lay largely in its function as an important site of political development and maturity.

Their Garveyite experience was shaped as much by the day-to-day activities of the local division as the directives and initiatives emerging from the Parent Body in Harlem. This reality also applied to other Garvey supporters, who could not fathom leaving the UNIA even after the BSL's collapse and Garvey's conviction.[46]

Moreover, many women and men who had forged strong bonds with each other during the formative years of the UNIA remained deeply connected to Garvey and his Pan-African agenda. Their dedication surfaced in their letters to the *Negro World*, their dutiful attendance at local meetings, and their generous donations to Garvey's legal defense fund. "We, the Negro peoples of the world," one Virginia Garveyite instructed his comrades, "must put our trust in God and the Honorable Marcus Garvey and follow his footprints so that we will someday take our stand among the mighty nations of the earth. We can build a government of our own to be ruled by black men. As black men ruled in the past so black men can rule in the future."[47]

For UNIA loyalists, the launching of the Black Cross Navigation and Trading Company (BCNTC) in the spring of 1924 provided a counterpoint to critics who insisted the movement had no chance of repeating its previous success. Like the BSL, the Black Cross line focused on trade and passenger service. Garvey promised that after its first ship transported "the first organized group of colonists to Liberia," additional vessels would be acquired to establish a "trade relationship between Negroes of Africa, the United States of America, the West Indies, and South and Central America."[48] A confident Garvey also assured his followers that the BCNTC would be in the position to employ a large number of black workers within a year: "There are hundreds of shiploads of cargo waiting for us in Africa, in the West Indies, [and in] South and Central America to convey back to the United States. Millions can be made for the race in the conveying of raw materials from one part of the world to the other, and the return to them of our finished products."[49]

The formation of the BCNTC revitalized UNIA divisions throughout the South. Writing to the *Negro World* in 1924, H. J. Ward, president of the West Munden

Division in Virginia, noted, "Many people that at one time stood up against the U.N.I.A. are now ready to embark for Africa, and many of those that were onetime members have taken on new life." Down the road from Norfolk, the UNIA division in Newport News experienced a similar revitalization of interest in the movement. When William Sherrill, the UNIA's assistant president-general, arrived in the city, local blacks crowded Liberty Hall to hear more about the progress of the UNIA's Liberian efforts. According to a reporter for the *Newport News Star*, "When we entered the hall in which the meeting was being held, we were struck with the fact that scattered about in the audience were men and women who joined the association when it first started; men and women who were just as enthusiastic now for the organization as they have ever been."[50]

This enthusiastic response to the UNIA's latest colonization plans was not confined to Virginia. Eager to start anew in Liberia, Garveyites in Blytheville, Arkansas, raised enough money to send two of their leaders, R. H. McDowell and J. B. Simmons, to the UNIA's 1924 annual convention. Following his constituency's orders, Simmons asked Garvey and the executive council to provide him with "some definite information concerning the ship that is expected to sail [for Liberia] on September 1."[51]

As long as blacks remained in the United States, many Garveyites believed, they would never achieve complete freedom. "The vast reservoir of intellect of my race in America," John Fenner, the president of the Richmond Division, bemoaned, "is going to waste. Why waste it when if we are granted the proper support in a country all our own we could well develop economically, industrially and make other achievements of merit?"[52] Similar thoughts consumed Sara Maclin of Memphis: "The Negro needs a flag and a country of his own. He can never expect to get any protection or recognition without a government of his own to back up his demands."[53] Agreed J. A. Shazier of Perkinston, Mississippi, "Africa is our motherland and it is up to us to help redeem it. We are the ones to re-establish the land and have an independent government. Let us work to that end as there is no better time than now."[54]

Offering more than just their words of support, UNIA followers in the South and elsewhere invested heavily in the BCNTC. Within months of the line's formation, capital investment in the company soared to more than $750,000. With strong backing from old and new Garveyites, the BCNTC purchased a vessel, the *General Goethals*, in the fall of 1924. On January 10, 1925, the ship, rechristened the *Booker T. Washington*, departed New York for an extensive voyage through the West Indies and Latin America. En route, BCNTC officials had a brief layover in Norfolk, where Garvey and his associates collected additional funds from black laborers thrilled that the organization had resumed its maritime commercial activities. Years later, one crew member remembered the ship receiving "a tremendous welcome from the Negro workers."[55]

Their enthusiasm stemmed from much more than race pride. As their letters to the *Negro World* indicate, southern Garveyites harbored deep concerns about the state of the economy, particularly the rapid pace of mechanization and the problem of labor redundancy. Few articulated this concern with greater clarity than Henry Harrison, a Norfolk longshoreman and ardent UNIA supporter. "The modern inventions," Harrison wrote, "have the greatest tendency to obstruct the earning power of the Negro people, as the majority of our race depends upon the white race for their livelihood." African American women in the domestic sector, he observed, "are constantly replaced by the electric iron, percolator, and the electric stove. . . . Anyone can plainly see that our women are being slowly eliminated of work." His prognosis for black working men was equally bleak. Capital's growing reliance on machines "has reduced the number of our men employed twenty-five or thirty per cent or more. The electrical trucks with trailers and derricks on the docks, the tractors on the farms, machinery in factories are slowly but surely obstructing the earning power of our men, and causing large numbers to be out of work." This surplus of unemployed workers "makes labor so cheap that it is impossible to get a salary at a rate in which we can live comfortable." Such circumstances, in Harrison's estimation, left workers with no choice but to support the "commercial and industrial enterprises of the UNIA."[56] But despite the chorus of black voices promoting the BCNTC, the line performed no better than its predecessor. Only five months after its first voyage, the mechanically troubled and greatly indebted *Booker T. Washington* suspended operations.

The line's failure coincided with another major loss for the UNIA. In early 1925, Garvey began serving a five-year sentence for mail fraud after losing his appeal. Critics celebrated his imprisonment and pending deportation as the dramatic end to a long political nightmare, while his supporters pledged their devotion to the UNIA. "The Honorable Marcus Garvey is in prison," James Rountree of Portsmouth, Virginia, declared in a letter to the *Negro World*, "but as long as God reigns we have no reason to despair. Our honored leader has been guilty of no crime and we have no reason to feel ashamed to support him and proclaim our allegiance to him and in the cause for which he is suffering. We know the price he is paying and we intend to support and encourage him until the end."[57] Notwithstanding these proclamations of support for Garvey, the UNIA was in serious trouble. The organization's most ambitious projects—the development of a settlement in Liberia and the establishment of a sustainable economic enterprise to provide employment opportunities for the masses of black workers—had failed miserably. Moreover, conflict within the Parent Body created a serious crisis of leadership that severely strained local divisions' relationships with the Harlem headquarters. Once again, southern Garveyites had to reassess the movement. Was the UNIA still a viable organization through which to pursue their struggle for political freedom and economic security? And to what extent should Garvey's legal status mandate a change in some of the organization's political tactics? Should local bodies continue to take direction from the Parent Body in New York, or should they assume a greater degree of autonomy? As they wrestled with these and other questions during the second half of the 1920s, UNIA divisions maintained a heightened visibility in many parts of the South. "The spirit of Garveyism is very rampant in the Southland," reported Samuel Haynes, the president of the Philadelphia UNIA and the high commissioner of the Virginia/North Carolina/South Carolina region. Haynes was especially ecstatic about the UNIA's growth in the Tar Heel State, where, as he proudly informed *Negro World* readers, the organization was "progressing by leaps and bounds." The Winston-Salem Division, which had been organized in the early 1920s, stood out as the "largest and most progressive" unit in the state. Its meetings at the Odd Fellows Lodge routinely attracted huge crowds. Much to Haynes's delight, the UNIA also made significant inroads in the nearby city of Greensboro, where youth added much-needed vitality to the local movement: "We have a wonderful club made of young boys and girls who are students of the various institutions in Greensboro."[58]

Several UNIA divisions pledged to devote more of their resources to addressing what they viewed as the most pressing problems facing their local communities, including limited health care facilities, insufficient municipal and social services, and inadequate educational opportunities for black youth. On the social welfare front, the work of the New Orleans Division was by far the most impressive in the South. The NOD organized a free medical clinic, set up an adult night school for leadership training and educational enhancement, and significantly augmented its social welfare programs. These self-help initiatives and community outreach programs did much more than assist blacks in navigating the demands of urban life. They also validated the UNIA as a socially engaged and civic-minded organization in the eyes of outsiders who found the Garvey movement far too detached from the everyday struggles of local people.

Though its community service projects expanded significantly during the second half of the 1920s, the NOD remained committed to the movement's nation-building efforts. New Orleans Garveyites used their community-oriented endeavors to advance one of the most important aspects of the political project of New Negro modernity: the redemption of the African American body politic in both the literal and figurative senses of the term.

On January 21, 1928, the NOD revealed its most ambitious project to date: the opening of "a first class-medical clinic for the poor of our community" in the back of the division's Liberty Hall, a midsized building local Garveyites had purchased in late 1926.[59] New Orleans had the highest black morbidity and mortality rates among U.S. cities with populations of more than one hundred thousand, a phenomenon white New Orleans blamed on African Americans' supposed moral laxity, sexual deviance, and unfitness for urban life. African American leaders, however, attributed the problem to deficiencies in the medical facilities available to blacks, the inefficient manner in which the local government distributed municipal services, and elected officials' general neglect of impoverished residents (both white and black).[60] These debates caught the attention of local Garveyites, who regarded the improvement of African Americans' physical and mental well-being as a central component of their political project and consequently opened the Free Community Medical Clinic in the fall of 1928. Logan Horton, a young African American doctor, served as the clinic's director, while the division's Black Cross Nurses volunteered to provide patient care. "Courtesy and efficient care will always be given to everyone," division leaders assured the local community.[61] Local black leaders praised the ambitious undertaking, and the *Louisiana Weekly*, the city's black newspaper, challenged other organizations to follow suit: "Too much credit cannot be given to this organization for its forward step towards the uplift of fallen humanity. This city and state needs many such clinics to cope with the rising death rate of the colored group in this section."[62]

The Black Cross Nurses auxiliary formed the heart and soul of the NOD. In addition to volunteering their services to the clinic, women in the auxiliary coordinated other aspects of the UNIA's health service program. Like thousands of black women in urban centers across the country, Black Cross Nurses disseminated information on disease prevention, promoted and observed National Negro Health Week, and sponsored weekly symposiums on diet, sanitation, and other disease-prevention measures.[63]

New Orleans Garveyites also attended to the intellectual needs and aspirations of black working women and men. In the fall of 1928, the division established an adult night school that offered classes in basic reading and writing as well as seminars for working women and men immersed in the associational life of their communities.[64] According to Doris Busch, a reporter for the NOD, "A course in public speaking and leadership" was offered for "those whose abilities and fraternal and social connections warrant the need of the course." The adult night school emphasized the need for working-class people to identify problems affecting their lives and then construct effective solutions to generate social change. The work of racial uplift, which entailed extensive investigation of social, economic, and political issues, should not be delegated solely to the black elite. As Lucille Hawkins announced in an advertisement for the NOD's "Education Month," "Everyone is expected to make a special study of race problems."[65]

Welcoming the opportunity to debate a wide range of issues, working women and men did not shy away from critical assessments of Garveyism's organizational weaknesses and strengths, the limitations of the UNIA's nationalist philosophy, and the most viable political strategies available to African Americans. One discussion opened by asking,

1. Is Garvey a Thief?
2. Is Garvey crazy?
3. Is Garvey a fake?
4. Is Garvey diplomatic?
5. How can Marcus Garvey get into Africa?
6. How can Negroes build for themselves a mighty nation?
7. Isn't the Negro's progress in the Western world a sufficient indication that he is going to enjoy equality with the white people within the next few years?
8. How does the U.N.I.A. propose to stop lynching?[66]

The NOD sought to present its members as rational, levelheaded activists willing to engage in complex discussions of how the modern black subject should navigate the cultural, social, and political terrain. Far from needing the intervention and guidance of the black cultural elite, working-class Garveyites were intellectually prepared to assert themselves on the world stage as political actors.

Seeing themselves as the standard-bearers for the southern wing of the UNIA, New Orleans Garveyites eagerly updated the larger Pan-African community on their various endeavors. "Great things are being carried on by the New Negroes in this section," Hawkins enthusiastically told the Negro World; "We are constantly on the firing line—the line that leads to true and lasting emancipation."[67] Indeed, the NOD had covered considerable ground in 1928. In addition to establishing the night school and medical clinic, UNIA followers had thrown their support behind various civil rights initiatives. NOD leader John Cary was outraged at the burdens African Americans bore in the political arena. Similarly, Virginia Young Collins recalled that her father, a staunch Garveyite, campaigned heavily against the poll tax. Conceiving Africa as a political idea rather than simply a geographical place, he viewed his civil rights work as very much a part of the UNIA's African Redemption program and frequently proclaimed to his daughter, "Africa is wherever Africans are."[68]

Throughout its existence, the NOD involved itself in political issues that seemed to belie the UNIA's public image. One such venture involved assisting the National Association for the Advancement of Colored People (NAACP) in one of its most important litigation efforts of the 1920s, a case involving a black sharecropper from Eros, Louisiana, whose two daughters had been brutally murdered by a group of drunken white men on Christmas Day 1928.[69] Predicting that the conviction of these murderers could have a far-reaching impact on the civil rights movement, the NAACP's Walter White instructed George Lucas, the president of the organization's New Orleans chapter, to reach out to local clubs, churches, labor unions, mutual aid and benevolent societies, and civic organizations for financial support for the organization's litigation work.[70]

The New Orleans UNIA answered the call. "Have received a few dollars from local sources," Lucas wrote to White, "among which is a check for twenty dollars from the local Branch of the U.N.I.A., and they promise more help."[71] A former member of the UNIA who had always maintained a good relationship with the local division, Lucas had steered clear of the vitriolic, personal attacks that had marred the relationship between Garvey and the NAACP's most prominent spokespersons. Neutrality, however, was not always easy. In both his writings and his public addresses, Garvey ridiculed the NAACP's liberal integrationist strategies and accused its leaders of lacking a genuine commitment to African Americans. "They would make it appear," Garvey warned, "that they are interested in the advancement of the Negro people of America, when in truth, they are but interested in the subjugation of certain types of the Negro race and the assimilation of as many of the race as possible in the white race."[72] In response, W. E. B. Du Bois dismissed Garvey as a "racist demagogue" who "easily throws ignorant and inexperienced people into orgies of response and generosity."[73] Even more vitriolic in his commentary, Robert Bagnall, director of branches for the NAACP, vilified Garvey as a "Jamaican Negro of unmixed stock, squat, fat and sleek, with protruding jaws, and heavy jowls, small bright pig-like eyes and rather bull-dog face," who was always "devising new schemes to gain the money of poor ignorant Negroes."[74]

Against this backdrop of escalating tension between two of black America's most visible groups, delegates at the UNIA's 1924 convention passed a resolution prohibiting members from joining the NAACP.[75] Nothing good, Garvey argued, could come from any alliance with the civil rights organization. But UNIA members in New Orleans arrived at a different conclusion, not only assisting the NAACP with the Eros murders but collaborating with the organization on several community service projects. To broaden their movement's appeal, Garveyites in Newport News and Norfolk, Virginia, also scripted a plan of action independent of the Parent Body in New York, initiating boycotts against discriminatory white businesses, organizing small-scale cooperatives, and collaborating with civic groups working to increase the black electorate. Much of the initiative for these projects came from Joseph B. Eaton, the president of the UNIA division in Berkeley, a small community on the outskirts of Norfolk. After moving from North Carolina to Berkeley in 1893, Eaton worked intermittently as a common laborer at the Navy Yard and the railroad depot before opening a dry goods store on Liberty Street in 1927. Involved in a variety of organizations, among them the UNIA, the NAACP, and the West Munden Civic League, Eaton promoted himself as the quintessential race man. "I am proud that I am Negro," he proclaimed, and "aside from my allegiance to my Supreme Creator, I place my race ahead of everything else in the world." Eaton's first major foray into local politics came in 1903, when as president of the West Munden Civic League he won city-sponsored improvements in the physical infrastructure of the black neighborhood. Five years later, he joined a group of African Americans defending their property from a railroad company seeking to buy additional land in West Munden. "Practically all my life," Eaton later reflected, "I have been nothing but a fighter."[76]

The UNIA garnered Eaton's greatest support, and he worked hard to keep the Berkeley Division afloat in good times and bad. He also defended the BSL and the BCNTC against their many critics and drove home the message of "Africa for the Africans" during his travels for the organization. Though unequivocal in his support of the UNIA's Pan-African politics, Eaton never wavered in his belief that blacks had the right to enjoy the privileges of American citizenship. Particularly during the second half of the 1920s, he and other Garveyites in the Hampton Roads area rejected the notion that involvement in the UNIA's emigration activity precluded pursuing of voting rights in the United States. Early in the summer of 1929, the Newport News Division established the Negro Political Union. Influenced by a community-wide drive to get African Americans involved in electoral politics, the union sought primarily to "unify the electorate" and thus "obtain through collective action what is impossible by individual efforts."[77] The Norfolk UNIA also threw its weight behind a local campaign to encourage blacks to pay their poll taxes. According to historian Earl Lewis, some within the movement scoffed at the idea of paying "$1.50 just for the privilege of voting for some white man," but others acknowledged the need to raise the number of qualified black voters.[78]

Under Eaton's leadership, Virginia's Garveyites also coordinated an economic response to business elites that infringed on African Americans' political rights. In 1931, the Berkeley Division "called for the 'boycotting' of certain merchants in our city because of their attitude toward our race, as to politics and also for their using certain disrespectful remarks about the Negro on Election Day. . . . I have not given one week's support to a white grocer since 1899 and advocated those methods to every Negro as far as general contact is concerned."[79]

Sporadic rather than sustained, the UNIA's political initiatives failed to transform power relations in Virginia as well as to prevent the steady exodus of blacks from the Garvey movement during the late 1920s. As the Great Depression tightened its grip on the African American community, the UNIA's influence declined considerably, not only in Hampton Roads but throughout the country. Worsening economic conditions not only limited southern Garveyites' ability to contribute to their division's various programs but also led many to question the wisdom of the organization's political agenda. The economic devastation created by the depression vividly revealed the limits of black enterprise as a strategy for collective economic advancement, while the episodic nature of the UNIA's political engagements lessened its attraction for African Americans, who were increasing their demands on the government. In response, a few divisions reflected critically on the need to shift the movement's direction. Noting that the local community had grown tired of the "monotonous repetition of previous programs," the Winston-Salem UNIA created the Colored Community Civic Circle to respond to the immediate needs of African Americans. The Civic Circle implemented an employment bureau, a bureau of information, a dressmaking department, a night school, and free legal service. Lest the division's service work be misconstrued as deviating from the UNIA's original mission, local leaders reiterated that the association had never been concerned solely with resettlement in Liberia: "The objects and aims of the organization was not to take them to Africa, as many have thought, but to lay a foundation in racial improvement, wherever they may chance to live."[80] Despite these and similar efforts, the UNIA struggled to retain old members, let alone attract new ones. A small cadre of committed nationalists carried the torch of Garveyism well into the civil rights and Black Power eras, but by the 1930s, most UNIA divisions functioned along the margins of black political life.

Though the ebbs and flows of the Garvey movement reveal a great deal about the ideological transformations in black political culture during the 1920s and 1930s, some New Negro organizations and intellectuals in the South found the depression and New Deal years less ideologically jarring than did their black nationalist counterparts. Some had already embraced a leftist perspective. Though the 1930s represented a watershed moment in terms of African Americans' relationship to the U.S. Left and organized labor, calls for a more labor-oriented civil rights struggle and a more strident critique of capitalism echoed in several black political and intellectual circles during the second half of the 1920s. As Garveyism faded, some New Negro activists and intellectuals had already begun to push black thought and politics in a more labor-oriented, leftist direction.

FIVE

The South Will Be Invaded

The same year that Marcus Garvey commenced his five-year sentence for mail fraud at the federal penitentiary in Atlanta, Abram Harris published a thought-provoking article in which he lamented the rising racial consciousness in black America. "Conflicting race psychologies," he argued, "vitiate any reapproachment between white and black workers and thus render impossible the unanimity of feeling and purpose necessary for independent working-class action in politics." Harris challenged his forward-thinking peers to take the lead in curing the "black masses" of the "color psychosis" that had developed as a result of their involvement in "reactionary organizations" such as Garvey's Universal Negro Improvement Association (UNIA): "If the Negro's ever-increasing self-assertion is not guided by Negro intellectuals possessed of catholic vision, it will build within the present order a self-illuminating black world oblivious to things white."[1]

Not everyone shared Harris's perspective. Far less concerned with the growing assertions of race pride emanating from African Americans, Thomas L. Dabney, a close friend of Harris during their undergraduate years at Virginia Union University, put forth a different reading of the political landscape. Opposed to the idea that the black masses required intellectual guidance from above, Dabney denounced what he viewed as myopic and often inadequately researched representations of African Americans as insufficiently class-conscious. A keen observer of U.S. labor relations, Dabney had witnessed firsthand the unwavering devotion of hundreds of black workers to trade union politics even when such devotion failed to translate into meaningful improvement in their material circumstances. "That Negro workers are amenable to the philosophy of trade unionism," he opined, "is attested by the fact that more than 200,000 Negroes belong to trade unions."[2] To deepen his readers' understanding of this important dimension of black working-class activism, Dabney devoted a great deal of his intellectual work to examining African Americans' complex relationship to organized labor. Of the many unions he examined in his writings, few intrigued him more than A. Philip

Randolph's Brotherhood of Sleeping Car Porters (BSCP). Organized in the summer of 1925, the Brotherhood focused on three important goals: improving the material conditions of porters and maids who worked for the Pullman Palace Company; gaining recognition as their representative body; and wiping out all vestiges of racial paternalism within and beyond the world of labor.[3] Though media coverage of the Brotherhood focused primarily on its activities in New York and Chicago, the BSCP was no stranger to black southerners. As Dabney discovered during a 1928 research trip, "In far Southern cities like Knoxville, Tennessee, Jacksonville, Florida, and Atlanta, Georgia, prominent Negroes and rank and file porters spoke in high terms of the Brotherhood and Mr. Randolph."[4] Unwilling to stand on the sidelines as various leaders and intellectuals debated the most effective strategies to improve African Americans' economic condition, BSCP followers in the South embraced the union's political vision and its emphasis on the unionization of African American workers. In Norfolk, for example, Brotherhood members defended the BSCP's unionization strategy as providing black Americans with "their only chance for economic emancipation."[5] Linking up with the Brotherhood provided black southerners with much more than an organizational vehicle for improving their economic status. It also connected them to a vibrant intellectual world in which women and men debated everything from political economy to religion. For many black southerners, the entry point into this world was the *Messenger*. Randolph and his colleague, Chandler Owen, had founded the *Messenger* monthly in 1917 with the goal of providing a socialist perspective on African American politics and culture as well as international issues. The cofounders eventually added Theophilus Lewis, George Schuyler, and James Ivy, among other talented writers and critics, to the staff. The magazine never abandoned its focus on literature and the arts, but after Randolph founded the BSCP in 1925, the *Messenger*'s labor section became more focused on that union's battle against the Pullman Company. As they sought to better understand how the union's message applied to their everyday lives, many BSCP members and sympathizers turned to the *Messenger* for political guidance and information about union developments. Unlike their counterparts in Chicago, New York, and St. Louis, Brotherhood districts in the South did not regularly hold mass meetings. Moreover, the Brotherhood's key spokesperson, Randolph, rarely ventured to the South during the union's early years. As a result of these regional dynamics, the information contained in the *Messenger* proved quite useful for Pullman porters based in the South yet interested in the inner workings of the organization, the comings and goings of Randolph, and the BSCP's negotiation efforts with the Pullman Company.

Much to its credit, the *Messenger* also offered intellectual stimulation and entertainment for BSCP members. Despite a limited budget, the journal featured provocative cultural critics and political thinkers unafraid to push readers out of their comfort zones. Thus, the *Messenger*'s monthly arrival became a highly anticipated event for some BSCP members in the South. As one Dallas follower wrote in 1927, "Among my Xmas mail, there was nothing that pleased me more than to receive a December copy of the *Messenger*, sent to me by one of the Brotherhood." Signing his letter "Sunny South," the correspondent praised the contributions of J. A. Rodgers and Richard F. Paige, even though the latter's agnostic stance on religion troubled the writer: "Several statements in different articles became so much a part of me, until they are almost my constant companions (as any good thought will be)."[6] Not just the *Messenger* but the Brotherhood as well became interwoven into the political and social lives of other black southerners between 1925 and 1928.

One of the most amazing things about the Brotherhood's initial success in the South was the willingness of its early supporters to withstand constant harassment from the Pullman Company and law enforcement officials. To counter the Brotherhood's activities, Pullman sent black agents to speak out against the union, transferred veteran porters to less desirable routes in retaliation for their involvement with the BSCP, and coerced porters into signing petitions of allegiance to the Employee Representation Plan (ERP), the company union. According to a 1927 report from the Brotherhood chapter in Jacksonville, Florida, "The members of the district are going through some of the worst sort of intimidation ever perpetrated by the Pullman Company. Everywhere they are being threatened by the superintendent and the stool pigeons. This district has been visited constantly by the Negro agents, who are holding meetings where the chief sport seems to be damning the Brotherhood of Sleeping Car Porters."[7]

Despite relentless opposition from the Pullman Company as well as certain segments of the black community, the BSCP maintained a small yet dedicated cadre of supporters in the South. Between the Brotherhood's founding in 1925 and the highly controversial postponement of its 1928 strike, the union established a visible presence in several southern cities. Its emphasis on the inextricable link between the Pullman porters' fight for economic justice and the black community's struggle for racial equality broadened its appeal beyond the world of labor.[8] In Dabney's assessment, "A very significant thing about Negro opinion on the porters' organization is that they regard it not as a struggle of the porters but as a struggle of the whole race. In other words many Southern negroes feel that the race should rally to a man in the struggle of the porters so as to better the social status of our group."[9]

Beyond their sense of racial obligation, some African Americans gravitated to the Brotherhood as a consequence of their strong views on the benefits of unionization. Though the postwar political climate presented numerous challenges for black labor organizers, a segment of the population remained resolutely committed to class struggle. To shift labor relations in their favor, they participated in strikes, supported existing and new labor unions, and promoted collective action. Commenting on the state of working-class protest in 1925, cultural critic George Schuyler reminded his northern readers that black labor activism in the South had a rich and enduring legacy: "Contrary to the general opinion of the Southern Negro being more backward, he is the more forward in organizing his labor power."[10] The validity of Schuyler's regional perspective would be greatly tested as the BSCP squared off against one of the nation's most powerful businesses.

Established in 1867, the Pullman Company profited immensely from its luxury sleeping cars, which were attached to many of the passenger trains crisscrossing the United States during the Roaring Twenties. To travelers who purchased a Pullman ticket, the company promised first-class comfort and safety. Of course, a critical component of that "first-class" experience was the high-quality service rendered by the African American porters. These men constituted a significant percentage of the Pullman Company's African American workforce, which by the 1920s totaled twelve thousand. Pullman's status as the single-largest employer of African Americans, along with its financial support of important black American cultural and social institutions, led some observers to regard the company as an unblemished friend of the African American community, deserving the community's gratitude and devotion. To protect its public image as well as stymie dissent within its ranks, the Pullman Company created the ERP in 1920. The ERP's stated purpose was to provide workers with a vehicle through which they could report their labor grievances; however, many BSCP leaders dismissed "the Plan" as the worst form of welfare capitalism. "This is the Company's union," Randolph complained in the summer of 1925; "the Negro officials of the union have no rights which the Company is bound to respect. This fact is fully and clearly shown by a number of cases adjusted under the Employee's Representation Plan. It is merely calculated to impress the Porters with the idea that they have a union when in reality they only have a fake union, a sham, a union which is of no earthly benefit to them because it is owned and controlled body and soul by the Pullman Company."[11]

Randolph singled out the ERP but also had issues with the Pullman Porters Benefit Association of America (PPBAA), which had been created in 1915. The PPBAA provided disability, sick, and death benefits to all black male Pullman workers who paid their annual dues (twenty-eight dollars for men under age forty-five and thirty-two dollars for those above it). According to historian Beth Tompkins Bates, "Porters valued the sense that PPBAA members looked after one another because it was one of the few safety nets available."[12] Under the leadership of Perry Parker, the PPBAA maintained a close relationship with the Pullman Company, which financed the association's administrative costs and its annual conventions. These gatherings drew members from all over the country, including such southern cities as Tampa, Jacksonville, New Orleans, Birmingham, Nashville, Dallas, and Richmond.[13] Over time, a vocal group of PPBAA members became disenchanted with the association's close relationship with company officials.

No one recognized the limitations of the PPBAA and the ERP more than Ashley Totten, a Pullman porter who in 1925 reached out to Randolph in the hopes of persuading the *Messenger* editor to speak to a group of porters about forming an independent union. The partnership seemed ideal for Randolph, an outspoken advocate of labor who lacked an institutional base in trade union politics. On June 25, Randolph, Totten, and Roy Lancaster gathered at the home of longtime Pullman porter William H. Des Verney to deliberate on the "many problems confronting the porter employees of the Pullman Company."[14]

A month after their summit at Des Verney's home, Randolph and his associates announced the formation of the BSCP, which on August 25 held its first mass meeting in Harlem. More than five hundred porters filed into the beautifully decorated auditorium of the Imperial Lodge of Elks on 129th Street, where they heard addresses from Randolph, Lancaster, Schuyler, and W. J. Orr of the Locomotive Engineers Union. Randolph declared the Brotherhood's principal objectives: the implementation of "240 hours or less in regular assignment as a basis of their monthly pay, with compensation for overtime; pay for 'preparatory time' in making ready the car to receive the passenger before the train leaves the terminal station"; and the elimination of double shifts. Randolph also called for an end to the paternalistic relations that had defined interactions among porters, the company, and its passengers.[15]

With its broad political agenda, the Brotherhood gained a strong following in several cities in the North and Midwest, most notably New York and Chicago. Growing numbers of Pullman porters broke ranks with the ERP and aligned with the Brotherhood. Elated over the union's progress, Frank Crosswaith, a labor organizer and one of the Brotherhood's most vocal supporters, celebrated the union's initial growth as indicating a monumental ideological shift in black America:

> In the short space of four months, more than 45 percent of 12,000 Pullman Porters
> of the nation have rallied to the bugle call of unionism and class solidarity. These
> Negro workers are breaking traditions and establishing the fallacy too long accepted
> as true, that Negro workers can't be organized and that they constitute the "scabs"
> of America. They have established the unmistakable fact that a new type of Negro is
> now facing America, and America must heed his presence.

After documenting the Brotherhood's early progress, Crosswaith revealed the union's even more robust and geographically expansive recruiting agenda: "Not content with the remarkable success of 1925, the Brotherhood is out to eclipse its record for that year by energetically pressing forward a program in 1926 which should win the genuine admiration of everyone truly interested in the struggles and triumphs of all workers." Toward this goal, he continued, "organizers will be sent into every state where Pullman porters are located." According to Crosswaith, Randolph had already solidified plans for a trip to the "Far West," and in the coming months, "The South will be invaded."[16] That daunting task went to Des Verney, a native of Savannah, Georgia, who had worked as a Pullman porter for thirty-seven years. Forfeiting his seniority rights and his pension, he had recently resigned from his job to assist the BSCP in "the great cause of emancipating the Pullman porters."[17] Few men, if any, better understood the inner workings of the Pullman Company and the lengths to which management would go to undermine the Brotherhood's recruitment activities. Despite his knowledge of the difficulties ahead, Des Verney leaped at the opportunity to carry the Brotherhood's message to various corners of the South.

Early in 1926, he embarked on his southern tour, which included stops in Savannah, Atlanta, Charleston, Jacksonville, New Orleans, Richmond, and Montgomery. On isolated street corners, in the waiting rooms of railroad stations, and in dimly lit dives, Des Verney shared the Brotherhood's program with interested porters and maids. He also reached out to wide sectors of the black community, particularly those that had been inundated with Pullman propaganda. Several black institutions recently had become mouthpieces for the ERP. Late in the summer of 1925, for example, the Improved Benevolent Protective Order of Elks had used its annual convention in Richmond to promote the ERP as an ideal form of collective action for black workers. "Unionism," the Elks declared, "is calculated to do our people all sorts of harm and injure them with the employing class in America. . . . We recommend that the methods used by the great industrial organizations of the country in relation to employee representation plans be used as a pattern to form organizations of workers within our group, wherein the interests of both employer and employee will be preserved."[18] Similar commentary on the value of the ERP emanated from other institutions in the black community. On his first organizing drive down south, Des Verney discovered that "presidents of colleges throughout the South have been warned by the company that no students of their institutions will be given work during the summer months if they allow anyone to speak to them in reference to the brotherhood organization."[19]

This move was hardly surprising given the growing militancy of black college youth, who, like the BSCP, were fighting white paternalism. From Fisk University in Nashville to Florida A & M in Tallahassee, black students rebelled against draconian disciplinary codes, philanthropic and governmental efforts to homogenize the curricular offerings of black colleges, and the acquiescence of conservative black leaders to the white establishment.[20] Very much aware of black youth's rising militancy, Pullman officials worked hard to limit black collegians' contact with the Brotherhood, efforts that frustrated Des Verney but did not destroy his resolve to plant "the seeds of the brotherhood" in the South.[21]

Des Verney and the Brotherhood had the backing of two of the region's most important black newspapers, the *Norfolk Journal and Guide* and the *Savannah Tribune*. Since the BSCP's formation, the two weeklies had reported on its progress, kept their readers abreast of Randolph's activities, and promoted the benefits of independent unionism. Challenging those who condemned the Brotherhood as detrimental to the race, the *Savannah Tribune* welcomed the union as a much-needed addition to the black political arena. It also dismissed the company union model as insufficient. Calling the porters' pay "wretched," the *Tribune* shot down the idea that Pullman management adequately cared for its workers: "For the small pittance given them, they are compelled to render hours of service that would in no manner be tolerated by any other set of workers in this country."[22]

Even more extensive in its coverage of the BSCP than the *Tribune*, the *Norfolk Journal and Guide* published several stories on the Brotherhood in the months before Des Verney's tour of the South. Writers reported on mass meetings in Chicago and New York, complaints against the ERP, and the Pullman Company's relentless harassment of BSCP leaders and members. Providing a counter to those who claimed that the Brotherhood could not penetrate the South, the *Journal and Guide* ran a February 13, 1926, feature on the union's progress with a particular focus on Des Verney, who, the paper reported, had "made exceptional progress among a ridiculously conservative group, and is now preparing to leave Jacksonville to carry the battle into New Orleans and vicinity."[23]

As Des Verney wrapped up his southern tour, Randolph focused on getting the Pullman Company to the negotiation table through the mediation provisions of the recently passed Railway Labor Act, a landmark measure that promoted collective bargaining, arbitration, and mediation to resolve labor disputes. It granted railroad workers the right to "organize and bargain collectively through representatives of their own choosing." On their recruitment trips and in the *Messenger*, Brotherhood leaders particularly emphasized the act's provision that

> if any dispute shall arise among a carrier's employees as to who are the representatives of such employees designated and authorized in accordance with the requirements of this chapter, it shall be the duty of the Mediation Board, upon request of either party to the dispute, to investigate such dispute and to certify to both parties, in writing, within thirty days after the receipt of the invocation of its services, the

name or names of the individuals or organizations that have been designated and authorized to represent the employees involved in the dispute, and certify the same to the carrier. Upon receipt of such certification the carrier shall treat with the representative so certified as the representative of the craft or class for the purposes of this chapter.[24]

Claiming to have the support of more than 50 percent of Pullman porters, the BSCP solicited the services of the Railway Mediation Board. On October 7, 1926, the Brotherhood requested the board's assistance in securing a conference with the Pullman Company over wages, working conditions, and union recognition. To many black southerners, the union's struggle against Pullman amounted to a spiritual battle between good and evil in which every person of "good morals" should fight for the advancement of not just the porters but the race as a whole. Framing the Brotherhood's unionization efforts in moral terms, an unidentified porter from the South praised Randolph as "a man among men because he has no price; he cannot be bought or sold—so brothers, pay your dues and be led by your honorable leader A. Philip Randolph. I feel that through the powers handed down to this man by the Supreme and Almighty God, Justice will conquer and injustice will lose. As I can see it, way down in my heart, we are on the right road to success and progress."[25]

On its road to success and progress, the BSCP endured a great deal of opposition from the Pullman Company, the ERP, and elected officials. Informants routinely reported the activities of BSCP recruiters and sympathizers to Pullman, which in turn relied on law enforcement officials to support its union-busting efforts. Nowhere was this partnership between Pullman and the state more visible than Jacksonville. Though far from a hotbed of political radicalism, the North Florida city definitely radiated some of the political energy of the New Negro movement. It had been a center of robust electoral activity in the immediate postwar years, boasted active UNIA chapters, and claimed a very vibrant cultural scene. To build up the Brotherhood in his hometown, Randolph dispatched one of his best organizers, Bennie Smith, in March 1927. Smith arrived in Jacksonville and checked into the Richmond Hotel, located in the heart of the black neighborhood La Villa, and according to the *Pittsburgh Courier* "was very successful in getting new members."[26] Pullman Company officials responded by sending representatives to the city. Among them was C. C. Webb of Chicago, who reached Jacksonville on April 20 for the express purpose of disrupting the BCSP's work. Webb not only warned Pullman porters to stay away from the Brotherhood but also alerted local authorities to Smith's activities. On the morning of May 18, two detectives ordered Smith to report immediately to police headquarters downtown. Smith did so and met with police chief A. J. Roberts. Roberts announced that Jacksonville would not tolerate distribution of the *Messenger*, which he declared was a communist propaganda tool that preached social equality between the races. Roberts then ordered Smith to leave the city immediately.[27]

The next day, W. H. Mitchell, one of the Pullman Company's local black officials, made three trips to Smith's hotel room to warn that "if he remained in Jacksonville he would do so at the risk of his life." On May 22, Smith sent Randolph a telegram in which the organizer said that despite the "grave seriousness" of the situation and the "personal danger" involved, he would remaining in Jacksonville "and meet the consequences." "The Brotherhood's cause," Smith insisted, was "so righteously important that a firm stand should be taken. . . . I am willing to make the supreme sacrifice."[28]

Randolph responded by ordering Smith to "leave immediately." Smith somewhat reluctantly complied.[29] Word of the events in Jacksonville spread as the *Pittsburgh Courier*, the *New York World*, and other northern black newspapers condemned Jacksonville authorities' actions. The *Jacksonville Journal*, however, challenged the portrayal of the city as antiunion, contending that objections to Smith's activities resulted not from his work on behalf of the BSCP but rather from his distribution of the *Messenger*: "Mr. Smith's mission in Jacksonville" was "in his personal financial interest and involved the distribution among colored people of Jacksonville of a peculiarly scurrilous and inflammatory collection of literature."[30] An infuriated Randolph denounced these charges as "absolutely untrue" and excoriated the *Journal*'s coverage of the matter and perpetuation of the Pullman Company's lies. "The brotherhood challenges anyone to produce a single piece of literature distributed by Mr. Smith in Jacksonville among colored people which was scurrilous or inflammatory. The Brotherhood also challenges anyone to produce a single piece of literature by Mr. Smith which did not relate directly to the organization of the Pullman Porters."[31]

The Smith incident confirmed Jacksonville's status as a key battleground in the fight between the Pullman Company and the Brotherhood. Throughout the union's formative years, Pullman routinely sent spies to the Florida city to undermine the BSCP's endeavors. But John W. Darby, the secretary-treasurer of the union's Jacksonville district, refused to back down. A married father in his early fifties, Darby had worked as a Pullman Porter for more than fifteen years. His knowledge of both the company and the city proved useful as he worked to transform Jacksonville into a Brotherhood stronghold. Shortly after Smith's departure, Darby reported that "the Brotherhood in Jacksonville is in excellent condition and the members have not been affected by the lying propaganda of the company and its hired snoopers." In the face of Pullman's threats to fire Darby and his men, he declared, "The real red blooded porters of the Jacksonville division have pledged their honor that they mean to stick with the brotherhood all the way, for they are confident that victory is assured if the porters and maids will just be women and men enough to hold out to the bitter end."[32]

The Brotherhood also elevated its status among African Americans in Virginia, where the *Norfolk Journal and Guide* again led the way in defending the union against its white opponents. The *Guide*'s relationship with the Brotherhood shifted noticeably in the summer of 1927, when the U.S. Mediation Board threw out the BSCP's case after the Pullman Company refused to participate in arbitration. The newspaper subsequently took a much harder stance against the company. "It is impossible to escape the conclusion," opined the *Journal and Guide*, "that both moral and statutory law is on the side of the Brotherhood and against the Company."[33] Though cautious in its language, the *Journal* joined the *Pittsburgh Courier*, the *Oklahoma Dispatch*, the *Crisis*, and other black periodicals in standing fully behind the BSCP's efforts to gain union recognition.

The BSCP's institutional supporters in Norfolk also included Grace Church and St. John's African Methodist Episcopal Church, both of which opened their doors to Des Verney when he visited the Tidewater region in late August.[34] In his address at Grace Church, he restated the porters' labor grievances, clarified misconceptions about the Brotherhood's larger political agenda, and reiterated the union's need for community-wide support across class lines. The *Messenger* later noted that Des Verney's efforts in "the Virginia territory have been crowned with unlooked for success."[35]

Encouraging news also emerged from New Orleans, where the Brotherhood leaned on the organizing skills of Oneida Brown, a local civil rights and labor activist whose husband was porter John C. Brown. Oneida Brown deplored the wages paid to Pullman porters and declared, "The standard of living in this country continues to rise and the needs of the people must be met . . . and that can only be done by receiving reasonable wages."[36] Her biggest challenge as a recruiter entailed convincing the porters to move against their employer. "The Pullman Company," she explained, "holds a big stick over the heads of these men and we are bending all our energy towards meeting them." To counter the company's intimidation tactics, Brown turned to those porters whose work brought them into contact with BSCP members in other parts of the country: "Our men who have the advantage of running to New York and Los Angeles and other points east and west, are untiring in their effort to acquaint the men who have short runs with the wonderful work being done by the leaders of the Brotherhood." Although the district's membership rolls were not expanding at the rate Brown and other Brotherhood officials desired, she still foresaw victory: "It will not be long before the New Orleans District will be one of the strongest supporters of the Brotherhood, both numerically and financially."[37]

Very much committed to the BSCP's regional expansion, Randolph began plans for a southern tour. Since the Brotherhood's formation in 1925, Randolph's only trip to the South had been a visit to North Carolina, where he lectured in Durham, Raleigh, and Asheville during the spring of 1926. Traveling to Dixie carried particular risks for such a staunch critic of racism and labor exploitation, but Randolph increasingly felt pressured by his southern constituency's clamor for his presence. On November 26, 1927, the *Pittsburgh Courier* unveiled Randolph's plans to tour the South at the beginning of the next year. Now was the time, the paper insisted, for Randolph to engage the people of the Southland and counter the ERP representatives in the region. "Realizing that the Pullman Company recruits most of its new men from the heart of Dixie," the *Courier* noted, "Randolph, general organizer of the Brotherhood of Sleeping Car Porters and editor of 'The Messenger,' is to shortly invade the section in a speaking tour designed to build up sentiment favorable to the porters' union."[38] Randolph's itinerary included New Orleans, Atlanta, Durham, and Jacksonville, all of which stood to reap immense benefits from his visits. Along with fielding questions about the state of the Brotherhood's negotiations with the Pullman Company, Randolph could infuse local districts with greater energy. As Brown explained, "There are still a large number of men who are not interested, or who have not made up their minds to join the organization, men of family who are just barely making enough to keep themselves going properly yet they hesitate. Mr. Randolph could be of great assistance in convincing them that they are standing in their own light." Because the Great Mississippi River Flood earlier in the year had limited porters' mobility, Brown thought that the BSCP leaders needed to bring their message to the South: "The deplorable thing about our district is that a large number of men have short runs and do not know what the Brotherhood stands for, they are afraid to inquire for fear someone might think they belong to the organization. . . . It is this class of people that a mass meeting by one of the representatives would benefit."[39] News of Randolph's impending visit circulated rather quickly throughout the South, where BSCP members and longtime readers of the *Messenger* planned extensively for his arrival. Their fervor quickly caught the attention of Pullman spies, along with a few politicians. Jacksonville mayor John Alsop threatened to jail Randolph "and anybody else who has anything to do with his meeting."[40] Fearing for Randolph's safety, the city's BSCP leaders advised him to cancel his visit. Racial tensions had remained high in the city in the wake of Smith's visit. Pullman agents had spent two weeks there in November, meeting with law enforcement officials and portraying the BSCP as a dangerous threat to the status quo.[41] Randolph ultimately called off his trip, leading his followers in New Orleans to tell the *Messenger*, "We were terribly disappointed when Mr. Randolph cancelled his engagement with us due to the letter he received from the Mayor of Jacksonville, Fla. Those of us who have not heard him were looking forward to a big treat and a tremendous boost for our district. The men were making arrangements to entertain him and to impress him how we of the southland feel towards the movement and to pledge him our hearty support."[42] Conspicuously silent on the matter, Randolph never explained the cancellation, but it is likely that he feared that a run-in with local politicians or law enforcement officials would compromise the union's progress on the next big item on its agenda: a strike vote.

In light of the limited powers of the Railroad Mediation Board and the Interstate Commerce Commission, Randolph increasingly viewed a strike vote as the only way to get the Pullman Company to the negotiating table. To demonstrate the rank and file's readiness to walk off the job, Randolph announced plans to conduct a strike vote among Pullman porters and maids. Ever the diplomat, Randolph worked hard to prove the union's militancy to its members without alienating sympathizers troubled by the thoughts of a massive walkout. As he explained, "A strike vote doesn't mean that the porters will necessarily strike. A strike vote is intended to show to what extent the men are committed to their demands, how firmly they believe in their cause, and how many are willing to strike if necessary."[43]

Entering the national debate over the Brotherhood's latest threat, the *Norfolk Journal and Guide* published a sympathetic editorial on Randolph's leadership and the BSCP tactics: "Every effort the Brotherhood has made to utilize the agencies set up by the Government to deal with controversies arising between interstate transportation companies and their employees has met with failure, but the approach has been dignified, straightforward, and comprehensive in citation of causes." Although the editors believed that a strike would be suicidal given the economic climate, the paper encouraged Brotherhood members to stay the course: "The porters must resolve themselves to stick through the fight; they will ultimately win much for which they are contending if they will remain in the fight; to falter or to faint will mean virtually their re-enslavement for a hundred years."[44]

In April, porters and maids voted 6,053–17 in favor of a walkout, which officials scheduled for June 8. Hotly debated in many of the major black newspapers, the BSCP's vote elicited considerable discussion and organizing down south. Brown, Darby, and other stalwarts updated members and sympathizers on upcoming events while contesting false information from the Brotherhood's chief nemeses. Under the watchful eye of Pullman spies, BSCP organizer S. E. Grain spent three weeks in Norfolk, encouraging members, before traveling to Richmond in hopes of adding to the ranks of Brotherhood supporters. Perhaps feeling as if black America had placed too much emphasis on literary and cultural achievements, he stressed the material needs of black working women and men: "The Negro has grown to be great intellectually, but economically he is still a babe, and will remain a babe until the toilers of our race, which is 98%, organize for a higher wage." For the race to develop economically, all of black America would have to buttress the Brotherhood's work: "We ask the people of Richmond and the South in general to get behind the organization. Help them morally and financially. They are struggling against a 5 million dollar corporation."[45]

On the eve of the proposed walkout, Brotherhood members in Norfolk reiterated their confidence in Randolph, who had come under even greater criticism from conservative black leaders, particularly those aligned with the Pullman Company. As had been the case for black labor activists in the area since World War I, BSCP members turned to the *Norfolk Journal and Guide* to defend both their leader and their actions: "We the Pullman porters of the Tidewater zone," they declared, "wish to express our faith and confidence in the Brotherhood of Sleeping Car Porters and its leaders." Believing that their actions had been unfairly maligned as reckless, the porters noted their awareness of the difficulties involved in their challenge to the Pullman Company. "We understand," the men confessed, "that no fight, as ours can be won overnight."[46] Victory required patience as well as the courage to blaze a new path to economic and political independence.

To further demonstrate their confidence in themselves, Randolph, and the Brotherhood, the Norfolk porters denounced the *Pittsburgh Courier* and its editor, Robert L. Vann, who had supported the Brotherhood for two years but now became one of the union's most vehement critics. Proving once again that the power struggles of the New Negro era frequently pitted black workers against not just capital but also prominent black spokespersons, BSCP members in Norfolk claimed the right to choose their own leaders: "For three hundred years the white people have been able to pick Negro leaders for Negroes. We wonder if Mr. Vann knows that if one pays the fiddler one can call the tune. So we, the Pullman porters, at this stage are paying the fiddler and we expect to call the tune. We are not going to let anyone call the tune for us." The black struggle for racial and economic justice, they seemed to argue, had entered another phase: "The masses now understand that the Pullman porters' fight is their fight, the Brotherhood is the only Negro Economic organization in the country, and we must not allow it to fail. For if we fail it will plainly show the yellow streak and that inferiority complex not only with Pullman porters and maids but also with the entire race." Moving the conversation beyond the issue of tactics and timing, the Norfolk BSCP reminded readers of one of the Brotherhood's central tenets: "No group can rise without an economic backing."[47]

Sensing that the moment was brimming with radical possibilities for black working people, Brotherhood members in Norfolk and across the nation awaited the next move from leaders at the union's headquarters. An undecided Randolph weighed his options as the union's rank and file declared their readiness to strike, while others recommended that he exercise caution. On June 7, William Green, the president of the American Federation of Labor, urged Randolph to call off the strike. Similar advice came from other supporters, who sympathized with the porters' cause but believed that a walkout would lead to the union's demise. With the long-term survival of the union in mind, Randolph decided to call off the strike. Nearly three weeks later, the *Baltimore Afro-American* published Randolph's statement insisting that the strike's postponement had provided the BSCP with considerable leverage, enabling "the Brotherhood to see and study the plans of the Company to break the porters' strike." This preview, he argued, would be useful if the Brotherhood subsequently made good on its threat to strike, which Randolph reiterated was not out of the question. Randolph also argued that "the postponement has enabled us to maneuver the powerful American Federation of Labor on the side of the Brotherhood of whose power the company is too well aware." Finally, Randolph noted that the threatened walkout "has gotten the Brotherhood a million dollars worth of publicity. This publicity is breaking down the backbone of the Company."[48] For the remainder of the year, Randolph continued to suggest that the Brotherhood might call a massive strike at any time.

As Randolph dangled that possibility before Pullman officials, Dabney explored the question of whether black southerners would support the walkout. Like many other labor journalists, Dabney regarded the political rise of the Brotherhood as one of the most fascinating developments of the New Negro era. In his judgment, only the UNIA had "caused so much comment and speculation among American Negroes and the nation generally" as the BSCP. Indeed, the Brotherhood had been the subject of intense debate in the pages of the *Chicago Defender*, the *Pittsburgh Courier*, the *Baltimore Afro-American*, and other black newspapers. Much of the news coverage centered on the union's activities in the North, but Dabney offered a rare southern perspective on the Brotherhood. Dabney argued that black southerners would overwhelmingly have backed the strike: "Pullman porters, naturally, do not talk very freely on the matter. Yet I venture the assertion that at least 75 percent of the Pullman porters in the South would not do anything to hamper a strike of the Brotherhood, while more than 50 percent would actively support a strike. Furthermore a large number of other Negroes would support a strike for the Brotherhood. This is not mere guessing. Some have told me without the asking that they would support the porters' strike." In addition, Dabney revealed, "The average Southern white person with whom I talked seemed more concerned with the racial phase of the porters' struggle than the economic phase." In this view, "the porters' union means an uprising of 'smart niggers' bent on getting out of their proper place by arrogantly asserting their manhood." Thus, Dabney insisted, white attempts to suppress the Brotherhood had as much to do with race as class: "The average Southern person cannot accept manhood and initiative in the Negro. It is the business of the Negro to accept the advice of the white man."[49]

By highlighting African Americans who embraced the BSCP and refused to "accept the advice of the white man," Dabney provided a counter to those who sought to portray the Brotherhood as a group of radical northerners who had no real influence in the South. As Dabney was probably well aware, the *Pittsburgh Courier* had recently published an article under the headline "Southern Porters Oppose Union Movement." Though the headline suggested regional opposition to the movement, the article focused solely on a group of Jacksonville porters who had approved a resolution declaring,

> We, the undersigned Pullman porters of Jacksonville realizing the condition that
> we are placed in by the so-called movement to organize the Pullman porters, and
> feeling that said movement has lowered the standard of some of the porters of our
> district, and caused loyal men to be blamed, take this method of showing our loyalty
> to the company and our appreciation for all that has been done for us. We further
> denounce the so-called movement of Brotherhood of Sleeping Car Porters. We are
> aware of the fact that quite a few were misled by a false and radical styled leader, but
> we promise and swear to do all in our power to defeat the object of this so-called
> leader.[50]

The resolution had been signed by 302 of Jacksonville's 340 porters, many of whom had endorsed the resolution out of fear rather than political conviction.[51]

Targeted by his fellow porters as "one of the misled," Darby refused to abandon the BSCP. Even as company officials threatened to fire him, he still spoke zealously about the union: "We have come a long way and victory is just around the corner, if we will just hold out and pay our dues and assessments and do all we can for this good and just cause." Likewise, Brown vowed to "continue the fight until victory is won." The New Orleans district, she acknowledged, had endured its share of disappointments, but the men in the Brotherhood "have by no means lost faith." Brown counseled patience: "This is but one of the many struggles that honest labor has had to undergo before it came into its own. The proper sentiment is necessary and in order to have that it sometimes takes not only months, but years in the accomplishment, but, just as other great movements, through struggle and long suffering, have finally won, the cause of the [working] man through the strong fight of the Brotherhood will finally prevail."[52]

This perspective proved necessary as the momentum the BSCP had built in the three years after its founding came to an abrupt halt as a result of the combination of the strike's postponement and the onset of the Great Depression. The Brotherhood's membership numbers fell across the country, and financial difficulties led to the demise of the *Messenger*. The May–June 1928 edition, which included a letter from the New Orleans District declaring that the monthly was "very much in demand," marked the end of one of the most important publications of the New Negro era.

The impact of the *Messenger*'s demise extended beyond the BSCP's members. The monthly had predated the union and had brought black southerners and other subscribers not only key information on the New Negro movement but also fiction, book reviews, and essays from writers based in the South. Two of those writers, Thomas Dabney and cultural critic James Ivy, confronted questions that consumed many women and men committed to the work of the BSCP: Could a progressive black labor movement thrive in the South, and to what extent could African American workers draw support from white liberals? Had the intensity of white supremacy rendered black southerners devoid of the necessary class consciousness to mobilize against capital, or was this myopic representation of African American workers just one of many stereotypes advanced by an uncommitted white Left? Looking at the ways in which Dabney and Ivy grappled with these and other questions provides a much-needed perspective on how New Negro intellectuals engaged the contemporary politics and future of the South.

SIX

New Negro Southerners

On his summer breaks from teaching at Union High School in Hampton, Virginia, budding literary critic James Waldo Ivy routinely traveled to New York City to partake in the rich intellectual life of Harlem and Greenwich Village, catch up with old college classmates, and temporarily escape the indignities of Jim Crow Virginia. Though he lived in the South, Ivy was hardly a stranger to New York's vibrant intellectual scene. A graduate of Virginia Union University, Ivy regularly contributed to the *Messenger*. On the strength of his book review section alone, Ivy garnered the respect of such noted thinkers as Claude McKay, Abram Harris, and the perpetually cantankerous George Schuyler. Writing to W. E. B. Du Bois in the summer of 1927, Harris praised Ivy's "literary powers," which needed to be "snatched from the deadening school life in Hampton."[1] Not one to easily hand out complements, Harris identified his fellow Virginia Union alumnus as one of the brightest cultural critics of the New Negro generation. Indeed, Ivy's "Book Bits" section, which covered subjects ranging from the utility of college fraternities to the literary merits of southern Renaissance writers such as Emily Clark and Julia Peterkin, provided *Messenger* readers with refreshingly original perspectives on race, culture, literature, and politics. Ivy's diverse intellectual palette meshed perfectly with the *Messenger*'s eclectic style. Moreover, his political sympathies complemented the monthly's activist agenda. Though Ivy explored a variety of literary and political topics, most of his writings betrayed a strong leftist sensibility. In ways both subtle and direct, the Danville, Virginia, native identified strongly with the political and economic struggles of black working women and men. His deep concern for their plight surfaced in his challenges to the uplift ideology of the black elite, his denunciation of racist white trade unionists, and his razor-sharp critiques of the much-celebrated "critical school" of New South writers.

Many of Ivy's views were echoed by Thomas Lewis Dabney, another Virginia Union alumnus who wrote for the *Messenger*. Initially plugged into the New Negro radical circuit during his undergraduate years, Dabney gained recognition during the second half of the 1920s for his astute political commentary in the *Labor Age*, the *Socialist Review*, the Urban League's *Opportunity*, the *Modern Quarterly*, and Hampton Institute's *Southern Workman*. His writings on political economy and American labor relations marked him as an expansive thinker frustrated by the theoretical limitations of both race-first and class-first perspectives within New Negro thought. Notwithstanding Dabney's embrace of socialist principles, his unflinching commitment to democratic praxis complicated his relationship with the American Left. His familiarity with the organizing struggles of black working people coupled with his aversion to elitist notions of leadership, even if emanating from self-described radicals, to sour him on the idea of a revolutionary vanguard leading the "black masses" into the socialist promised land. Thus, despite his frustrations with white organized labor, Dabney promoted trade union politics as the most viable and democratic vehicle through which black workers could fight the interlocking systems of class privilege, racism, and labor exploitation. If black workers were to improve both their material condition and their political standing, he believed, a consolidation of their power at and beyond the workplace was mandatory. "Unionism," Dabney insisted, "adds dignity to labor and imparts self-respect to the workers. . . . It forms the economic basis for a wholesome psychology toward both work and leisure." His perspective was shaped not only by his intense study of "the industrial phase of the Negro problem" but also by his close encounters with "the advanced section of Negro workers who are embracing trade-union philosophy."[2]

Dabney and Ivy not only complicate the widely held perspective that New Negro discourse "shifted from political radicalism to romantic culturalism" with the onset of the Harlem Renaissance but also offer insight into the persistence of social democratic aspirations during the interwar period.[3] As Howard Brick notes in *Transcending Capitalism*, "The anticipatory sense of a coming new era continued in the aftermath of war, albeit tempered by a rocky journey through several years marked by crosscurrents of hope, disappointment, militancy, and setback."[4] Brick's claims about the persistence of "war-inspired aspirations to economic or industrial democracy" definitely hold true when examining the postwar writings of Ivy and Dabney.[5] In the *Modern Quarterly*, the *Messenger*, and other venues, the two men evaluated the future of trade union and left-wing politics as well as alternatives to the capitalist market economy. The relative ease with which Ivy and Dabney discovered outlets for their writings on political economy and labor relations signaled an important shift in black intellectual life. The "class question" as it related to the "Negro problem" consumed the thoughts of black social scientists, journalists, and political activists throughout the 1920s. On street corners, in private homes, and in a slew of publications, black women and men debated the merits of a capitalist versus socialist-based economy.

Though Rod Bush, Jeffrey Perry, Francille Wilson, Marlon B. Ross, Jonathan Holloway, and Charles P. Henry, among other scholars, have brought this vibrant intellectual milieu into sharper focus, the multiple streams of New Negro thought have by no means been fully exhausted.[6] In fact, the writings of Dabney and Ivy bring to the fore several underexplored themes: the importance of historically black colleges in nurturing black progressive thought during the 1920s; the seriousness with which African American southerners approached the labor question; and the regional differences in how black writers assessed the trustworthiness of southern white liberals.

One of the defining features of both Ivy's and Dabney's work was their detailed attention to the South. Particularly during the second half of the 1920s, they produced remarkably insightful essays on the South's racial politics, the shifts in its economic structure, and the intellectual renaissance unfolding in Chapel Hill, Nashville, New Orleans, and Richmond. Their rootedness in the region undoubtedly contributed to their analytical depth and nuance. Unlike many of their New Negro contemporaries who judged the South from afar, Ivy and Dabney remained residents of Virginia for much of the 1920s, giving them a different vantage point from that of their northern counterparts. Perhaps nowhere was this more apparent than in their provocative assessments of the southern literary renaissance, a movement built around the creative works of DuBose Heyward, Julia Harris, Emily Clark, Paul Green, and Julia Peterkin. These writers garnered a great deal of praise among New Negro critics, particularly Alain Locke. Consistent with his integrationist agenda, Locke envisioned New Southerners and New Negroes as potential coworkers in the struggle to create a more democratic society. To forge this bond, Locke encouraged African American writers and artists to reach out to their enlightened "cultural cousins" living south of the Potomac: "Let the New Negro therefore welcome the New South in the confident hope that the New South will welcome the New Negro."[7]

Such commentary struck Dabney and Ivy as intellectually unsophisticated and politically naive. Both men were well aware of an emergent group of white southerners willing to challenge the repressive nature of southern society. Dabney and Ivy routinely wrote about the new crop of southern intellectuals who directed a critical eye toward the region. "There is a resolute minority in the South," Ivy noted, "that is intelligent and above all, realistic; they are certainly not afraid of facing the facts, which the old type Southerner would never do."[8] Such liberals definitely deserved New Negroes' attention, but Ivy believed that it was equally important for African Americans to recognize the resiliency of white supremacy. His growing impatience with those who failed to do so appeared in his review of Edwin Mims's *The Advancing South*, which generated tremendous conversation among white and black liberals. "In recent years," Ivy wrote, "the rapid industrialization of the South has been responsible for the infiltration of capitalist ideas to the detriment of Confederate ideology. But do not for a moment believe that the South has suffered a change of heart, for she has not, despite Professor Mims' discovery that some Southerners are actually civilized."[9] Dabney took a similar position, urging his readers to understand the complex nature and limitations of the South's changing landscape. Dabney, too, viewed the South's "trend toward liberalism" as "the result of the economic orientation of Southern life." The rise of liberal voices was to be expected, he reasoned, but would not lead to an improvement in the material lives of the South's laboring majority.[10] Ivy and Dabney were committed not simply to documenting societal change in the South through intense study and research but also to communicating what those changes meant for the region's African Americans and particularly its working women and men.

Better understanding how Ivy and Dabney arrived at their positions on a variety of issues related to race, region, and class requires looking at Virginia Union, the institution that had the most profound impact on their postwar intellectual trajectory. Located in West Richmond, Virginia Union traces its roots back to the emancipation era, when the American Baptist Home Mission Society established National Theological Institutes in Richmond and Washington, D.C. Later known as Wayland Seminary, the D.C.-based Institute had a much smoother start than its Richmond counterpart, which from 1867 to 1870 held classes in a former slave holding pen known as Lumpkin's Jail. The two schools consolidated in 1899 to become Virginia Union. Despite external pressure to mold its curricular offerings along the lines of Tuskegee Institute, Union claimed a progressive group of faculty members deeply committed to supplying students with the intellectual training necessary to maximize their individual gifts. Of Union's constellation of stellar instructors, no one received greater praise than Joshua Baker Simpson. A professor of the classics and theology, Simpson elicited praise from Union's most accomplished graduates, including Charles Johnson, Charles Thompson, and Abram Harris.[11] Nearly two decades after graduating from Union, Harris remained indebted to Simpson's teachings, which Harris credited with introducing him to the study of economics: "In spite of the fact that he often antagonized people, no student ever went into Simpson's classroom and came out without a burning desire to know, and that in my judgment is the essence of good teaching. For him teaching was a great art and he knew that whereas the methods of others were an aid the true artist must often create his own methods. He had no patience with the educational theory that the way to teach men was to make every answer simple and easy. Learning for him was a severe discipline."[12]

Leaving an indelible mark on the women and men who enrolled in his courses, Simpson belonged to a distinguished group of "master teachers" whose pedagogical endeavors had a discernable impact on black collegians of the New Negro era. The names that loomed the largest among this group were Simpson, Benjamin Mays and Samuel Archer of Morehouse, and Benjamin Brawley of Shaw University. These seminal intellectuals defined their legacy not just by the scholarship they produced but also by the students they trained. In the words of historian Vincent Harding, their pedagogical agenda sought not just to provide students "with factual information but to tap the magnificent but underdeveloped faculties of their imagination."[13] This important aspect of the black professor's vocation was eloquently articulated in Brawley's fascinating 1926 article, "The Profession of the Teacher":

> To take our boys and girls, our young men and women and to lead them into the knowledge of truth; to acquaint them with the master-minds of the ages; to help them to be clean of heart and pure of spirit; to teach them to have self-respect without arrogance and chivalry without pride; to help them to have faith even if they see wrong all around them. This is no mere business, no simple matter of office routine. It is the highest task that God can give a mortal.[14]

Like Brawley, Simpson regarded teaching as an integral component of his larger calling. Therefore, he pushed his Union students beyond their intellectual comfort zone, demanded their absolute best, exposed them to a wide range of literature, and treated them with the utmost respect.

Fortunately, Union's extracurricular activities buttressed many of the intellectual values Simpson and other professors promoted in their classrooms. Every Saturday evening, for example, the Gamma Chi Literary and Debating Society featured stimulating exchanges and orations on subjects ranging from women's suffrage and birth control to government ownership of railroads. Over the years, the Gamma Society amassed a distinguished group of participants, including Charles Johnson and Chandler Owen.

Not long after his arrival on Union's campus in the fall of 1915, Dabney plunged into this vibrant intellectual culture. His interactions with such esteemed professors as Simpson, religious scholar Miles Mark Fisher, and John W. Barco opened him to new ways of imagining his place in the world. Dabney also benefited from his alliances with a small yet dedicated group of students committed to pushing their peers and the larger Richmond community to new levels of political engagement. Their most immediate goal was to transform the university into a site of intense political thought and activism. Toward this end, campus activists formed a college chapter of the National Association for the Advancement of Colored People (NAACP). Chartered in June 1914, the Virginia Union NAACP garnered support from such accomplished students as John Malchus Ellison, William Colson, Nathaniel Davis Oyerinde, and George William Clement Brown.[15] Much more than a local extension of the national NAACP, the Union branch developed into an important incubator of New Negro thought and political expression for many students, stressing race pride and black cultural awareness, group unity, cross-regional collaboration among young African Americans, and the necessity of consistent political engagement. In its formative period, the Union chapter protested local screenings of *The Birth of a Nation*, raised funds for the NAACP's antilynching work, implemented cultural programming to enrich students' educational experiences, and sought to raise the consciousness of African Americans beyond Union's campus.[16] Intimately involved in these student-led initiatives, Dabney gained invaluable political experience within the institutional matrix of the NAACP. His leadership responsibilities as chapter vice president and sales agent for the *Crisis* proved crucial to his political maturation as well as his emotional well-being. Dabney and some of his colleagues greatly admired the political work and literary achievements of both James Weldon Johnson and W. E. B. Du Bois. As Dabney later wrote to Du Bois, "When I was a poor struggling student at Virginia Union, I sold the *Crisis* and supported the NAACP, without which I would have died in despair. I owed my spiritual existence to the *Crisis* under your editorship and the NAACP under the guidance of the late James Weldon Johnson."[17] To repay what he regarded as his mounting debt to the NAACP, Dabney vowed to turn the Union chapter into a major agent for transformative social action in Richmond.[18]

The U.S. entry into World War I temporarily suspended Dabney's lofty plans for the Union branch. On June 5, 1917, the twenty-three-year-old Dabney walked into a registration office in Mechanicsville, Virginia, and added his name to the list of able-bodied men eligible for military service.[19] Shortly thereafter, he departed for France, joining thousands of African Americans fighting for the Allied powers. The war years shifted Dabney further to the left, deepening his commitment not just to racial equality but also to economic justice for those working women and men whose labor proved so central to U.S. mobilization efforts.

By the time Dabney returned home in 1919, he was an avowed socialist, though he remained committed to completing his undergraduate studies at Virginia Union. Much to his frustration, however, family concerns delayed his reentry for two years. His parents, Reuben and Virginia, depended heavily on his financial support, while his younger brother, Leonard, who had also served in the war, faced serious medical issues. The emotional strain of Dabney's financial responsibilities was apparent in his correspondence with James Henry Dooley, a Richmond businessman from whom he occasionally solicited financial assistance:

> My parents are poor—and they have only one son to whom they can look for help. There are three of us, but one of my brothers is helpless—suffering from an acute case of tuberculosis in the left hip which he contracted in France, where he served twelve months during the late war. He has been confined to bed ever since August when he was sent back home. I served about twenty months in the army, 16½ months of which I served in France.[20]

To support his struggling family, Dabney sold copies of Marcus Garvey's *Negro World*, the *Crisis*, and the *Messenger* in Richmond and surrounding areas, an endeavor that not only provided him with money but also kept him abreast of developments throughout the African diaspora.

In 1921, Dabney finally reenrolled at Union and immediately found a group of campus activists who shared many of his political commitments and intellectual passions. Harris and Ivy particularly encouraged Dabney's growing fascination with Marxian political analysis and iconoclastic literature. Dabney was seven years older than Ivy, but the two men were especially close, sharing not just intellectual pursuits but also living quarters. They engaged in a variety of intellectual projects, including the 1921 formation of the Club for the Study of Socialism, an affiliate of the Intercollegiate Society. At the same time, Harris launched the *Union Gazette*, an independent student newspaper, and the campus saw the creation of Open Forum, celebrated in some circles as the "most liberal and advanced organization ever formed by the students." Both provided safe spaces where young women and men could showcase their intellectual acumen, debate domestic and foreign policy, enumerate the many wrongs of the current economic system, and gain exposure to new and exciting ideas. Union's liberal atmosphere proved a great boon to both Ivy and Dabney, and in 1923, they started their own newspaper, the *Critic*. According to Ivy, the *Critic* gained a large following for its irreverent approach to student life and university politics: "We gave everything going on around campus hell. Whenever we posted a new edition of the *Critic* students would cluster around reading it." Ivy and Dabney found literary inspiration from the *Sunday Call*, the *Iconoclast*, the *Messenger*, and the *Appeal to Reason*. "Anything that was iconoclastic," Ivy remembered, "I became interested in." Ivy and Dabney were particularly drawn to writers who "helped to tear down or criticize . . . the supposed sanctified institution of the United States of America."[21]

Not just making waves among their peers, Ivy and Dabney eventually caught the attention of several Union professors and graduates, including Chandler Owen. Though federal intelligence agents kept close tabs on Owen whenever he visited

Richmond, most Union administrators welcomed his presence on campus.[22] According to Ivy, "Union was proud of its alumni if it made any sort of achievement. So a famous preacher would be welcomed if he came back, and also a radical like Owen if he came back."[23] On one occasion, Owen spoke to one of Ivy's classes and then held a meeting at which he extolled the virtues of socialism. He also encouraged students to write for the *Messenger*, already a favorite among Ivy, Dabney, and their socialist friends.[24]

Ivy and Dabney also identified strongly with youth activists from around the world. Universities emerged during this era as important movement centers for civic-minded youth, and student activists in Cuba, China, Korea, Indonesia, India, and Japan participated in labor strikes, organized boycotts, challenged imperial governments and dictatorships, and aligned themselves with various communist, socialist, nationalist, and anticolonial organizations.[25] These student-led initiatives left a lasting impression on activist youth in the United States, particularly those affiliated with the National Student Forum. Organized in 1922, the Forum sought to unite liberal and leftist students around the nation, protect and expand academic freedom at colleges and universities, lend support to antiracist and anticolonial movements, and elevate American youth's political consciousness and social awareness. A constant point of emphasis in the Student Forum's nationally distributed weekly, the *New Student*, was the need for collegians to become more aware of their power and the world around them. "The average student," one editorial lamented, "is either ridiculously modest to the point of believing that he has neither power nor influence . . . or else he believes his influence is limited to setting the style in clothes and conversation." Though many students fell short of the paper's radical standards, some were engaged in important political work. Youth activists at Harvard, Brown, Temple, Bryn Mawr, and Farmingdale State College, among other universities, organized labor conferences, challenged the dismissal of progressive professors, demanded changes in their universities' curricula, and fought for greater control over student councils and campus newspapers. Well aware of these developments, African American college students strategized about how to carve out a sphere of influence within the civil rights community and the larger youth movement. "The consensus of opinion among student leaders is that it is time for us actually to do something," wrote J. Alpheus Butler of Howard University; "it is obviously up to the Negro youth, the Negro student, to show the way."[26] Howard students' rising militancy led to the formation of a college branch of the National Student Forum as well as the founding of the Federation of Negro Students in April 1923. Leading that charge was Glenn Carrington, a student of Locke's. Carrington served as the editor-in-chief of the student newspaper, the *Hilltop*, as well as vice president of the university's student government. A Richmond native who had graduated from Virginia Union's high school division in 1921, Carrington trumpeted black youth as the vanguard of a coming revolution. As he observed at the annual convention of the Federation of Negro Students, "A new blood is being poured into the veins of youth."[27]

Carrington's optimistic outlook developed in response to political initiatives at Howard as well as his interactions with undergraduates at Fisk, Lincoln, and Virginia Union. As a member of Howard's Kappa Sigma Debating Society, Carrington had frequent contact with some of the brightest young minds in black America. On April 27, 1923, for example, he traveled to his hometown to debate members of Union's Gamma Society on the question of whether France was justified in occupying Germany's Ruhr Valley in an effort to collect war reparations authorized by the Versailles Treaty.[28] On this and other visits to Union, Carrington had extended conversations with students about how to empower themselves politically, socially, and economically.

Enmeshed in this vibrant network of black youth activists, Ivy and Dabney institutionalized their connection with Carrington and other collegians through involvement with organizations such as the Federation of Negro Students and the Intercollegiate Society. Like their counterparts across the country, they envisioned themselves as part of a new generation of thinkers equipped with the intellectual skills, political contacts, and cultural confidence to shape the world in their own image.

After graduating from Union, Dabney and Ivy had to decide whether to remain in the South or join the thousands of other African Americans who were venturing north. Other Union men had launched their careers in New York, Chicago, and Pittsburgh, and Dabney and especially Ivy had important contacts who could help facilitate the transition to the North. During his summer breaks in New York, Ivy had rubbed elbows with some of the leading thinkers in black America, including Claude McKay and Chandler Owen, who had encouraged Ivy to relocate to New York and contribute to the *Messenger*. The offer piqued Ivy's interest, but both he and Dabney elected to remain in Virginia. Following his 1925 graduation, Ivy accepted a teaching position at Union High School in Hampton Roads, where he taught Greek, English, and French. One of his students, Hylan Lewis, went on to become a noted anthropologist and praised Ivy as a first-rate teacher.[29] Though he preferred the stability of his teaching job, Ivy welcomed the chance to contribute to the *Messenger*. To the respected monthly, Ivy brought brilliant prose, intellectual curiosity, and confidence in the singularity of his literary voice. Taking advantage of the freedom provided by the magazine's editors, Ivy touched on a vast array of topics, among them sex and marriage and the future of global capitalism. His broad intellectual palette and biting wit ensured that the *Messenger*'s book review section was never predictable or dull. However, Ivy's writings consistently highlighted the deep layers of emotional depth and beauty among the African American working class. In no small part as a consequence of his interactions with African American workers in Hampton Roads, Ivy looked favorably on their progress: "The future of Negro labor is in some ways quite encouraging, yet there are many obstacles to be overcome; many fallacies to be exploded; prejudices to live down. Yet Negro labor is forging ahead, this is significant." If Negro labor were to continue its forward march, Ivy believed that the African American leadership class needed to deal with the race's proletarian character. As he explained in his glowing review of Charles Wesley's seminal study *Negro Labor in the United States, 1850–1925,* "Ninety-nine percent of the Negroes in this country are laboring people. Yet the majority of our Negro leaders proceed upon the assumption that we are a race of bourgeois: comfortable, middle-class shopkeepers. It is this notion which is at the back of our so-called leaders' aloofness to the black worker and his problems; it, too, is responsible for the exasperating aping of the upper-class by our so-called rich."[30]

Not content with simply browbeating the black elite, Ivy's writings also cast a critical eye on the white labor movement. He repeatedly lashed out at what he perceived as the provincialism of white workers, who in his view played the biggest role in the failures of the American labor movement. "It is the American laborer's selfishness, coupled with his extravagant sense of Nordic superiority, that makes him resist attempts at the organization of Negroes into unions, or even their admission into existing white unions. He doesn't see beyond his eyelashes that the little material benefit which accrues to the Negroes as a result of organization is nothing in comparison with the larger benefits coming to labor as a whole." Because of his frustration with white workers, Ivy found himself at odds with leftist thinkers predicting the dawn of a new era in labor relations and economic arrangements. As he wrote in a review of Scott Nearing's *Where Civilization Is Going,* "there are no assured proofs that we are at the front door of this socialist Utopia."[31]

This did not mean that Ivy wrote off the current economic order as impervious to change. Like many social progressives throughout the Atlantic world, Ivy promoted cooperatives as a way of achieving a more equitable distribution of the nation's wealth: "I firmly believe that in co-operation and co-operative societies lies one of the solutions for the Negroes' present economic plight. We could have grocery stories, clothing stores, coal yards, and what not, run on the co-operative basis. They would save us money, give more of our people employment, and lay the foundation for a sounder economic order."[32]

En route to building a reputation as one of black America's most perceptive social critics, Ivy rooted himself in the political culture of the black South. Yet he remained intimately connected to the institutional networks of the northern

Left. The *Messenger*, along with the tutelage of McKay and Schuyler, played an important role in the development of Ivy's political voice.[33] These transregional networks also sustained Dabney's early career. Never restricting himself to one particular career path, Dabney worked intermittently as a teacher, a journalist, and a labor organizer during the second half of the 1920s. Immediately after graduating from Virginia Union in 1924, he accepted a position as principal of the Buckingham Training School in Dillwyn, Virginia, seventy miles west of Richmond. The school symbolized African Americans' commitment to expanding their children's educational, economic, and political opportunities within a rural context.[34] The Buckingham Training School offered Dabney not only a salary but also invaluable experiences that shaped his intellectual trajectory. His daily interactions with schoolchildren and their parents, fellow teachers, and county boards exposed him to the unique challenges and opportunities facing the rural South.

Though deeply appreciative of the learning experiences in rural Virginia, Dabney's mounting interest in labor politics quickly pulled him in another direction. After one year at Buckingham, he left Central Virginia for Upstate New York. In the fall of 1925, with financial support from the American Fund for Public Service and the NAACP, Dabney enrolled at Brookwood Labor College. Located on the outskirts of Katonah, New York, Brookwood was the brainchild of socialist A. J. Muste, who opened the school immediately after World War I. Initially conceived as a community school for local residents, Brookwood transformed into a labor college specifically designed to train workers for trade union leadership. "Well to the left" of adult educational institutions such as New York City's New School for Social Research, Brookwood developed into "one of the most important sites of cooperation between organized labor, pacifism, and progressive intellectuals during the 1920s." The school admitted native-born whites, a few African Americans, and immigrants from Europe, Latin America, and Asia. Its pedagogical agenda was largely shaped by one question: "What can a resident school do to enable American workers to work more effectively in the American labor movement?" With the goal of assisting organized labor in its pursuit of social and economic justice, Brookwood professors and administrators implemented a rigorous curriculum intended to produce activists skilled in public speaking, labor journalism, media relations, and labor and community organizing. In Dabney's first year at Brookwood, he studied U.S. and international labor history, English, economics, public speaking, social psychology, labor journalism, trade union organizing and administration, and parliamentary law. Immersing himself in the cultural activities of the student body, Dabney even participated in a student-produced play centered on the social and labor lives of a fictive coal mining family. His close contact with students from all over the world, combined with his extensive coursework, convinced him that

Brookwood was "destined to become a potent factor in the labor movement for the social betterment of the working class in America."[35]

After graduating from Brookwood in 1926, Dabney began publishing articles in the *Southern Workman*, the *Messenger*, and *Opportunity*, expounding on the theories and lessons he had learned. The *Southern Workman* proved a particularly welcoming home, and his pieces for the journal explored modernizing efforts in the rural South, labor relations, global youth activism, foreign affairs, and American race relations.[36] Since its inception at Hampton Institute in 1872, the *Southern Workman* had espoused a political philosophy that emphasized interracial cooperation and capitalist accumulation within the context of the existing Jim Crow system. It routinely ran features on black landownership, the progress of black businesses, the state of African American education in the rural South, and the programs of the Commission on Interracial Cooperation. The monthly's political tone was decidedly moderate, but increasingly during the interwar years, it welcomed writers and scholars who hardly fit the category of racial accommodationists, including Howard Thurman, Rayford Logan, and Allison Davis. Consistent with larger intellectual developments in the world of southern reform and North Atlantic thought, Dabney focused on the rural hinterlands in his first two pieces for the *Southern Workman*. Using Central Virginia as his case study, he challenged the idea of the rural South as isolated and disconnected from the monumental transformations taking place in the larger world. As if writing a rural analogue to Locke's urban-centered account of New Negro life, Dabney identified the proliferation of rural conferences, the establishment of county training schools for black youth, and educators' growing attention to the "careful and scientific study of rural problems" as evidence of "a new awakening" in the southern countryside.[37]

Sharing many progressives' concerns about the atomistic nature of rural life, Dabney duly noted the progress of black education in locales such as Buckingham County, where private and state support had led to the creation of two schools for African Americans. The growing number of rural conferences and fairs also caught his attention: "Through these conferences a sort of social consciousness is being developed among rural people which is indispensable for group co-operation and advancement. This is a great accomplishment for any rural community, for farmers are by occupation very individualistic."[38] Despite these accomplishments, however, Dabney recognized the vast problems still facing black rural communities—social isolation, poor farming techniques, inadequate social services, and the gross imbalances in educational opportunities among black and white children.[39] Dabney sought to draw attention to the challenges confronting rural people as well as their collective and individual efforts to overcome those obstacles.

His quest for a deeper understanding of the rural hinterlands eventually led him to Europe, a magnet for many Americans studying the U.S. countryside. As historian Daniel Rodgers notes, "The problem of the folk" along the edges of modernity had been a focus of intellectuals and reformers in both the United States and Europe during the Progressive and interwar eras.[40] Moreover, many U.S.-based intellectuals turned to Europe for additional insight into solving the social and political dilemmas of rural life. Early in the summer of 1925, Dabney traveled with Carrington and other American students to Soviet Russia to study problems and solutions pertaining to education, health, gender relations, and other topics. With the information gained from his travels, Dabney produced a fascinating account of the postwar improvements in Russia's social welfare services. Though circumspect in his language, he judged Soviet health care and welfare programs superior to those in the rural Jim Crow South.[41]

Dabney also wrote for the *Messenger* between 1926 and 1928, penning articles geared more toward organized labor than those published in the *Southern Workman*. Dabney dissected the inner workings of the U.S. labor movement, revealing both its weaknesses and its strengths. He offered meticulous detail regarding trade union politics, a perspective quite different from the *Messenger*'s more common satirical dismissals of the black leadership class. Dabney often focused on trade unions' governing structures: "One of the vital questions of the trade union movement," he wrote in 1926, "is that of democratic government. At present practically all power rests in the hands of officials of national and international unions. Some of these officials are dictatorial and indifferent to the interests of workers. Many are dishonest and spend much of their time making themselves and their friends secure in office. . . . [T]hey need an intelligent following to hold them in check." However, Dabney noted, the lack of democracy in the labor movement "is not due merely to the kind of officials in the trade unions but it is due in part to the inclination among the masses to worship leaders," an inclination Dabney declared to be the "product of group psychology." The average worker, he continued, "is well nigh helpless before both his boss and his union leader. As peculiar as this situation may seem, it is the very thing that the trade union movement is supposed to remedy for this relation between leaders and the workers must be changed."[42]

To remedy the situation, Dabney recommended the creation of institutional structures and pedagogical platforms to empower workers. Now more than ever, workers needed to "establish and control their own educational institutions." Dabney's advocacy of a labor-oriented educational movement dedicated to advancing the material interests of the working-class majority reflected his growing commitment to challenging institutions that provided political and ideological legitimacy to the prevailing social order. Such work was critical, Dabney believed, precisely because opposition to the collectivist principles and democratic vision of the labor

Left existed in every facet of public life. Far from a reformist, Dabney distinguished his vision from those uplift strategies associated with the Progressive era: "Workers' education does not mean merely educating the workers. It means providing a definite kind of education for the workers, for the tremendous social responsibility, which rests upon them as a group. This type of education transcends race, creed, nationality and sex. It has but one limitation and that is class. It is class education in that it is for workers only or those who have the workers' viewpoint." Moreover, according to Dabney, "Workers' education is not by any means limited to the schools. It is fostered by labor publications, lecturers, pictures, libraries and open forums." Dabney singled out the efforts of the Workers' Education Bureau and the League for Industrial Democracy, which, he noted, "are doing much work in the field of education for the workers."[43]

Though the labor Left definitely faced an uphill climb in its quest to democratize trade union bureaucracies, Dabney remained hopeful about building a democratic labor movement, particularly in the South. Much of his optimism arose from his encounters with black trade unionists as a lead researcher for the National Urban League. Dabney began working for the League in the summer of 1926, conducting most of the interviews for a national survey of blacks in the labor movement. Eager to further broaden his knowledge base, Dabney crisscrossed the country, interviewing both black and white trade unionists on the state of organized labor in their communities, the level of interracial cooperation among workers, and the general morale among skilled and unskilled laborers. On the southern portion of his tour, he encountered determined black trade unionists dedicated to the principles of class solidarity and collective action. These encounters subsequently influenced Dabney's journalistic endeavors, particularly his writings for *Labor Age*, the *Socialist Review*, and the *Locomotive Engineers Journal*, an important leftist publication whose contributors included Charles and Mary Beard, George Soule, and Paul Douglas.[44]

Much like Ivy, Dabney was drawn to black workers whose behavior challenged stereotypical images of African American laborers as politically apathetic and hostile to unions. As he explained in an article for *Labor Age*, "In principle and theory Negro workers to a considerable extent favor trade unionism. The philosophy of the labor movement has a tremendous appeal for them; but they have learned by bitter experience that the theory of trade unions is one thing and their practice is another." Echoing the African American trade unionists who frequented the American Federation of Labor's annual conventions during and immediately after the war years, Dabney argued, "There are cases where Negro trade union members were loyal and faithful to the organization, going out on strikes and supporting the campaigns for higher wages and better working conditions only to lose their jobs when the settlement was made with the employees."[45] Despite these betrayals, thousands of African Americans still belonged to local and national trade unions.

Familiarity with the organizing struggles and sacrifices of black working people gave Dabney a unique perspective on how the South might be pushed in a more progressive direction. Dabney and Ivy departed from the thinking of New Negroes who increasingly saw southern white liberals as the region's most likely redeemers. James Weldon Johnson, Charles Johnson, and Alain Locke invested considerable faith in a new crop of white writers and artists who challenged the "old assumptions and old gods" of the mythic South. Charles Johnson, for example, noted in the summer of 1926 that "simultaneously with the appearance of the 'New Negro' comes 'The Awakening South' with its emancipated liberals, its intellectual revolution and its industrial prosperity." Insisting that the South no longer be treated as a bastion of intellectual conservatism, Johnson alerted his readers to the emergence of "splendid journals like the *Southwest Review*, the New Orleans *Double Dealer*, the *Reviewer*, [and] *Social Forces*." H. L. Mencken praised *Social Forces*, edited by Howard Odum, as "full of dynamite," and it featured regular contributions from one of the region's most insightful journalists, Gerald Johnson. The two men understood the dangers involved in criticizing the region from within but viewed their bold critiques of the South's many political wrongs as vital to the South's rebirth. As Odum wrote in 1924, "The South needs criticism, and severe criticism." This new critical spirit was not the only magnet drawing Charles Johnson and other New Negroes to white New Southerners. "Most interesting of all," Johnson opined in 1926, "is the queer turn of fortune, which reveals in such superb examples as Julia Peterkin's *Green Thursday*, Dubose Heyward's *Porgy*, T. S. Stribling's *Birthright*, and Howard W. Odum's *The Negro and His Songs*." To this list of the South's most impressive creative achievements, Johnson soon added the "movingly human plays of Paul Green."[46]

Over the next few months, Johnson and other *Opportunity* contributors published a series of reviews that assessed the larger implications of the southern renaissance. In a review of Mims's *The Advancing South*, Locke called for members of the black intelligentsia to incorporate into their writings the "progressive South" of George Gordon Crawford, Odum, Green, Gerald Johnson, John Eagan, Ashby Jones, Will Alexander, and Julian Harris, arguing that these New Southerners shared cultural and political sensibilities with New Negroes:

The New Negro and the New South have more than interesting parallelisms, they have many ideals, loyalties and objectives in common. Each seeks an emancipation from the old obsessions of the Southern traditions—a revolution of mind and social attitude sought as a necessary preliminary to any really vital reform; each demands a change of leadership based on concrete, constructive programs and a philosophy and policy of class cooperation and mass education; each is economically and not politically pointed; each strives to raise a stagnated but richly endowed folk tradition to the level of free-flowing and creative expression; each hopes to freshen and purify brackish group emotions through new, dynamic processes of cultural and spiritual release. Art for the minority, education for the masses, self-direction, self-criticism, self-determination in both, are the common creed and common spirit of these two movements; which only the most enlightened on either side will be able for a half generation or so to see and recognize. These movements and the constructive efforts they represent should therefore have not only the moral support of our intelligent sympathy but the practical help of our active participation. It should be one of the articles of faith of the young Negro movement to believe in the New South.[47]

But Ivy and Dabney had a quite different perspective. Attuned to the literary and political developments taking place in Chapel Hill, Nashville, Richmond, and Atlanta, the two men closely monitored the intellectual endeavors of white women and men who positioned themselves as the region's new voices. Ivy never positioned himself as a regional expert but devoted more attention to southern literature than any other *Messenger* writer. His first foray into the world of southern literature was a detailed analysis of James Branch Cabell's literary contributions. One of the most celebrated writers of the postwar period, Cabell sparked controversy with the publication of his eighth novel, *Jurgen: A Comedy of Justice*. Featuring objects and motifs from the Arthurian legend, the novel's title character is a poet turned pawnbroker who undertakes fantastical journeys through the mythical Poictesme. Employing literary techniques prevalent in such later works as John Steinbeck's *Cup of Gold* and William Faulkner's *Mayday*, Cabell's book offers his readers a titillating fiction of ironic comedy from the perspective of a skeptical romantic.

Published in 1919, *Jurgen* became a topic of national discussion when the New York Society for the Suppression of Vice pushed to have the book banned for what its members deemed "lewd, lascivious, indecent" material. The controversy did wonders for Cabell's book sales, which increased astronomically during the first half of the 1920s. In Ivy's view, however, the controversy blinded critics and some supporters to *Jurgen*'s most important attribute: Cabell's literary genius. "The true, authentic, the flesh and blood Cabell is not known." Instead, he had been misinterpreted as a "ribald and smutty writer" who "concocts phrases of perfumed and esoteric smut." Such a view was especially prevalent "among the Ku Kluxers, Rotarians, and one hundred percent Americans." Ivy's words echoed those of his literary hero, Mencken, who identified Cabell as the writer "around whom the revival of literature in the South, if it is ever to come, must revolve." Like Mencken, Ivy judged Cabell a "great romantic writer with a wonderful command of English phrase and diction." Cabell avoided falling into the trap of sentimentalism and seasoned "his romanticism with the salt of irony, wit, and skepticism." His unique style, Ivy seethed, "is not understood by the *vulgus*; and since they get no joy out of it and can perceive no beauty therein, they proceed to slander, to hurl vile epithets, and to even succeed in suppressing Jurgen." And despite the fierce opposition to his work, Cabell continued "writing beautiful, polished sentences, and paragraphs and inventing romances of supreme charm and beauty."[48]

As the book editor for the *Messenger*, Ivy also lavished praise on Peterkin, Clark, and Green. Of Peterkin's work he wrote, "In *Green Thursday*, there was a magic of loving comprehension which appealed to the deepest humanity in us. Now in *Black April*, she again reveals her astounding talent in a sympathetic study of a certain class of South Carolina Negroes."[49] Ivy deemed Clark's *Stuffed Peacock* a "must read" for African Americans.[50] Though impressed by the literary talents of Clark, Peterkin, and other New Southerners, Ivy was far less sanguine about the political ramifications of their work than were Locke and James Weldon Johnson. Ivy's caution surfaced in a rather tepid review of Edward C. L. Adams's *Congaree Sketches*, a collection of folk tales that received quite a bit of attention because of Green's introduction, which James Weldon Johnson praised as "one of the finest approaches by the written word to interracial understanding and good will ever made."[51] Ivy agreed with Johnson's verdict on Green's insights, praising the introduction as "the best preface to any book by or about Negroes." To prove his point, Ivy excerpted for his readers one of the introduction's most discussed paragraphs: "Here at the end of this century's first quarter the United States is awakening to the fact that the destiny of the Negroes is its destiny, that black and white are inextricably mingled in blood and bone and intention, and that as the white men fails the Negro fails and as the Negro rises the white man rises."[52]

But beyond Green's introduction, Ivy had difficulty investing much more in Adams's book and in fact viewed it as evidence of white southerners' staunch racism: "Whites make caricatures of our elite because of their superiority complex and the insidious nonsense, engrained in them from childhood that there 'ain't no such animal' as an intelligent Negro."[53] Ivy recognized the need to acknowledge the distinctiveness of New South modernists such as Green and Odum but, unlike Locke, hardly saw them as coalition-building material.

The differences of opinion between Ivy and Locke are also evident in their opposing views on the Commission on Interracial Cooperation (CIC), which served as an institutional center for many white southern liberals. Characterized by the historian Patricia Sullivan as a "bold departure in the field of southern race relations," the CIC was founded in late December 1918. Under the leadership of Will Alexander, the CIC endeavored to "promote dialogue and interaction among black and white community leaders as the essential first step to constructive race relations."[54] Locke lauded the commission in a 1927 *Opportunity* essay, "Welcome the New South," declaring, "The inter-racial movement, halting and cautious as it has been, is nevertheless full of fine future possibilities." Even as many of his contemporaries questioned the CIC's failure to speak out against segregation and its weak record on labor, Locke hailed it as "the only possible constructive basis of practical reform."[55]

Ivy, in contrast, had serious issues with the CIC, noting in the summer of 1927, "I, for one, have little faith in these so-called inter-racial committees, for their Negro members are in so many cases hand picked 'darkies' who know their master's voice when they hear it, and who, consequently exercise much more of their energy in placating their white overlords than in stating and defending the real grievances of the Negro." Especially frustrating for Ivy was the CIC's unwillingness to contribute to the economic empowerment of the black working class: "According to the report of the committee for the year 1926, it has done some very commendable things for the Negro and the cause of racial justice in education, health and housing, institutional care and legal aid. I notice, however, that in the vital field of economic opportunity the committee has done nothing other than getting fifty Negroes jobs in a weaving plant in Newport News." He raged, "Negrophiles are today quite willing to contribute their thousands, and even their millions, to teach the Negro how to work; but none of them is willing as far as I know, to give these able recipients of their munificent educational bounties a chance to put their knowledge to good use by giving them ordinary decent jobs and a living wage."[56] Ivy's commentary captured his frustration with the CIC in particular as well as with white southern liberals in general.

Dabney took a similar tone in his essays on the South's progressive white writers, critics, and artists. Dabney explored the political implications of the work of Odum, Green, Alexander, and Guy Johnson in several articles published between 1926 and 1928. Dabney also closely monitored the CIC's activities, particularly its role in implementing race relations courses at more than two dozen southern white colleges, most notably the University of North Carolina at Chapel Hill, the University of Florida, and Vanderbilt. His *Southern Workman* essay on these courses revealed Dabney's complex relationship with the publication. On the one hand, his commitment to capturing the changing dynamics of southern society complemented the *Workman*'s editorial policy of presenting a more progressive South. On the other hand, Dabney strongly believed that many of the individuals, institutions, and organizations that the *Workman* upheld as sources of progressive change deserved a more critical appraisal and cautioned readers against placing too much faith in the Negro's popularity as a subject of critical inquiry on white college campuses. "The writer does not regard the present movement in the South to study the race problem as any radical change. It is promising and encouraging but the South is still conservative."[57] Dabney decried what he viewed as the limited attention devoted by these race relations "experts" to political economy. "The friend of the South," he later asserted in an article for *Modern Quarterly*, "is he who studies present-day Southern life critically and objectively and who supports interracial co-operation on the basis of the immediate material interests of the two races."[58]

Dabney was much less cautious in his private writings on southern liberals and their race relations work, condemning a political group that he viewed as undermining efforts to build a worker-led democratic movement. In a letter to V. F. Calverton, editor of *Modern Quarterly*, Dabney ridiculed liberals as "a positive menace of the revolutionary movement."[59]

Dabney's preference for limiting his critiques of southern liberals to the private realm reflected economic realities. Depression began to grip the black South in the late 1920s, and Dabney needed to support himself financially. His intermittent work as a freelance journalist, organizer for the American Negro Labor Congress, and researcher for the National Urban League hardly covered his personal expenses. "I have no money to travel," he complained to Calverton, "only enough to eat from day to day."[60] When he wrote more radical articles, mainstream publications refused to buy his work, leaving him only with reams of unpublished and incomplete manuscripts to show for his efforts. In 1929, therefore, Dabney returned to Buckingham Training School as both teacher and principal. While his work in the classroom consumed a great deal of his time, he continued to write for a variety of publications, most notably the *Norfolk Journal and Guide*.

Ivy also balanced his work as an educator and journalist, gaining a national following for his essays on race, labor relations, literature, and global politics. As the New Negro renaissance gathered steam, he tracked the historical contributions emanating from Carter G. Woodson's Association for the Study of Negro Life and History as well as the literary works of Claude McKay and other writers. Ivy had first come into contact with McKay during the summer of 1922, when Countee Cullen's white lover, Donald Duff, escorted Ivy to McKay's apartment to introduce the young man to the noted author. During the journey, Ivy "was racking my brain wondering what to do. I wanted to make an impression. . . . What we talked about that night, I don't remember, but we immediately became friends."[61]

Ivy subsequently became one of McKay's biggest champions in the black press. Early in 1928, McKay provoked a firestorm with his publication of *Home to Harlem*, which many black leaders saw as an embarrassment to the race. W. E. B. Du

Bois, for example, claimed that after consuming the "dirtier parts" of the novel's "filth," he felt "distinctly like taking a bath."[62] Ivy, however, took a different view, describing the novel as "dissect[ing] the ulcer of brothels of Harlem for our eyes to see and our mind to grasp." He appreciated McKay's creative foray into the world of "pimps, bulldykers, faggots, snoweaters, wild parties, razor fights, and sluttish women," finding it "beautiful but frank to the verge of cruelty."[63] Ivy also judged McKay's next novel, *Banjo*, to be a fine piece of literature.[64]

For his part, McKay appreciated and respected Ivy's literary taste but never fully understood the Virginia native's rootedness in the South. "Couldn't you get a job up North?" McKay queried in 1928. A year later, writing from Paris, McKay again asked, "Don't you make enough to take a trip abroad? So many of the Negro teachers and professors do Europe every summer."[65] McKay seems not to have grasped the fact that Ivy's regular pieces for the *Messenger* and the *Baltimore Afro-American* gave him substantial influence among the New Negro crowd. As George Schuyler noted, "So far as knowing about the black world, [Ivy] is so superior to the other people around."[66]

The vibrant black intellectual culture above the Mason-Dixon Line owed a great deal of its dynamism to independent South-based thinkers like Dabney and Ivy, regional publications like the *Southern Workman*, and intellectual training grounds like Virginia Union. But the economic challenges and political shifts brought about by the Great Depression strained many New Negro institutions and movements, including the *Messenger*, which folded in 1928. The depression also affected African Americans themselves. "No living group," Dabney wrote later that year, "is facing a more acute situation in the matter of employment than the American Negro." He continued, "While employment is a grave problem for the Negro, both North and South, the present shift in the economic status of the Southern Negro has by far greater social implications." Many whites had developed what Dabney called a "new work psychology" and had become willing to perform jobs previously dismissed as "beneath the dignity of a gentleman."[67] Like the men and women they studied, Dabney, Ivy, and other New Negro activists had to find ways to adjust to the changing times.

SEVEN

Stormy Weather

Legal victories against the Jim Crow system were few and far between for black southerners, but on March 14, 1927, civil rights activists in New Orleans had cause for a major celebration. On that day, the U.S. Supreme Court declared New Orleans's 1924 residential segregation ordinance unconstitutional. Celebratory commentary on the court's decision in *Tyler v. Harmon* echoed throughout black America, from Los Angeles to New Haven, Connecticut. Officials of the National Association for the Advancement of Colored People (NAACP) in New Orleans were especially ecstatic over the decision. For the past three years, the group and its dynamic president, George Lucas, had invested considerable time and energy into mobilizing the community around the branch's litigation efforts. Divisions between the city's Uptown blacks and creoles of color had limited the effectiveness of local civil rights initiatives. The housing segregation case, however, brought the two groups together in an impressive display of goodwill and unity.

Having put aside their differences for the larger goal of ending racism in the housing market, these two sectors now intensified their work in the civil rights arena. "This victory," Lucas informed NAACP executive secretary James Weldon Johnson, "has served to awaken our people here as never before."[1] But the optimistic spirit generated by the court decision quickly dissipated as the Great Mississippi River Flood further confirmed the precarious nature of black existence in the Jim Crow South.

Torrential rains combined with the collapse of levee systems along the Mississippi River brought immeasurable human suffering to the South during the first five months of 1927. Throughout the Mississippi Delta, floodwaters washed out entire towns, uprooted hundreds of thousands of people, and further imperiled the black poor who were already at the mercy of ruthless planters.[2] An examination of African Americans' plight during this disaster reveals a great deal about the South's entrenched racism as well as blacks' determination to survive. It also provides important insights into the inner workings and institutional strength of various black organizations. The flood had major effects on New Negro activists as well as the masses of African Americans—for example, reducing the runs of Pullman porters in the South and thus limiting their contact with leaders of the Brotherhood of Sleeping Car Porters (BSCP) in the North and West and forcing the Universal Negro Improvement Association (UNIA) to confront the limitations of its self-help philosophy in light of the fact that the vast majority of blacks lacked basic civil rights protections. The Great Flood tested the political resolve and strength of the New Negro crowd. Could its leaders generate a collective response that pushed the federal government to action as well as organize their communities' resources to meet the immediate needs of the Delta's black victims?

Between mid-August and early October 1926, three deadly storm systems rocked the Upper Midwest. Swollen by record rainfall, the Mississippi River's tributaries in Illinois, Minnesota, Indiana, and Nebraska rose to unprecedented levels. Flooding from the Floyd, Nokasippi, Neosho, and Illinois Rivers washed out bridges, railroads, and power plants. Nationally distributed newspapers kept readers updated on both the rising river levels and the human casualties. In late September, the *New York Times* informed readers of eight flood-related deaths in Hawarden, Iowa, as well as the drowning of a young girl in Illinois.[3] Down south, many wondered, privately and publicly, whether the region was adequately prepared for the storm. Would the levees withstand the deluge or buckle under the pressure of the raging waters? Did state and local governments have an effective evacuation plan for their citizenry? And if so, to what degree did those plans protect the region's black populace, particularly those laboring in the cotton fields?

Spokespersons for the Mississippi River Commission and the US Army Corps of Engineers assured the nation that the levees along the Mississippi were in good shape. In mid-December, Tennessee, Kentucky, Alabama, Mississippi, and Arkansas endured two weeks of violent rainstorms. The Big Sandy River, the Cumberland River, the Yazoo River, and the Tennessee River inundated surrounding towns and cities. Flood levels ranged from 6 inches (Little Rock, Arkansas) to 10.3 inches (Nashville, Tennessee).[4]

Two days after Christmas, the floodwaters temporarily receded, but January brought more rain to many parts of the region, increasing the pressure on the already strained levee systems. Levees in Arkansas succumbed to the rushing waters from the White and Little Red Rivers on February 4, flooding more than 150,000 acres and leaving five thousand people homeless. Two weeks later, a deadly tornado ripped through Louisiana, Alabama, and Mississippi, causing forty deaths and four hundred thousand dollars' worth of property damage.[5] More severe weather came the South's way in March as record snowfall blanketed North Carolina, Virginia, and Tennessee; tornadoes killed more people in the Lower Mississippi Valley; and rain continued to pound the Delta.

The situation in the Mississippi Delta was particularly distressing. Black laborers worked to fortify the battered levee systems, but on April 15, 1927 — Good Friday — parts of Mississippi, Arkansas, Tennessee, and Louisiana received between six and fifteen inches of rain. From Cairo, Illinois, to the mouth of the Mississippi, the *New York Times* reported, "the most menacing flood in years was sweeping down the Mississippi River and its tributaries."[6]

The next day, a twelve-hundred-foot levee near Cairo collapsed, deluging more than 175,000 acres of land. On Easter Sunday, surging waters demolished levees along the Arkansas and White Rivers, leaving thousands in the most desperate of situations. And still the terrible weather persisted. The levees at Mounds Landing, near Greenville, Mississippi, collapsed on April 21. First among the casualties were the African American workers who had been assigned to fortify those levees: their lifeless bodies drifted in the floodwaters alongside dead animals, abandoned cars, and all kinds of debris and wreckage.[7]

By the time the storms ended in May, flooding had affected an area of twenty-seven thousand square miles, displaced 700,000 people, killed 250 people, and caused property damage estimated at $350 million. Across the Delta, local and state governments authorized the rapid erection of refugee camps in Little Rock, Memphis, Greenville, Vicksburg, New Orleans, and elsewhere. More than 300,000 of the refugees who found temporary shelter, food, and medical assistance in these tent cities were African Americans. After visiting the refugee camps in May, the NAACP's Walter White wrote, "The most impressive thing about the camps was the incredible melancholy of the colored refugees. There was no laughter, no music, no Negro light-heartedness. They sat in silent apathy, or talked in low tones."[8]

When refugees did speak, much of their talk involved starting anew in another part of the South or even the North. Searching for a glimmer of hope, some African Americans speculated that the deluge was part of God's plan for deliverance. Maybe now, some reasoned, black families could find a dramatically different life. At a tent city in Memphis, an Arkansas sharecropper told White,

I've worked for my boss nearly all my life and my children and grandchildren have worked for him. Year after year, I have raised the best crops I could and spent as little for supplies as I could. I have never complained though I knowed he wasn't treating me right. But when the flood came and I had to wade in water up to my neck holding my grandchildren high over my head to save them. I appealed to this white man to help me save my family and he said to me "don't you bring your troubles to me." I will never go back to Arkansas again.[9]

But relocation was difficult. The National Guard patrolled the refugee camps where African Americans had taken shelter, stationed there to safeguard the economic interests of a planter class determined to maintain its bountiful supply of cheap labor. Whites tightly restricted African American movement, leading northern civil rights activists to accuse the tent cities of maintaining a system of virtual slavery in which blacks were required to work from sunup to sundown and were unable to leave the encampments without permission from their current employers. The stories coming out of Greenville, a Delta town that hosted more than fifty thousand black refugees, were particularly troubling. Will Percy, a powerful planter who headed the city's relief efforts, worked black residents and refugees to the brink of exhaustion. Consistent with power arrangements in the Delta, blacks bore a disproportionate amount of the work burden, unloading goods from incoming boats, preparing food, feeding livestock, sorting and distributing supplies, cleaning buildings, and performing other tasks. Moreover, refugee laborers subsisted on the very poor diet of meal, lard, and coffee, since most whites believed that "luxury items" such as vegetables, meat, and sweets would only spoil the labor force.[10]

African Americans began to express outrage at the situation. Writing to the *Chicago Defender* in early May, an African American in Greenville asked, "Why are hundreds of thousands of our people herded in camps, instead of being provided for in houses, where they and their families can be helped as are the white refugees, and live together as families should do? Why must colored people only be forced to work on the levees for $1 per day at the point of a gun before they can get rations?" Frustrated by these stories, veteran activist Ida B. Wells-Barnett called her people to action: "Nobody else is going to do anything about it if we don't. . . . The only way to bring public opinion to action is for those whose race is suffering to cry aloud, and keep on crying aloud until something is done." Finding no hope in "President Coolidge, Secretary Hoover, [or] the National Red Cross," Wells-Barnett urged African Americans to use their electoral strength to effect change. "It will require the combined influence of all our people in the North, East and West, where our votes count, to put a stop to the slavery that is going on right now in the government camps in Arkansas, Mississippi, and Louisiana."[11]

The NAACP was already on the offense. Months earlier, the organization's executive council had sent White to tour some of the camps and had begun seeking information from Lucas and other southern NAACP officials. On May 13, Lucas reported "that a perfect state of slavery exists in many camps in Mississippi, Arkansas, and Louisiana."[12] White, too, "found Negroes penned in concentration camps from which they were not permitted by National Guards to emerge without the consent of their planters." Moreover, refugees were being charged for Red Cross supplies, and "when they were unable to pay, many of them lost everything they owned, the 'debt' was assumed by the landlord of the near plantation, and the Negro taken under guard to the plantation to work out his debt."[13]

For the rest of the spring and well into the summer of 1927, the NAACP blitzed the national media with reports on the cruel and inhumane conditions endured by black refugees, situating the problems in the context of previous economic relations. Though Congress had barred debt peonage—forced unpaid labor as a form of repayment for outstanding debt—in 1867, many black southerners remained trapped in such a system, usually as a result of sharecropping and frequently "with the full connivance and encouragement of state and local authorities."[14] Many African American leaders used their commentary on the flood to argue that the federal government no longer could or should turn a blind eye to this (re)enslavement of black laborers. In a July article in the *Negro World*, veteran black journalist T. Thomas Fortune declared,

> The Mississippi Flood showed the uplift agencies of the country, as well as the protective agencies of the federal government, that a system of slavery has grown up in the Mississippi River states which it is necessary to run down and root out. They now know and can have no excuse for not doing the work of correction, redress and protection which the victims call loudly for and are entitled to receive as a matter of constitutional right and as an act of human justice. The white employers of labor in the Southern States must not be allowed to develop another condition of Negro slavery which might grow into a cause for another civil war.[15]

African Americans also coordinated self-help initiatives to alleviate black suffering. The *Norfolk Journal and Guide*, the *Chicago Defender*, and other publications delivered this message to their readers: remedying the horrific situation would require pooling individual, familial, and community resources.[16]

Numerous black organizations mobilized their resources to assist victims of the Mississippi flood. In many areas, their relief endeavors built on communication and institutional networks created during the previous decade. Such was the case in New Orleans, where the local UNIA division and the NAACP branch coordinated relief drives. Under the leadership of the Black Cross Nurses, the New Orleans UNIA attended to the needs of Louisiana's flood victims, seeking assistance via the *Negro World*:

> At this time, we request the members of the Universal Negro Improvement Association the world over to know that thousands of its members, active and otherwise, are severely suffering from flood disasters along the Mississippi Valley. Critical conditions exist among our people. For humanity's sake we are appealing to all of

our brothers and sisters to help with food and money and whatever possible for the sufferers.[17]

Garveyites in Florida, California, New York, and other states immediately responded with money, clothing, and other materials, earning tremendous appreciation from New Orleanians: "The New Orleans Division wishes to give thanks through the *Negro World* to the divisions and chapters throughout the United States who did what they could to help out the suffering of the Mississippi. . . . Those of the organization who helped will have our everlasting gratitude."[18]

With the NAACP's New York headquarters focused primarily on pressuring the federal government to address the exploitation of black laborers in camps, Lucas and the group's New Orleans chapter spearheaded a similar national relief drive among members. Clothing, supplies, and money came from Fresno, California; Grinnell, Iowa; New York City; Marshall, Texas; Columbia, South Carolina; Wilmington, Delaware; and Alliance, Nebraska; among other locales. A women's club in New Haven, Connecticut, donated more than three hundred dollars, while the Federation of Colored Women's Clubs in Buffalo, New York, sent a check for one hundred dollars. African American churches, too, responded, with New York's Mount Olivet Baptist Church contributing $114.25 and Second Calvary Baptist in Columbia, South Carolina, donating $25.30. And Lucas and other NAACP activists on the ground in the region made sure that donated clothes, supplies, and funds quickly reached flood victims in Louisiana and Mississippi.[19]

The speed with which the New Orleans branch relayed information to the national media, coordinated fund-raising drives in other cities, and delivered goods and money to needy families testified to the strengthening of black America's transregional networks between the outbreak of World War I and the flood. When NAACP branches in the West and Northeast forwarded monies to Lucas, they were giving to someone about whom they had read in the pages of the *Crisis* or whom they had met at the NAACP's national conferences. They knew Lucas to be a dedicated servant of the black freedom struggle who was worthy of their trust.

However, these relief drives also illuminated the limitations of self-help strategies as well as the absence of a powerful movement capable of challenging the political dominance of the ruling elite. No major social policy initiatives addressing the well-established patterns of racial and class inequality that had been magnified during and after the flood emerged from either the White House or Congress. Thus, racism and labor exploitation remained firmly entrenched in the everyday lives of millions of black southerners.

This reality caused many African Americans to reflect on their future in this country. A decade had passed since the United States engaged in a war with the alleged goal of making the world safe for democracy, but the vast majority of blacks remained mired in impoverished conditions, unable to vote, and subjected to a judicial system in which equality under the law applied only to whites. As W. E. B. Du Bois raged in the summer of 1927, "Let us be frank and open with ourselves. The American of Negro descent is still a slave in the United States."[20] Across the storm-ravaged Delta and beyond, Du Bois's blunt commentary resonated deeply, particularly among African Americans feeling the effects of the nation's deepening economic crisis.

Structural changes engendered by rising levels of white and black urbanization, demographic shifts in occupational patterns, and the reorganization of capital resulted in drastic changes in black employment opportunities in the late 1920s. Complaints that African Americans were being squeezed out of the labor force reached a fever pitch as traditional "Negro jobs" increasingly went to unemployed whites. Traveling through Florida, Alabama, and Louisiana in March 1927, Detroit Garveyite J. A. Craigen was stunned:

> Conditions in the South, as I see them, call for the serious attention of all who are engaged in this life of Negro leadership. Formerly in the South . . . Negroes did most of the laborious and menial tasks that were to be done; but today where Negroes once were farmers, white men of foreign extraction have taken their places; where Negroes were the servants, white men and Mexicans have supplanted them; where Negro girls were the maids and nurses, we find the poor white girls who have left the farms are succeeding them; where Negro men did the ditching, chauffeuring, barbering, plastering and brick masonry, we find that schools have been opened and white boys are being taught the arts of driving automobiles, of barbering, plastering and brick masonry, and Negroes are openly dismissed to give way to white men. Therefore, we find that these conditions necessitate sound study on the part of those who assay to lead. The question is not to point out the injustice of the other fellow, because the first law of nature, which is self-preservation, compels him to provide for his own, but it is up to the Negro leaders to blaze the way in directing the course of action that will eventually and permanently benefit the masses by saving them from the danger of annihilation that faces them.[21]

Craigen was hardly alone in his despair about the economic plight of black southerners. Sociologist Gordon Blaine Hancock of Virginia Union University was equally convinced that the race faced a critical situation: "The survival of the Negro in this country," Hancock lamented, "is not a foregone conclusion to thoughtful men! More and more unemployment is going to be a phenomenon of our [mechanized] industrial order and it takes no prophet to see that the burden will fall upon the Negroes."[22]

As the stock market plunged and depression gripped the country, the economic situation for black southerners and the nation as a whole further worsened. The four months following the stock market crash of October 1929 saw the nation's unemployment rolls skyrocket from 500,000 to nearly 2,000,000. Over the next three years, that number reached an astonishing 11.8 million as factories and mines shut down, agricultural prices plummeted, and banks collapsed, one after another.[23]

Throughout the South, blacks struggled to secure employment. "I walked from house to house," one Charlotte woman complained, "begging for something to do and could not even find washing or scrubbing."[24] More often than not, these unsuccessful searches for work forced the unemployed to local relief centers, where they endured even greater levels of humiliation. Writing to the *Negro Worker* in 1931, an unemployed Atlanta laborer described a local soup kitchen's disregard for the black poor: "Everyday hundreds of unemployed, starving Negroes and whites, go there with their two cents to get a can of slop. . . . When a Negro does get past the insulting red tape and question cards he got to fill out, then he finds that he must have two cents and a tin can in order to get a cupful of stinking mixed vegetables and a hunk of stale bread, while whites get their choice of soup or milk and even some of them have coal delivered to their homes."[25]

Better-positioned members of the black working class who had escaped the hardships of the postwar recession also sung the depression blues. "When the Depression came," Albert Gibson of Miami recalled decades later, "us people who had a little money went down with the banks. At the time of President Hoover, we were standing in line for a six-pound sack of flour and a can of soup. Some days you went and stood all day, and didn't get anything."[26] To make matters worse, several city governments barred African Americans from participating in certain trades as a consequence of the rise in white unemployment. On a research trip to Jacksonville, Florida; Savannah, Georgia; and New Orleans, historian Lorenzo Greene noted how the "merciless struggle for bread" combined with political expediency resulted in the passage of laws prohibiting blacks from working on various city projects and in predominantly white neighborhoods.[27]

These policies combined to exact a heavy toll on black communities. As the aggregate income of African Americans plummeted, black institutions struggled to stay afloat. Several NAACP branches in the South lapsed into inactivity as economic hardships shifted members' priorities. "It is exceedingly hard," David Harrell, the president of the Portsmouth, Virginia, branch wrote in 1933, "to stimulate enough interest in the people of this city to make them feel that they are justified in contributing anything to the best interest of the NAACP."[28]

Sustaining membership was also a problem for the UNIA. Firmly integrated into the institutional structures of the black South during the 1920s, the UNIA had achieved a level of popularity that most organizations could only envy. Even after the political embarrassment and internal conflicts brought about by Garvey's imprisonment in 1925, thousands of black southerners still held the organization and its leader in high regard. Such resilience boosted many UNIA leaders' confidence in the association's ability to overcome the challenges of the Great Depression. In 1929, the secretary of the New Orleans UNIA declared, "Despite the industrial handicap through which the colored folk in this section have been passing, the New Orleans Division is yet keeping the fires of loyalty and progress burning." Two years later, however, the secretary's tone was decidedly different: "The people have very little or no money at all. The president, Mr. John Cary Jr., is doing his best to make the New Orleans Division what it used to be and to financially straighten her out with the Parent Body." But neither the New Orleans Division nor many others would ever return to "what it used to be." By 1931, one Miami Garveyite was longing for the "by gone days when Liberty Hall was the center of attraction and served to stimulate the spirit of race pride, and respect for the standard of honor which prevails in high places."[29] Once an institutional center of the New Negro movement, the UNIA had clearly become a shell of its former self.

Garveyites and other New Negro activists had to figure out how to respond to the economic downturn and the new sites of resistance developing within the African American community. Did the current reality call for new political strategies or a deeper commitment to old ones? Should racial uplift ideology and self-help philosophy be discarded, given the profound structural crisis in global capitalism? And if so, what were the most effective ways to reorient black political culture to a more leftist praxis? The political challenges and opportunities of the depression years occasioned a radical shift in the political thinking and attachments of some New Negroes. For others, including Thomas Dabney and James Ivy, political continuity rather than discontinuity marked their activist endeavors following the collapse of the New Negro movement. The two men surged forward in their intellectual and political activities during the 1930s and 1940s. Less than a year after his return to Buckingham Training School, Dabney led a group of six hundred black teachers in a fight for salary equity. A wage scale passed by the Virginia Assembly in early 1930 granted white teachers "a minimum of $60 per month plus as much as $50 more per month based on their qualifications, while their black counterparts would receive a minimum of only $45 per month and not more than an additional $25 based on qualifications." An outraged Dabney, who served as the president of the Buckingham County Colored Teachers' Association, mobilized teachers in twenty-five counties and five cities to sign a petition condemning the salary disparity. Speaking to black teachers, he argued, "Your grocer, doctor, landlord, and the like do not sell their products and wares according to the color of their customers, but according to the general market price of such articles. . . . It is manifestly unjust to have to buy according to economics while earning money according to color!"[30] With the backing of the *Norfolk Journal and Guide*, he called for a mass movement against the "wretchedly low salary paid to the average Virginia Negro teacher." "We have a perfect right," Dabney insisted, "to expect justice and fair play from our state government." He countered those who counseled acquiescence to the status quo due to fear of losing their jobs and their social standing by pointing out that teachers' low salaries frequently resulted in perpetual financial insecurity: "We should not be satisfied with merely white collar jobs. We should love learning, but we must also value money. Under the capitalist economy your well being depends on money." Utilizing the organizing and media relation skills he had acquired at Brookwood Labor College in the 1920s, Dabney counseled, "We cannot afford to delay action in this matter. If ever we needed to organize and act as a solid mass, it is now. . . . Remember that cowards never win the battles of life. Do your own thinking! Use your head! If you can not do either you are not fit to teach the children of Virginia."[31]

Unsuccessful in his fight for equal pay, Dabney found himself blacklisted by Virginia's public schools. Late in the summer of 1933, he reached out to former classmate Abram Harris for assistance in securing employment with the Negro Industrial League, a lobby group organized by John A. Davis in 1933 to pressure New Deal agencies to address the needs and concerns of African Americans. Dabney's growing frustration was apparent in his letter to Harris: "I have been blacklisted by the Virginia school officials and will probably be unable to secure a position in the state public system. . . . I might as well enter the labor field where my training can be utilized in the interest of Negro labor." Unable to secure a position with the Negro Industrial League, Dabney cobbled together an existence as a freelance journalist (he was a regular contributor to the *Norfolk Journal and Guide* well into the 1960s) and instructor at Virginia College and Seminary in Lynchburg.[32]

Ivy also joined the effort to equalize Virginia teachers' pay. He published articles in the *Norfolk Journal and Guide* exhorting the African American community to stand behind men and women who educated their children.[33] In addition, he remained actively engaged in the literary world. Taking a position at Hampton Institute as an English professor in the 1930s, he revived his "Book Bits" review section for the *Crisis*, for which he worked as a writer and editor until the 1960s. Unafraid to chart his own ideological course, Ivy remained one of black America's sharpest political commentators and defied easy categorization. While deeply committed to improving the lives of black workers through unionization and collective action, Ivy had serious issues with what he identified as dogmatic Marxist approaches to American race relations. Economics, he wrote in the *Baltimore Afro-American*, "is by no means the sole cause of race prejudice." Ivy tended to follow Du Bois's ideological worldview, a position that put him at odds with some of his intellectual peers, who favored the Communist Party's approach. To those who had issues with his political inclinations, particularly his critical approach to the party, Ivy quipped, "If fact finding is reactionary then I plead guilty."[34]

Like Ivy and Dabney, Sidney Burt had taken leftist positions in the 1920s, particularly regarding the need to organize black workers, and did not undergo any major ideological shifts during the depression and New Deal eras. After attending the 1917 American Federation of Labor convention, Burt lost patience with the organization's racist politics and became one of the founders of the National Brotherhood Workers of America in 1919. Though the Brotherhood faded into oblivion by the early 1920s, the self-determinist principles that undergirded the organization remained a part of Burt's political career. A highly respected railroad laborer, he presided over several trade unions, most notably the Brotherhood of Railroad Carmen of America, winning praise from the *Norfolk Journal and Guide* in 1948: "Under his leadership the local has been instrumental in bringing about better working conditions — not only at the Seaboard Airline Railway shops, where he has been employed for 36 years — but in several plants of this area."[35] He also served as the leader of the Jefferson Ward Civic League, routinely stressing the need for African Americans to exercise political and economic autonomy. Burt's advocacy of the need to pay poll taxes and vote and to field black labor organizers clearly illustrated that the spirit of the New Negro movement never loosened its grip on his political imagination.

The same can be said of James B. Nimmo, a Miami Garveyite from 1919 to 1929 who became a New Deal–era labor activist.[36] Nimmo's organizational affiliations included the Miami Laundry Workers' Union, the Transport Workers of America, and Shipbuilders Union, which was affiliated with the Congress of Industrial Organizations. Though Nimmo's politics shifted toward the left during the 1930s, he remained indebted to the UNIA and its many political lessons. Until his death in 1992, Nimmo praised the organization not only for enriching the political lives of black Miamians, particularly Bahamian immigrants struggling to negotiate life in Jim Crow Florida, but also for facilitating his radicalization during the New Negro era.[37]

A similar perspective shaped Sylvia Woods's views on her experiences in the Garvey movement. Her father was a New Orleans Garveyite, and Woods's political path eventually brought her into the world of revolutionary politics. After moving to Chicago with her husband, Henry, during the depression years, Woods became a labor organizer for the United Auto Workers. Those experiences pushed her farther to the left, and she eventually held various leadership positions in the

Communist Party. Claude Lightfoot remembered her as a champion of the people who combined radical social critique with a generosity of spirit that endeared her to many black Chicagoans.[38] Southside Chicago and the needs of its most vulnerable citizens consumed much of Woods's life, but she never forgot her roots and the models of working-class and female leadership the New Orleans UNIA had provided. Much like Nimmo, she later credited her connection with the UNIA "as the beginning of my realizing that you have to fight for freedom."[39]

In the Whirlwind

The ways in which the Garvey movement and other New Negro organizations maintained an esteemed place in the memory of Sylvia Woods and other activists bring to mind Black Arts writer, Kalamu ya Salaam, a New Orleans native. His 1978 poem "Whirlwind Storm Warning UNIA" opens with a powerful statement on the historical links between New Negro–era politics and Black Power activism, collapsing the distance between then and now.

> Garvey meant us
> when he said look for me
> he meant not an individual
> a person, a messiah or some christ
> come sneaking like thief at
> midnight but rather a bold collective
> of conscious, capable and committed bloods
> breaking cold day like new firey sun.[1]

Salaam's poem uses a figurative genealogy to illuminate the similarities between past and present political moments. It gives voice to activists and intellectuals of the 1960s and 1970s who envisioned themselves as bringing to fruition the political vision put forth by Marcus Garvey and other New Negro figures. In some cases, this genealogy was not just figurative but also literal. The leaders and foot soldiers of the civil rights and Black Power movements included the children and grand-children of Garveyites, courageous women and men who as youngsters had attended meetings of the Universal Negro Improvement Association (UNIA), hawked publications such as the *Negro World*, or listened in 1927 when Garvey told his beloved followers in New Orleans to "look for me in the whirlwind." These heirs included Virginia Young Collins and Randolph T. Blackwell, whose political trajectories offer important insight into the complex legacy and enduring influence of New Negro political culture.

A native of Plaquemines Parish, Louisiana, Virginia Young Collins was raised in an intensely political household in which her parents preached the importance of civic engagement and race pride. Her father, William Young, was a porter who became an insurance agent as well as a part-time preacher who was heavily involved in the UNIA. Twelve in 1927, when Garvey was deported from the United States, Collins remembered quite vividly Garvey's impact on both her family and community. Nearly every Sunday afternoon, the Young family flocked to the UNIA's Liberty Hall in New Orleans, where moving political speeches, good music, and beautiful displays of pageantry uplifted the spirits of hundreds. Collins also learned a great deal from her father's involvement in voter registration drives, and her immersion into the diverse black political world of the 1920s strengthened her confidence in her ability to meaningfully contribute.[2]

During the New Deal era, Collins linked up with the Southern Conference for Human Welfare, which was founded in 1938 by a biracial coalition of leftists who sought to eliminate all forms of racial and class oppression. Like other members of the group, Collins supported unionization drives, pushed for the elimination of poll taxes, and fought for equal access to public accommodations. As she matured personally and politically, Collins became affiliated with other groups, among them the Voter Education Project, the Revolutionary Action Movement, and the Youth Crusader Corps. Her political journey brought her into close contact with other activists who had roots in the New Negro movement.[3]

One of those activists was Randolph T. Blackwell. Much like Collins, Blackwell had been nurtured in a politically involved household. Blackwell's hometown, Greensboro, North Carolina, claimed a very vibrant UNIA division, and his father, Joseph Blackwell, preached the message of race pride, self-help, and Pan-African unity and attended UNIA meetings, bringing along his son. Randolph Blackwell also canvassed neighborhoods selling Garveyite publications. The family's organizational affiliations shifted during the New Deal era, however: Joseph Blackwell "had not particularly liked Du Bois . . . or the NAACP up to this point, having been highly influenced by the Garvey movement," but during the 1930s, Randolph Blackwell recalled, his father began "to ease his attitude towards the NAACP."[4] The younger Blackwell also worked closely with the NAACP, but the UNIA and its populist sensibilities continued to influence Blackwell's public life.[5]

Blackwell was particularly interested in the ways in which race and class intersected to shape the life chances and experiences of black workers. A graduate of North Carolina A & T University and Howard University Law School, Blackwell taught economics at Winston-Salem State University between 1953 and 1961.[6] However, he devoted much of his public career to applying his intellectual lessons to the real world. As a student at North Carolina A & T in 1948, Blackwell ran for a position on the North Carolina State Assembly, condemning the exploitative practices of the city's business elite as well as black middle-class leaders estranged from serious political engagement. Such fiery rhetoric brought Blackwell public attention but few votes.[7]

He lost the race but remained involved in politics. The following year, Blackwell lent his organizing efforts to Brody McCauley's campaign for a seat on Winston-Salem's city council. The owner of a popular local eatery/poolroom, McCauley hardly qualified as "respectable" in many elite circles, but Blackwell and other Young Turks approached the campaign as a way "to involve people who had not been traditionally thought of as voting citizens." McCauley's campaign pulled "the guys out of the poolrooms and bars and [got] them registered."[8] This deep commitment to empowering laboring people guided Blackwell's work during the 1960s with the Voter Education Project, the Citizen's Crusade against Poverty, and the Southern Rural Action Program. As the civil rights movement gathered steam, Blackwell helped develop institutional structures and financial resources through which the black rural poor could achieve a greater degree of material comfort and human dignity. The cornerstone of his plans was the Southern Rural Action Program. Subsidized by the United Autoworkers and the U.S. Office of Economic Opportunity, the Atlanta-based program sought to increase rural black southerners' economic autonomy through the creation of light industries in impoverished areas such as Plains, Georgia; Mound Bayou, Mississippi; and Greensboro, Alabama. Under Blackwell's leadership, the program organized nine garment factories, four brick manufacturing plants, three silk-screen printing shops, two roof truss operations, and a bakery. "Poor people have the resources in their possession," Blackwell believed, "that can be employed to change their economic condition."[9] Talking to a reporter for *Ebony* magazine, Blackwell evoked the language of self-determination that he had imbued as a Garveyite child: "I'm damn frightened of living in a world where all blacks have to depend upon white people to exist. I'm not saying that we all need to be manufacturers, but we sure need to have some."[10] Blackwell often specifically cited his family's roots in the Garvey movement to explain his political outlook.[11]

Blackwell's and Collins's political careers buttress the idea that the historical significance and legacy of the New Negro era extends beyond the cultural and literary arena. The democratic impulse and egalitarian vision that defined many aspects of the New Negro movement remained a part of African American social and political thought for years to come. As activists encountered new challenges and struggles, they turned to the political victories and defeats of the 1920s for historical perspective and navigational guidance.

In addition, the organizational developments and political activities of the New

Negro era figured significantly in the creation of a black political infrastructure and the formation of a black nationality. After the NAACP's 1929 national convention, W. E. B. Du Bois offered some perspective on the organization's accomplishments during the preceding decade: "The significance of what we have done is not so much the advancement made as the foundation we have begun to lay."[12]

Du Bois's commentary applies to many of the political actors discussed in this volume. With the conviction that they stood on the verge of great political, cultural, and economic achievements, southern New Negroes set out to refashion the world with the same sense of confidence and urgency that drove many of their New York and Chicago counterparts. Their literary and political endeavors transformed New Orleans, Norfolk, Miami, Savannah, Jacksonville, and other southern cities into important centers of New Negro politics and culture. More than mere outposts of organizations headquartered in the North, southern branches of such important New Negro groups as the UNIA and the Brotherhood of Sleeping Car Porters contributed to the political milieu. James Ivy, Thomas Dabney, and other black intellectuals created an impressive body of work that benefited immensely from their residency in Virginia, enabling them to cast a critical eye on key issues in a distinctly different manner from their colleagues in New York, Washington, or Chicago.

But New Negro southerners were not disconnected from developments in the North. To build bonds with politically engaged blacks in the larger African diaspora, many southern activists identified strongly with Marcus Garvey, A. Philip Randolph, and Claude McKay, among other New Negro figures. Southerners also read and wrote for the *Negro World* and the *Messenger*, traveled north for political conventions and conferences, and followed intellectual developments taking place in Harlem and Southside Chicago. At the same time, New Negroes in the North derived great inspiration from their counterparts working, living, and organizing in the South, and engagement with southern activists and organizations shaped northerners' views on such issues as the relationship between blacks and organized labor, the trustworthiness of white liberals, and the radical potential of black colleges and universities.

Du Bois and other critical thinkers understood that the South was much more than a bastion of white supremacy; it was also a dynamic region that supplied the postwar period with some of its most courageous fighters for racial equality and economic justice. Students at the South's black colleges, for example, battled conservative white administrators who restricted social opportunities, compromised the intellectual rigor of coursework, hired racist white teachers, and succumbed to pressure from racist philanthropists and politicians who sought to maintain the status quo. These students brought several important questions to the center of black political discourse: What role would black universities play in training the next generation of African American leaders? Would African American colleges produce future freedom fighters or defenders of the status quo? And how much control would the radical, liberal, and conservative wings of the black leadership class have over the direction of black higher education? Du Bois, for one, defended black collegians' political endeavors as not only necessary but profoundly revolutionary. On the heels of a 1925 student strike at Nashville's Fisk University, he proudly announced,

> At last we have real radicalism of the young—radicalism that costs, that is not mere words and foam. Hitherto so much of what we called radicalism has been simply internal jealousy. We struck and jibed at our own brothers and felt brave. This was the case with Garveyism which from start to finish was simply a scurrilous attack of Negroes on Negroes. This was the case with the young black Socialists who started out ten years ago to attack capitalism and ended by attacking every Negro whose head appeared above the mired mass. But here is the real radical, the man who hits power in high places, white power, power backed by unlimited wealth; hits it and hits it openly and between the eyes; talks face to face and not down "at the big gate." God speed the breed![13]

Situating the college rebellions of the 1920s within a larger political context, Du Bois identified black collegians in the South as the African American community's most potent line of defense against wealthy capitalists determined to strengthen their sphere of influence in higher education. "The Bourbon South," Du Bois hissed, has "always wanted to not simply separate the world into white and black, but to enter the black world at will and order 'niggers' about."[14]

Unlike many of his contemporaries, who all but ignored the student rebellions of the 1920s, Du Bois poured tremendous energy into covering and interpreting events at black colleges, particularly Fisk and Hampton. His investment reflected not just his interest in black higher education but also his ability to imagine the South as a key battleground for black self-determination. His position undoubtedly derived from his numerous encounters with black college students who indeed viewed themselves as the revolutionary vanguard of the New Negro movement. Du Bois's ability to position the South as an incubator for some of the era's most radical political actors may also have resulted from his contact with the black southerners who labored to start NAACP branches, subscribed to the *Crisis*, stopped by his office in New York, challenged the racist politics of the American Federation of Labor, battled their employers on the job, and put their lives on the line to advance the black freedom struggle.

Like Du Bois, the New Negroes discussed in this book envisioned the South as a space from which they could launch their fight against white racism and economic injustice. Between the outbreak of World War I and the onset of the Great Depression, they challenged the exploitative practices of employers and the racism of the American Federation of Labor, promoted the Pan-African politics of the UNIA, sought to democratize electoral politics, and put forth new paradigms for studying the so-called Negro problem. Few of these political activists lived to see the fruits of their efforts, but they indeed helped to sow the seeds of change.

NOTES

Abbreviations

Marcus Garvey Papers   Robert A. Hill, ed. *The Marcus Garvey and Universal Negro Improvement Association Papers*. Vols. 1–6. Berkeley: University of California Press, 1983–89.

NAACP Papers-LC   National Association for the Advancement of Colored People Papers, Library of Congress Manuscript Division, Washington, D.C.

NAACP Papers-MF   *Papers of the National Association for the Advancement of Colored People*. Frederick, Md.: University Publications of America, 1982–.

NJG   *Norfolk Journal and Guide*

NW   *Negro World*

NYT   *New York Times*

Introduction

1. *New York Age*, September 20, 1919.

2. For primary data on the National Brotherhood's activities consult the United States Railroad Administration files in Grossman, *Black Workers*, Reel 10, Frames 770–85; *Messenger*, August, December 1919; *Marcus Garvey Papers*, 1:467. Brief mention of the NBWA can also be found in Spero and Harris's seminal text, *Black Worker*, 117–19.

3. *Messenger*, August 1919.

4. Ibid., December 1919.

5. Ibid., August 1919.

6. *Marcus Garvey Papers*, 2:121.

7. For a broader discussion on New Negroes' complex relationship to modernity, see Baker, *Modernism*; Gates, "Trope"; Hutchinson, *Harlem Renaissance*; Spencer, *New Negroes and Their Music*; Favor, *Authentic Blackness*; Maxwell, *New Negro, Old Left*; Foley, *Spectres of 1919*; Ross, *Manning the Race*; Nadell, *Enter the New Negroes*; Carroll, *Word, Image, and the New Negro*.

In my exploration of black southerners' quest for citizenship, economic security, and literacy during the New Negro era, I have relied on Houston Baker's definition of Afro-modernity: "The general effects of African, African diasporic, and Afro-American people's 'strike toward freedom,' their move toward a cosmopolitan mobility of citizenship, work, cultural reclamation and production that enhance the lives of a black majority globally conceived" (*Turning South Again*, 34).

8. The idea of the South as a site of cultural backwardness, political repression, and racial horror finds expression in the utterances of such notable Harlem Renaissance pro-

tagonists as Nella Larsen's Helga Crane, Rudolph Fisher's King Solomon Gillis, and Jean Toomer's Ralph Kabnis. See Rudolph Fisher, *City of Refuge*; Larsen, *Quicksand*; Toomer, *Cane*. For the regional politics of the Harlem Renaissance's literary productions, see Griffin, "*Who Set You Flowin'?*"; Lawrence Rodgers, *Canaan Bound*, 70–96; Nathan Grant, *Masculinist Impulses*.

9. *NW*, March 9, 1929.

10. Stansell, *American Moderns*, 7.

11. In fleshing out this particular issue, I have found the work of historian Charles Payne quite useful. Payne argues that southern blacks in the civil rights movement possessed a "dialectical worldview sensitive to how contradictions in social structure shape contradictions in people, and also sensitive to people as at least potentially changing and evolving." This worldview, he continues, "militated against thinking about people in one dimensional terms" (*I've Got the Light of Freedom*, 314). Suggested but not explicitly stated in Payne's analysis was how black southerners' humanism may have guarded them against theoretical and political dogmatism.

12. *NW*, November 17, 1927.

13. Significant insight into the contested history of interracial unionism in the American South can be gleaned from Gutman, "Negro and the United Mine Workers"; Rachleff, *Black Labor in the South*; Rosenberg, *New Orleans Dockworkers*; Arnesen, *Waterfront Workers of New Orleans*; Arnesen, "Following the Color Line"; Letwin, "Interracial Unionism"; Norwood, "Bogalusa Burning."

14. See Iton, *Solidarity Blues*.

15. Earl Lewis, *In Their Own Interests*, 46–58; Foley, *Spectres of 1919*.

16. For more on the NAACP's work during the New Negro era, see Eisenberg, "Only for the Bourgeois?"; Reich, "Great War."

17. Several New Negro activists, most notably Randolph, Owen, Hubert Harrison, and Cyril Briggs, denounced the NAACP for what they perceived as its stubborn unwillingness to move beyond its reformist agenda. A great deal of their criticism was directed toward W. E. B. Du Bois, whom they deemed out of touch with the realities of the black masses. As historian Paula Pfeffer explains, "Just as Booker T. Washington had seemed too conservative to the young Du Bois, Du Bois now seemed too conservative to the young Socialists" (*A. Philip Randolph*, 9).

18. Baker, *Modernism*, 71–98.

19. See Moses, *Golden Age*; Moses, *Black Messiahs and Uncle Toms*; Moses, *Afrotopia*; Stein, *World of Marcus Garvey*; Gaines, *Uplifting the Race*; Bush, *We Are Not What We Seem*; Dean E. Robinson, *Black Nationalism*. My analysis of the labor arena as a site of black nationality formation builds on the work of scholars who situate African Americans' complex articulations of nation within very specific local, material, and ritualistic contexts. Two studies in particular have had a profound impact on my interpretive framework: Glaude, *Exodus!*; Walker, *Noble Fight*.

20. See Hunter, *To 'Joy My Freedom*, 219–40; Arnesen, *Waterfront Workers of New Orleans*; Haiken, "'The Lord Helps Those'"; Leslie Brown, *Uplifting Black Durham*, 223–43. For primary materials on black working-class activism in the South, see Arnesen, *Black Protest*; Foner and Lewis, *Black Worker*, 5:417–28.

21. Foley, *Spectres of 1919*, 66.

22. Dawson, *Black Visions*, 258–67.

23. See Bair, "Renegotiating Liberty"; Vought, "Racial Stirrings in Colored Town";

Rolinson, *Grassroots Garveyism*; Harold, *Rise and Fall*; Hahn, *Political Worlds*; Duncan, "'Efficient Womanhood.'"

24. *NW*, December 31, 1929.

25. Bates, *Pullman Porters*; Bynum, *A. Philip Randolph*, 101–56.

26. Foner and Lewis, *Black Worker*, 7:207.

27. *Messenger*, December 1927.

28. Dabney, "Southern Students Study Race Relations," 400.

29. Clyde Taylor, "Oscar Micheaux," 226; Baldwin, *Chicago's New Negroes*; Baldwin and Makalani, *Escape from New York*.

30. Clyde Taylor, "Oscar Micheaux," 132.

31. My understanding of the "black South" as a geographical and cultural space draws on Bond, "Negro Looks at His South"; Toomer, *Cane*; Du Bois, *Souls of Black Folk*; Du Bois, *Black Reconstruction*; Sterling A. Brown, *Sterling A. Brown's A Negro Looks at the South*; Griffin, "*Who Set You Flowin'?*"; Payne, *I've Got the Light of Freedom*; Carmichael, *Ready for Revolution*, 277–322; Patterson, *Zora Neale Hurston*; Smethurst, *Black Arts Movement*, 319–66; Davis, "Reclaiming the South"; Baker, *I Don't Hate the South*.

32. Killens and Ward, *Black Southern Voices*, 1.

33. W. E. B. Du Bois, "Behold the Land," in *W. E. B. Du Bois: A Reader*, 545.

34. Richard Wright eloquently articulates this perspective in *Black Boy*:

Never being fully able to be myself, I had slowly learned that the South could recognize but a part of a man, could accept but a fragment of his personality, and all the rest—the best and deepest things of heart and mind were tossed away in blind ignorance and hate. I was leaving the South to fling myself into the unknown, to meet other situations that would perhaps elicit from me other responses. . . .

Yet deep down, I knew that I could never really leave the South, for my feelings had already been formed by the South, for there had been slowly instilled into my personality and consciousness, black though I was, the culture of the South. So, in leaving, I was taking a part of the South to transplant in alien soil, to see if it could grow differently, if it could drink of new and cool rains, bend in strange winds, respond to the warmth of other suns, and perhaps, to bloom. . . . And if that miracle ever happened, then I would know that there was yet hope in that southern swamp of despair and violence, that light could emerge even out of the blackest of the southern night. (284–85)

35. Toomer, *Cane*, 81.

36. *Crusader*, December 1919.

37. *Marcus Garvey Papers*, 3:376.

38. Over the past fifteen years or so, scholars in a wide range of disciplines have called for a more expansive understanding of what constitutes the South. For example, in a special issue of *American Literature*, "Global Contexts, Local Literatures: The New Southern Studies," Tara McPherson writes, "We need to think of Southernness and Southern geography as at best provisional, relational—as spaces that shift with various border crossings . . . This means that we need to reorient southern studies from an axis of us versus them or blue vs. gray to think about the South more broadly . . . as a hinge point between the Americas. We need to think in terms of transit zones, not closed-off borders" ("On Wal-Mart and Southern Studies," 696). More on the development of the field of new southern studies can be found in Baker, *Turning South Again*; McPherson, *Reconstructing Dixie*; Jon Smith and Cohn, *Look Away!*; Kreyling, "Toward 'A New Southern Studies'";

Cobb and Stueck, *Globalization and the American South*; Duck, *Nation's Region*; Richardson, *Black Masculinity*; Peacock, *Grounded Globalism*.

39. Gilmore, *Defying Dixie*, 5, 6.

40. McKee and Trefzer, "U.S. South in Global Contexts," 69.

Chapter 1. The Hour Has Come

1. American Federation of Labor, *Report of the Proceedings of the Thirty-Seventh Annual Convention*, 278.

2. Earl Lewis, *In Their Own Interests*, 46–58; Arnesen, *Waterfront Workers of New Orleans*, 217–28; Haiken, "'The Lord Helps Those.'"

3. Arnesen, *Black Protest*, 27. For a broader view of labor activism during and immediately after World War I, see McCartin, *Labor's Great War*; Montgomery, *Fall*, 370–78.

4. See Williams, *Torchbearers for Democracy*.

5. Lentz-Smith, *Freedom Struggles*, 2.

6. For detailed information on the Great Migration, see Henri, *Black Migration*; Gottlieb, *Making Their Own Way*; Marks, *Farewell*; Grossman, *Land of Hope*; Trotter, *Great Migration*; Earl Lewis, *In Their Own Interests*; Alferdteen Harrison, *Black Exodus*; Sernett, *Bound for the Promised Land*; Phillips, *AlabamaNorth*; Best, *Passionately Human*; Wilkerson, *Epic Story*.

7. *Crisis*, June 1917.

8. *The Vindicator*, September 12, 1918.

9. *Crisis*, May 1917.

10. National Association for the Advancement of Colored People, *Report*.

11. Sullivan, *Lift Every Voice*.

12. Arnesen, *Black Protest*, 141.

13. Their bold actions incurred the wrath of not only employers but also local law enforcement officials. Arguing that these strikers were interfering with the city's wartime mobilization efforts, Savannah's police department immediately swung into action, arresting fifty of the strikers under the city's work-or-fight law. These events did not go over well in the black community. Civil rights leaders and labor activists lambasted the local police department, insisting that the actions of law enforcement officials constituted a misuse of police power and a blatant violation of one of the most important provisions in the work-or-fight law: the exclusion of strikers from arrest. The police actions had clearly sought to intimidate the longshoremen into a quick submission, but the strikers stood their ground (*Savannah Tribune*, August 24, 1918).

14. See Horton, *Race*; Schneirov, *Labor and Urban Politics*.

15. *Savannah Tribune*, March 23, 1918.

16. American Federation of Labor, *Report of the Proceedings of the Thirty-Seventh Annual Convention*, 3.

17. Ibid., 3.

18. Foner and Lewis, *Black Worker*, 5:418–19.

19. U.S. Census, 1920.

20. U.S. World War I Draft Registration Cards, 1917–18, available at ancestry.com.

21. *NJG*, March 3, 1951.

22. Ibid., September 22, 1917.

23. Foner and Lewis, *Black Worker*, 5:419.

24. American Federation of Labor, *Report of the Proceedings of the Thirty-Seventh Annual Convention*, 280.

25. Foner and Lewis, *Black Worker*, 5:418.

26. Work, "Effects."

27. *New York Age*, November 22, 1917.

28. *Marcus Garvey Papers*, 1:467–68. No monies were allocated for more black organizers in Virginia, North Carolina, or Florida. Nor were any funds set aside to address the needs of black workers employed on the railroads of the Southeast. Neither the executive council nor Gompers veered away from their customary handling of the race question and African American workers. Gompers's refusal to take a bold, proactive stance on the matter of racial discrimination meshed perfectly with his politics of prudential unionism.

29. Foner and Lewis, *Black Worker*, 5:420.

30. Perry, *Hubert Harrison*, 356.

31. Only one month after the United States officially entered the war, officials at the Charleston Navy Yard's clothing factory announced plans to employ only white women for six hundred new openings. Wasting no time in aligning itself with the cause of African American workers, the local NAACP committed its resources to defending black women's right to the same employment opportunities as their white counterparts. The association's executive secretary and most outspoken leader, Richard M. Mickey, viewed the hiring controversy as an opportunity to widen black women's employment options as well as galvanize various segments of the black community. Of the opinion that the diversification of black women's employment options advanced the larger goals of the race, Mickey exerted tremendous energy to secure positions for black women. During the dispute with the clothing factory, local blacks received vital advice and legal counsel from James Weldon Johnson and W. E. B. Du Bois, NAACP executive secretary Roy Nash, and Grimké. Transregional connections forged by the NAACP also linked black Charleston to the Midwest, where one civil rights activist closely monitored labor developments in the South Carolina city. Interpreting the clothing factory's discriminatory hiring policies as a crucial labor and civil rights issue that had profound implications for African Americans across the nation, R. Augustine Skinner, secretary of the Minneapolis NAACP, dispatched letters of protest to select members of the U.S. Congress. Well aware of black southerners' limited political power, the Minnesota activist hoped that Republicans' fear of losing the northern black vote would move them to protect the interests of black workers. To a certain extent, this strategy proved effective. Not long after the NAACP's national office and its northern branches launched their letter-writing campaign, correspondence from the nation's capital began pouring into the organization's headquarters in Manhattan. Claiming that blatantly discriminatory hiring policies undermined the country's war efforts, several Republican congressmen, most notably Minnesota's Knute Nelson, Clarence B. Miller, and Harold Knutson, agreed to assist the NAACP in its efforts. See James Weldon Johnson to Richard Mickey, April 13, 1917, Knute Nelson to R. A. Skinner, June 26, 1917, Harold Knutson to R. Augustine Skinner, July 6, 1917, "Committee of Colored Citizens," Charleston, S.C., May 10, 1917, all in Box G-196, Folder 11, NAACP Papers-LC.

32. Touré F. Reed, *Not Alms but Opportunity*, 81.

33. *New York Age*, February 9, 1918.

34. Foner and Lewis, *Black Worker*, 5:421.

35. American Federation of Labor, *Report of the Proceedings of the Thirty-Eighth Annual Convention*, 205.

36. None of the African American trade unionists in attendance at the Buffalo convention made it to Minnesota.

37. American Federation of Labor, *Report of the Proceedings of the Thirty-Eighth Annual Convention*, 175.

38. Records of the National War Labor Board, Case File 2.

39. Foner and Lewis, *Black Worker*, 5:424.

40. American Federation of Labor, *Report of the Proceedings of the Thirty-Eighth Annual Convention*, 263.

41. *Savannah Tribune*, March 2, 1918.

Chapter 2. Now Comes the Test

1. *NYT*, November 17, 1918.

2. Quoted in Dubofsky, *Hard Work*, 121.

3. J. E. Cutler to Marlborough Churchill, August 15, 1919, Case File 10218-361-87, Military Intelligence Division, Records of the War Department General and Special Staffs.

4. See Bush, *We Are Not What We Seem*; James, *Holding Aloft*; Foley, *Spectres of 1919*; Martin, *Race First*; Pfeffer, *A. Philip Randolph*; Solomon, *Cry Was Unity*, 22–37; Hubert H. Harrison, *Hubert Harrison Reader*; Perry, *Hubert Harrison*.

5. "Open Letter," Box C-414, Folder 5, NAACP Papers-LC.

6. Ibid.

7. Arnesen, *Brotherhoods of Color*, 55.

8. According to L. A. Gabriel, every member of Local 1000 also belonged to the Key West branch of the NAACP, which had been organized in 1913 (L. A. Gabriel to James Weldon Johnson, January 26, 1919, Box C-414, Folder 5, NAACP Papers-LC).

9. This was not the first time that Gabriel had alerted Johnson to a labor situation in the South Florida city. Only six months earlier, Gabriel had been embroiled in a battle over the exclusion of black carpenters from a government project to construct army cantonments (Foner, *History*, 191).

10. L. A. Gabriel to James Weldon Johnson, January 26, 1919, Box C-414, Folder 5, NAACP Papers-LC.

11. James Weldon Johnson to L. A. Gabriel, February 28, 1919, in ibid.

12. James Weldon Johnson to John J. Joyce, February 28, 1919, in ibid.

13. John J. Joyce to John R. Shillady, March 4, 1919, James Weldon Johnson to L. A. Gabriel, March 12, 1919, both in ibid. In his letter to Shillady, O'Connor noted the recent formation of Local 1000 but promised to provide assistance: "I am making arrangements to send one of our representatives to Key West, and when he goes there he will do everything possible to assist the workers of that port. These men were only organized a few weeks when they went out on strike. However, it is our purpose to do everything we can to help them and when Mr. Herman Fricke goes to Key West he will undoubtedly make such recommendations as will be of greatest benefit to them" (T. V. O'Connor to John R. Shillady, March 11, 1919, Box C-414, Folder 5, NAACP Papers-LC).

14. *Marcus Garvey Papers*, 1:467.

15. Foner and Lewis, *Black Worker*, 5:417–27.

16. *Marcus Garvey Papers*, 1:467.

17. Jeannette Carter, Woman Wage Earners Association, Carter Collection, Folder 4.

18. Carter believed that women needed to take the lead in improving their labor condi-

tions. "It is no longer deemed wise nor expedient," she stated, "for women to wait for men to do for them what woman should do for woman" (ibid.).

19. *New York Age*, March 8, 1919.

20. *Richmond Planet*, June 20, 1909, June 30, 1917.

21. Grossman, *Black Workers*, Reel 10, Frame 770.

22. Foner and Lewis, *Black Worker*, 5:419.

23. Arnesen, *Brotherhoods of Color*, 48.

24. Lewis H. Brown and Edward D. Thompson to W. S. Carter, in Grossman, *Black Workers*, Reel 10, Frame 783.

25. Lewis H. Brown and Edward D. Thompson to J. R. Franklin, in ibid., Reel 10, Frames 778, 785; *Messenger*, August, December 1919.

26. *Washington Post*, June 5, 1919; *Richmond Times-Dispatch*, June 6, 1919.

27. *Virginia Pilot*, June 5, 1919.

28. *Washington Post*, June 5, 1919; *Richmond Times-Dispatch*, June 6, 1919.

29. *New York Call*, June 12, 1919.

30. *Richmond Planet*, June 14, 1919.

31. *NYT*, June 10, 1919.

32. Foner and Lewis, *Black Worker*, 5:424–25.

33. *Crisis*, September 1919.

34. *NYT*, June 14, 1919.

35. Foner and Lewis, *Black Worker*, 5:435.

36. *NYT*, June 14, 1919.

37. Foner and Lewis, *Black Worker*, 5:447.

38. *Messenger*, August 1919.

39. *Marcus Garvey Papers*, 1:467.

40. Gompers, *Samuel Gompers Papers*, 188.

41. Randolph and Owen argued that the NBWA's impressive growth in membership influenced proceedings at the AFL's Atlantic City convention. Countering the claims of moderate black leaders who asserted that their inside negotiations with the AFL had been responsible for the convention's progressive resolutions, Randolph and Owen attributed the AFL's less hostile attitude toward blacks to its concerns about the NBWA's growing influence. "It was the power of the organization," they insisted, "more than anything else, which drove the American Federation of Labor to adopt its changed profession toward the Negro labor" (*Messenger*, August 1919).

42. Ibid., December 1919.

43. Tuttle, *Race Riot*; Abu-Lughod, *Race, Space, and Riots*; Voogd, *Race Riots and Resistance*; Whitaker, *On the Laps of Gods*; Krugler, *Year of Racial Violence*.

44. *Messenger*, December 1919.

45. *NYT*, June 18, 1919.

46. *Messenger*, December 1919.

47. The NBWA's crucial role in enriching the political culture of New Negro radicalism has been overshadowed by the African Blood Brotherhood. Organized by Cyril Briggs, Richard B. Moore, and W. A. Domingo in 1919, the African Blood Brotherhood has been elevated by many scholars as the quintessential New Negro radical group. Bush, for example, asserts that the Brotherhood "came closest to developing a political line that was appropriate for building a revolutionary black working-class movement" (*We Are Not What We Seem*, 102).

For comparison sake, I believe that the NBWA resembles the League of Revolutionary Black Workers, which was comprised of industrial workers and radical political theorists. Organized in 1969, the League, like the NBWA, developed in response to the entrenched racism within the trade union movement. On the League of Revolutionary Workers, see Geschwender, *Class, Race, and Worker Insurgency*.

48. For a broader and more nuanced reading of New Negro–era gender politics, see Ula Yvette Taylor, *Veiled Garvey*; McDuffie, *Sojourning for Freedom*, 24–57.

49. Ross, *Manning the Race*, 24.

50. See also Hornsby-Gutting, *Black Manhood and Community Building*.

51. Looking primarily at the Communist Party, Gilmore reinforces this point in *Defying Dixie*: "Because the South represented the least industrialized and unionized part of the United States, the region weighed heavily on Communist minds. In 1920, 9 million African Americans lived within the confines of the Old Confederacy, the border states of Kentucky and Oklahoma, and the mid-Atlantic states of Maryland and Delaware. Only 1.5 million African Americans lived outside those bounds. If southern African Americans became Communists, they could lead the revolution in their region" (30).

52. *Messenger*, February 1920.

53. Ibid., July 1918.

54. Ibid., September 1919.

55. For detailed accounts of the 1919 Elaine, Arkansas, race riot, see Stockley, *Blood in Their Eyes*; Whitaker, *On the Laps of Gods*; Woodruff, "New Negro."

56. Woodruff, *American Congo*, 81.

57. *Crusader*, January 1920.

58. Norwood, "Bogalusa Burning."

59. *Messenger*, February 1920.

60. Spero and Harris, *Black Worker*, 118.

Chapter 3. Making Way for Democracy

1. Charles A. J. McPherson to NAACP, November 9, 1920, Part 4, Reel 1, Frames 445–46, NAACP Papers-MF.

2. Perman, *Struggle for Mastery*.

3. G. W. Williams to John Shillady, July 15, 1919, Part 4, Reel 1, Frame 188, NAACP Papers-MF.

4. *Messenger*, August 1920.

5. *Savannah Tribune*, April 27, 1918.

6. Adolph Reed Jr., *Stirrings in the Jug*, 19.

7. *Vindicator*, August 20, 1918.

8. C. L. Henderson to Walter White, May 17, 1919, Part 4, Reel 1, Frames 168–69, NAACP Papers-MF.

9. Ibid., Frame 167.

10. Lebsock, "Woman Suffrage and White Supremacy"; Wilkerson-Freeman, "Women and the Transformation"; Terborg-Penn, *African American Women*, 143–58; Wilkerson-Freeman, "Stealth"; Schuyler, *Weight of Their Votes*; Ortiz, *Emancipation Betrayed*; Nikki Brown, *Private Politics and Public Voices*.

11. Jeannette Carter, n.d., Woman's Suffrage, Carter Collection, Folder 5.

12. Nikki Brown, *Private Politics and Public Voices*, xi.

13. See Arnesen, *Black Protest*, 141–44; Nikki Brown, *Private Politics and Public Voices*, 30–65.

14. Addie Hunton, "Hampton," October 25, 1920, Part 4, Reel 1, Frame 415, NAACP Papers-MF.

15. *NYT*, September 20, 1920.

16. *Florida Times-Union*, September 25, 1920.

17. *NYT*, September 19, 1920.

18. *Florida Times-Union*, September 20, 1920.

19. Lebsock, "Woman Suffrage and White Supremacy," 85.

20. *Florida Times-Union*, October 17, 1920.

21. Gross, *Colored Amazons*, 126.

22. Addie Hunton, "Hampton," October 25, 1920, Part 4, Reel 1, Frame 412, NAACP Papers-MF.

23. Addie Hunton, "General Statements," October 25, 1920, in ibid., Frame 414.

24. Addie Hunton, "Hampton," October 25, 1920, in ibid., Frame 413.

25. Addie Hunton, "Phoebus," in ibid., Frame 411. Fields's response lends credence to Schuyler's claim that "southern black manhood was fortified by defending black women voters" (*Weight of Their Votes*, 34).

26. Addie Hunton, "Phoebus," Part 4, Reel 1, Frame 412, NAACP Papers-MF.

27. Ibid.

28. Butler W. Nance to Moorfield Storey, September 17, 1920, in ibid., Frame 480.

29. *Crisis*, November 1920.

30. Charles A. J. McPherson to NAACP, November 18, 1920, Part 4, Reel 1, Frame 483, NAACP Papers-MF.

31. *Richmond Planet*, March 20, 1920.

32. *NYT*, June 6, 1920.

33. *Richmond Planet*, April 29, 1920.

34. John Parker, the North Carolina Lily-Whites' nominee for governor, predicted that the Republicans would heroically redeem the South—without the assistance of "Mr. Nigger" (quoted in Gilmore, "False Friends and Avowed Enemies," 222).

35. Richard B. Sherman puts forth an excellent summary of the Republican Party's dilemma during the 1920s: "The new spirit among the Negro population complicated the Republican political situation. On the one hand was the desire to crack the solid South, a development that seemed to require even greater neglect of Negroes and acceptance of lily-whiteism. On the other hand was the growing militancy and racial consciousness of Negroes. More strenuously than ever they demanded their constitutional rights, while the new concentrations of Negroes in the North represented a potential voting power that had to be considered" ("Republicans and Negroes," 65–66).

36. *NYT*, June 6, 1920.

37. Ibid., May 26, 1920.

38. Ibid.

39. Ibid., July 23, 1920.

40. Ibid. The *Times*'s prediction proved largely correct, as Harding won only Tennessee among the former Confederate states.

41. Devore, *Defying Jim Crow*, 182–86; Donald L. Grant, *Way It Was*, 336–38.

42. *Crisis*, October 1920.

43. *Crusader*, October 1919. For more on Burroughs's politics, see Harley, "Nannie

Helen Burroughs"; Karen A. Johnson, *Uplifting Women and the Race*; Savage, *Your Spirits Walk beside Us*, 163–204.

44. *NYT*, April 29, May 9, 1920. Perhaps no campaign shocked whites more than the nomination of African American J. H. Blount for the Arkansas governorship.

45. For more on black Richmond, see Elsa Barkley Brown, "Womanist Consciousness"; Kimball and Brown, "Mapping the Terrain"; Alexander: *Race Man*.

46. Mass Meeting Flyer, Box G-210, Folder 10, NAACP Papers-LC.

47. *Virginia Pilot*, March 27, 1920. In May, Ferguson and Pollard served as delegates to the National Republican Convention.

48. In the 1920s, Pollard led the Citizens' Defense Committee in its efforts to desegregate housing in Richmond (J. Clay Smith Jr., *Emancipation*, 233–34); D. A. Ferguson to NAACP, October 5, 1920, Part 4, Reel 1, Frame 312, NAACP Papers-MF.

49. *Richmond Planet*, May 26, 1920.

50. D. A. Ferguson to NAACP, October 5, 1920, Part 4, Reel 1, Frame 312, NAACP Papers-MF.

51. Ibid., Frames 311–12.

52. *Crisis*, January 1921, 106–9.

53. "NAACP Press Release," November 9, 1920, Part 4, Reel 1, Frame 451, NAACP Papers-MF. Section 2 of the Fourteenth Amendment asserts that "when the right to vote at any election for the choice of electors for President and Vice-President of the United States, Representatives in Congress, the Executive and Judicial officers of a State or the members of the Legislature thereof, is denied to any of the male inhabitants of such State, being twenty-one years of age, and citizens of the United States, or in any way abridged, except for participation in rebellion, or other crime, the basis of representation therein shall be reduced in the proportion which the number of such male citizens shall bear to the whole number of male citizens twenty-one years of age in such State."

54. *NYT*, December 6, 1920.

55. Mrs. S. S. Humbert to the NAACP, November 9, 1920, Part 4, Reel 1, Frame 420, NAACP Papers-MF.

56. Clara D. Mann to William H. Hays, November 19, 1920, in ibid., Frame 484.

57. W. S. Turner to William Pickens, December 30, 1920, in ibid., Frame 564.

58. *NYT*, May 19, August 21, 1921.

59. D'Orso, *Like Judgment Day*; Jones, "Rosewood Massacre."

60. *NW*, October 8, 1921.

Chapter 4. On the Firing Line

1. Leon Howe to Bureau, July 8, 1921, Bureau Section Case File 198940-183, Records of the Federal Bureau of Investigation.

2. *Miami Herald*, February 10, 1975.

3. Ida Caroline Gibson, Petition for Naturalization, December 3, 1953, Florida Naturalization Records, 1847–1995, available at ancestry.com.

4. For recent studies on Garvey's global impact, see Vinson, *Americans Are Coming*; Ewing, *Age of Garvey*; Chery, "Kingdoms of the Earth."

5. *Spokesmen*, May 1927.

6. Ibid.

7. For more on the UNIA's early success in the Hampton Roads area, see Special Agent

Jones to Bureau, February 9, 1920, OG 185161, Records of the Federal Bureau of Investigation; *Spokesmen*, May 1927.

8. Bandele, *Black Star*; *Marcus Garvey Papers*, 1:452.

9. *Marcus Garvey Papers*, 2:117.

10. *Spokesmen*, May 1927.

11. *NW*, September 3, 1921.

12. Frank, *Purchasing Power*, 75.

13. *Marcus Garvey Papers*, 2:534, 518.

14. Ibid., 682–83.

15. W. W. Bailey to Bureau, December 31, 1919, OG 267600, Records of the Federal Bureau of Investigation.

16. C. B. Treadway to Frank Burke, August 11, 1919, OG 185161, in ibid.

17. E. J. Kerwin to Bureau, March 12, 1919, in ibid.

18. U.S. Census.

19. See *NW*, February 19, June 25, October 29, 1921, February 4, March 11, 1922.

20. U.S. Department of Commerce, Bureau of the Census, *Negroes in the United States*, 57.

21. *NW*, April 16, 1921.

22. Ibid., February 20, 1921.

23. J. M. Toliver to Bureau, July 16, 1921, Case File 198140-198, General Records of the Department of State; Harry Gulley to Bureau, January 24, 1923, case file 61-50-195, obtained by author from FBI through Freedom of Information Act.

24. New York Passenger Lists, 1820–1957, available at ancestry.com.

25. *NW*, April 12, 1921. Here, Johnson echoed the sentiments of local activists such as George Lucas, who as the president of the local NAACP spoke frequently on the need for greater unity and cooperation among various groups in black New Orleans.

26. *NW*, April 12, August 20, October 29, 1921; J. M. Toliver to Bureau, July 16, 1921, Case File 198140-198, General Records of the Department of State.

27. J. M. Toliver to Bureau, July 16, 1921, Case File 198140-198, General Records of the Department of State.

28. For more information on the NOD, see *NW*, April 12, October 29, 1921; Harold, *Rise and Fall*, 29–60.

29. Millie Charles, interview by Felix Armfield, July 2, 1994, Behind the Veil.

30. Arnesen, *Waterfront Workers of New Orleans*, 204–52.

31. Harry Gulley to Bureau, January 24, 1923, case file 61-50-195, obtained by author from FBI through Freedom of Information Act.

32. P-138 to Charles J. Scully, July 26, 1921, Bureau Section Case File 198940-205, Records of the Federal Bureau of Investigation.

33. See Sundiata, *Brothers and Strangers*.

34. *NW*, October 29, 1921.

35. Quoted in Colin Grant, *Negro with a Hat*, 329.

36. *NW*, July 8, 1922; U.S. Department of Commerce, Bureau of the Census, *Negroes in the United States*, 59.

37. *NW*, July 15, 1922.

38. Ibid.

39. Ibid.

40. Ibid.

41. *Richmond Planet*, July 8, 1922.

42. *Miami Herald*, July 2, 1921, February 10, 1975. Whites' abduction of Higgs was not an isolated event designed solely to weaken the UNIA but rather was intimately related to a larger pattern of white intimidation and violence against the black community. Viewing South Florida's black immigrant population as a disruptive force, state authorities monitored closely the activities of the immigrant-dominated UNIA.

43. *NW*, November 17, 1927.

44. Ibid., March 24, 1923.

45. Lynd and Lynd, *Rank and File*, 114.

46. Many of the UNIA's rank-and-file members had no illusions about the difficulties involved in achieving the organization's political goals. Years of organizational experience had instilled in many members a revolutionary patience that proved critical during difficult times.

47. *NW*, May 24, 1923.

48. Ibid., March 22, 1924.

49. *Marcus Garvey Papers*, 5:756–57.

50. *NW*, July 12, May 24, 1924.

51. *Marcus Garvey Papers*, 5:653.

52. John Fenner to Earnest Cox, June 17, 1925, Cox Papers, Box 2.

53. *NW*, July 25, 1925.

54. Ibid., February 7, 1925.

55. *Marcus Garvey Papers*, 5:757.

56. *NW*, March 21, 1925.

57. Ibid., October 31, 1925.

58. Ibid., September 29, 1928.

59. Ibid., January 21, 1928.

60. U.S. Department of Commerce, Bureau of the Census, *Mortality Rates*, 268; *Louisiana Weekly*, September 22, 1928; George Lucas to Robert Bagnall, December 14, 1926, Box G-81, Folder 7, NAACP Papers-LC.

61. *NW*, September 15, 1928.

62. *Louisiana Weekly*, September 22, 1928.

63. *NW*, March 9, 1929.

64. Ibid., November 3, 1928; Estella James, interview by author, January 12, 2002. Garveyites in Puerto Limón, Costa Rica; Colón, Panama; and New York City also built schools in their communities.

65. *NW*, November 23, March 9, 1929.

66. Ibid., January 12, 1929.

67. Ibid., March 9, 1929.

68. Rogers, *Righteous Lives*, 20.

69. *New Orleans States*, December 31, 1928.

70. Walter White to George W. Lucas, March 29, 1929, Part 12, Reel 14, Series A, Frame 539, NAACP Papers-MF.

71. George W. Lucas to Walter White, April 22, 1929, in ibid., Frame 600. The white men were found guilty of the murders and sentenced to life in prison.

72. Garvey, *Philosophy and Opinions*, 316.

73. *Century*, February 1923.

74. *Messenger*, March 1923.

75. *Marcus Garvey Papers*, 5:814.

76. *NJG*, January 19, 1935. Newport News Garveyites organized a laundry service in 1931, while two years later their counterparts in Norfolk opened a grocery store.

77. *NW*, June 15, 1929.

78. Earl Lewis, *In Their Own Interests*, 147.

79. *NW*, June 13, 1931.

80. Ibid., July 12, 1930.

Chapter 5. The South Will Be Invaded

1. Abram Harris, "White and Black World," 378, 381.

2. Dabney, "Negro Workers at the Crossroads," 10.

3. William H. Harris, *Keeping the Faith*; Bates, *Pullman Porters*; Bynum, *A. Philip Randolph*, 101–56.

4. *NJG*, June 30, 1928.

5. Ibid., May 5, 1928.

6. *Messenger*, June 1927.

7. Ibid., January 1927.

8. As BSCP organizer S. E. Grain informed a Richmond audience in the spring of 1928, "The Brotherhood could not lose if the Pullman Porters as a group and the Negroes in general could understand that the organization is not just a Pullman Porter's fight, but [also] a race fight" (*NJG*, June 2, 1928).

9. Ibid., June 30, 1928.

10. *Messenger*, August 1925.

11. Ibid.

12. Bates, *Pullman Porters*, 52.

13. The PPBAA openly denounced the BSCP. In fact, when the Brotherhood formed, the PPBAA declared that there was "no necessity for further organization" (*New York Amsterdam News*, November 18, 1925).

14. *Messenger*, December 1925.

15. *New York Amsterdam News*, September 23, 1925.

16. Foner and Lewis, *Black Worker*, 7:207.

17. *New York Amsterdam News*, November 25, 1925.

18. Dabney, "Negro Workers at the Crossroads," 9.

19. *New York Amsterdam News*, March 17, 1926. The Brotherhood did have support from one college president, Mary McLeod Bethune. Late in 1925, Bethune wrote to Randolph, "I have observed with genuine interest the progress of the movement to organize the Pullman Porters to contend for better wages and better working conditions. Your program, I note is sane and fair." Bethune disagreed with those who contended that the BSCP engaged in activities that imperiled the black community and instead maintained that "the organization is working towards a perfectly legitimate goal. I, therefore, give you my hearty personal endorsement and bid you Godspeed in your worthy efforts." Bethune closed her letter, "Please tell the men that they must not be dismayed by the opposition. Let it rather spur them on to lawful, loyal, united action" (*Messenger*, February 1926).

20. See Wolters, *New Negro On Campus*; James D. Anderson, *Education of Blacks*; Summers, *Manliness and Its Discontents*, 242–86; Lamon, "Black Community"; Holland, *Nathan B. Young*.

21. *New York Amsterdam News*, March 17, 1926.

22. *Savannah Tribune*, January 21, 1926.

23. *NJG*, February 13, 1926.

24. http://railwaylaboract.com/RLA.htm.

25. *Messenger*, April 1927.

26. *Pittsburgh Courier*, June 11, 1927.

27. Ibid.

28. Ibid.

29. Ibid.

30. *Jacksonville Journal*, June 6, 1927.

31. A. Philip Randolph to Editor, June 14, 1927, in Randolph, *Papers*, Reel 1.

32. *Messenger*, October 1927.

33. *NJG*, September 17, 1927.

34. Ibid., September 3, 17, 1927.

35. *Messenger*, December 1927.

36. Ibid., May–June 1928.

37. Ibid., December 1927.

38. *Pittsburgh Courier*, November 26, 1927.

39. *Messenger*, January 1928.

40. *Chicago Defender*, January 21, 1928.

41. *Messenger*, January 1928.

42. Ibid., February 1928.

43. *NJG*, March 31, 1928.

44. Ibid.

45. Ibid., June 2, 1928.

46. Ibid., May 5, 1928.

47. Ibid.

48. *Baltimore Afro-American*, June 23, 1928.

49. *NJG*, June 30, 1928.

50. *Pittsburgh Courier*, May 5, 1928.

51. *Messenger*, May–June 1928.

52. Ibid.

Chapter 6. New Negro Southerners

1. Abram Harris to W. E. B. Du Bois, July 11, 1927, Du Bois Papers.

2. Dabney, "Negro Workers at the Crossroads," 9.

3. Jarrett, *Representing the Race*, 80.

4. Brick, Transcending Capitalism, 54.

5. Ibid., 56.

6. Henry, "Abram Harris"; Wilson, *Segregated Scholars*; Ross, *Manning the Race*; Holloway, *Confronting the Veil*; Bush, *We Are Not What We Seem*.

7. Locke, "Welcome the New South," 375.

8. James W. Ivy, "Book Bits," *Messenger*, March 1928.

9. Ibid., May 1927.

10. Dabney, "Dominant Forces in Race Relations," 271.

11. Gilpin and Gasman, *Charles S. Johnson*, 65.

12. McGuinn, "Phylon Profile," 221.

13. Harding, "Is America Possible?"

14. Brawley, "Profession of the Teacher," 486.

15. N. D. Oyerinde to Mary Childs Nerney, January 10, 1915, Thomas L. Dabney to Joel E. Spingarn, September 6, 1915, Thomas L. Dabney to Mary Childs Nerney, October 25, December 4, 1915, all in Box G-211, Folder 17, NAACP Papers-LC.

16. Thomas L. Dabney to Mary Childs Nerney, October 25, 1915, in ibid.; Thomas L. Dabney to Roy Nash, December 1, 1916, G. W. C. Brown to Roy Nash, March 27, 1916, both in Box G-211, Folder 18, NAACP Papers-LC.

17. Du Bois, *Correspondence*, 3:279.

18. Ibid.

19. U.S. World War I Draft Registration Cards, 1917–18, available at ancestry.com.

20. Thomas L. Dabney to James Henry Dooley, November 4, 1920, Branch and Company Records.

21. Miles Mark Fisher, *Virginia Union University*, 64; James Ivy, interview by Theodore Kornweibel, "No Crystal Stair: Black Life and the Messenger Interviews," Theodore Kornweibel Interviews, Folder 1.

22. Kornweibel, *Seeing Red*, 76–99.

23. Ivy, interview.

24. Ibid.

25. See Boren, *Student Resistance*, 78–87.

26. *New Student*, March 10, 1923.

27. *Richmond Times*, March 24, 1924. According to the editors of the *Critic*, the Federation sought "to focus the attention of the Negro students upon national, racial and world problems. It seeks to develop a cosmopolitan view among students by breaking down the old tradition of narrowness and apathy manifested by some college groups. It conducts an open forum to which distinguished speakers are invited from time to time. Such questions as the League of Nations, the World Court, coeducation and the ethnological study of the race question are discussed" (Miles Mark Fisher, *Virginia Union University*, 64).

28. Carrington Papers, Correspondence, 1921–75, Box 3, Folder 4.

29. Hylan Lewis, "Pursuing Fieldwork," 124.

30. James W. Ivy, "Book Bits," *Messenger*, June 1927.

31. Ibid., December, September 1927.

32. Ibid., November 1927.

33. For Ivy's relationship with Schuyler, McKay, and Owen, see Ivy, interview; Long, "Interview," 72–73; McKay, *Passion of Claude McKay*, 145–47.

34. The Buckingham Training School demonstrates that the enterprising spirit of the New Negro extended beyond the urban terrain. In 1919, a group of African Americans led by the Reverend Stephen J. Ellis, initiated fund-raising efforts for a training school in Buckingham. Small personal contributions, coupled with donations from various churches and social groups, provided the seed money for the black community's purchase of nearly ten acres of land along with building material for the proposed school. The state refused Ellis's request for financial assistance; however, the General Education Board and the John F. Slater Fund supplied Ellis with funds to complete the school in 1924 (Dabney, "Rural Education").

35. Thomas L. Dabney, "Brookwood Labor College," *Messenger*, December 1926; Kosef, *Acts of Conscience*, 70; Kates, *Activist Rhetorics*, 81; Warburton Papers, Brookwood Labor College Series, Box 4, Folder 5.

36. See, for example, Dabney, "Rural Education"; Dabney, "Southern Students Study Race Relations"; Dabney, "Health and Welfare Work."

37. Dabney, "Colored Rural Life Conference," 224.

38. Ibid.

39. Dabney, "Rural Education," 79.

40. Daniel Rodgers, *Atlantic Crossing*, 318.

41. Dabney, "Health and Welfare Work."

42. Thomas Dabney, "Trade Union Movements," *Messenger*, November 1926.

43. Dabney, "Workers' Education," 91, 92.

44. Brick, *Transcending Capitalism*, 62.

45. Dabney, "Negro Workers at the Crossroads," 10.

46. Odum, "Editorial Notes," 730; Charles Johnson, "New South and the New Negro," 176; Charles Johnson, "Our Book Shelf," 324. In 1920, Mencken published "Sahara of the Bozart," in which he condemned the South as an intellectual and cultural wasteland: "For all its size and all its wealth and all the 'progress' it babbles of, it is almost as sterile, artistically, intellectually, culturally, as the Sahara Desert. If the whole of the late Confederacy were to be engulfed by a tidal wave tomorrow, the effect upon the civilized minority of men in the world would be but little greater than that of a flood on the Yang-tse-kiang. It would be impossible in all history to match so complete a drying-up of a civilization" (*Prejudices*, 70). But Mencken subsequently became attracted to the work of some southern artists and writers, and late in the fall of 1925, he alerted his readers to the South's shifting intellectual terrain: "Just what has happened down there, I don't know, but there has been an immense change of late. The old sentimental snuffling and gurgling seem to have gone out of fashion; the new southern writers are reexamining the civilization they live under, and striking out boldly" (*Chicago Tribune*, May 10, 1925).

47. Locke, "Welcome the New South," 374–75.

48. James W. Ivy, "Book Bits," *Messenger*, October 1926; Mencken, "South Begins to Mutter," 140.

49. James W. Ivy, "Book Bits," *Messenger*, May 1927.

50. Ibid., January 1928.

51. Quoted in Singal, *War Within*, 267.

52. James W. Ivy, "Book Bits," *Messenger*, September 1927.

53. Ibid., May 1927.

54. Sullivan, *Days of Hope*, 32.

55. Locke, "Welcome the New South," 375.

56. James W. Ivy, "Book Bits," *Messenger*, June 1927.

57. Dabney, "Southern Students Study Race Relations," 400.

58. Dabney, "Dominant Forces in Race Relations," 271.

59. Thomas Dabney to V. F. Calverton, n.d., Calverton Papers.

60. Ibid., May 7, 1927.

61. Ivy, interview.

62. *Crisis*, June 1928.

63. James W. Ivy, "Book Chat," *Baltimore Afro-American*, March 17, 1928; James W. Ivy, "Book Bits," *Messenger*, May–June 1928, 116.

64. James W. Ivy, "McKay's New Book Hits at Washington Society," *Baltimore Afro-American*, April 27, 1929.

65. Claude McKay to James Ivy, September 20, 1929, in McKay, *Passion of Claude McKay*, 148.

66. Long, "Interview," 73.

67. Dabney, "Conquest of Bread," 418.

Chapter 7. Stormy Weather

1. George Lucas to James Weldon Johnson, March 19, 1927, Part 5, Reel 4, Frame 782, NAACP Papers-MF.

2. For more on the Mississippi Flood of 1927, see Daniel, *Deep'n as It Comes*; Barry, *Rising Tide*.

3. *NYT*, September 20, October 3, 1926.

4. Ibid., December 26, 27, 1927.

5. Ibid., February 19, 1927.

6. Ibid., April 15, 1927.

7. *NJG*, June 4, 1927.

8. Walter F. White, "The Negro and the Flood," *Nation*, June 22, 1927.

9. Ibid.

10. *Chicago Defender*, June 4, July 2, 1927; *NJG*, June 4, 1927.

11. *Chicago Defender*, July 30, 1927.

12. George Lucas to James Weldon Johnson, May 13, 1927, Part 12, Series A, Reel 14, Frame 441, NAACP Papers-MF.

13. White, *Man Called White*, 80–81.

14. Litwack, *Trouble in Mind*, 140–41.

15. *NW*, July 9, 1927.

16. *Chicago Defender*, May 2, 14, June 25, July 2, 30, 1927; *NJG*, June 4, 25, 1927.

17. *NW*, May 14, 1927.

18. Ibid., July 16, 1927.

19. George Lucas, "Money Received for Flood," May 24, 1927, Part 12, Series A, Reel 14, Frame 443, NAACP Papers-MF; Andrew J. Ellison to George Lucas, June 30, 1927, Part 12, Series A, Reel 14, Frame 454, NAACP Papers-MF; George Lucas, "Money Received for Flood," 1928, Part 12, Series A, Reel 14, Frames 484–90, NAACP Papers-MF.

20. *Crisis*, August 1927.

21. *NW*, March 26, 1927.

22. Hancock, "Thinking in Ultimate Terms," 296–97.

23. U.S. Department of Commerce, Bureau of the Census, *Historical Statistics*, 65.

24. Foner and Lewis, *Black Worker*, 6:177.

25. *Negro Worker*, January 1931.

26. *Miami Herald*, February 10, 1975.

27. Lorenzo Greene, *Negro Wage Earner*, 309.

28. David Harrell to NAACP, March 28, 1933, Box G-210, Folder 1, NAACP Papers-LC.

29. *NW*, January 26, 1929, January 31, September 5, 1931.

30. J. Douglas Smith, *Managing White Supremacy*, 354.

31. *NJG*, January 23, 1932.

32. Thomas Dabney to Abram Harris, August 22, 1933, Du Bois Papers.

33. *NJG*, May 9, 1932.

34. *Baltimore Afro-American*, November 24, 1934.

35. *NJG*, January 10, 1948.

36. See Harold, *Rise and Fall*, 121–22.

37. *Miami Times*, February 21, 1985.

38. Lightfoot, *Chicago Slums to World Politics*.

39. Lynd and Lynd, *Rank and File*, 114.

Epilogue. In the Whirlwind

1. Salaam, *Revolutionary Love*, 59.

2. Rogers, *Righteous Lives*, 20; Germany, *New Orleans after the Promises*, 87–94.

3. Germany, *New Orleans after the Promises*, 87–94.

4. Randolph E. Blackwell, interview by William Chafe, 1973, William Henry Chafe Oral History Collection.

5. Grayson Mitchell, "Southern Rural Blacks Help Themselves," 78.

6. *NYT*, May 23, 1981.

7. Blackwell, interview.

8. Chafe, *Civilities and Civil Rights*, 26.

9. Randolph Blackwell, Southern Rural Action Project of the Citizens' Crusade against Poverty, "Progress Report," Citizens' Crusade against Poverty Records; Grayson Mitchell, "Southern Rural Blacks Help Themselves."

10. Grayson Mitchell, "Southern Rural Blacks Help Themselves," 87.

11. Ibid., 87.

12. David Levering Lewis, *Portable Harlem Renaissance Reader*, 762–63.

13. *Crisis*, April 1925.

14. Ibid.

BIBLIOGRAPHY

Manuscript Collections

Behind the Veil: Documenting African American Life in the Jim Crow South (Oral History Project). William R. Perkins Special Collections Library, Duke University, Durham, N.C.

Branch and Company Records. Virginia Historical Society, Richmond.

Calverton, V. F., Papers. Manuscript and Archives Division, New York Public Library, New York.

Carrington, Glenn, Papers. Schomburg Center for Research in Black Culture, New York Public Library, New York.

Carter, Jeannette, Collection. Moorland-Spingarn Research Center, Howard University, Washington, D.C.

Chafe, William Henry, Oral History Collection, William R. Perkins Special Collections Library, Duke University, Durham, N.C.

Cox, Earnest Sevier, Papers. William R. Perkins Special Collections Library, Duke University, Durham, N.C.

Du Bois, W. E. B., Papers. Special Collections and University Archives, University of Massachusetts Amherst Libraries.

Ellison, John Malchus, Papers. L. Douglas Wilder Library, Special Collections, Virginia Union University, Richmond.

General Records of the Department of Justice. National Archives, College Park, Md.

General Records of the Department of State. Record Group 59. National Archives, College Park, Md.

General Records of the Post Office Department. National Archives, College Park, Md.

Hancock, Gordon Blaine, Papers. William R. Perkins Special Collections Library, Duke University, Durham, N.C.

Kornweibel, Theodore, Interviews. Schomburg Center for Research in Black Culture, New York Public Library, New York.

National Association for the Advancement of Colored People Papers, Manuscript Division, Library of Congress, Washington, D.C.

Odum, Howard, Papers. Southern Historical Collection, Wilson Library, University of North Carolina, Chapel Hill.

Records of the Federal Bureau of Investigation, Record Group 65, National Archives, Washington, D.C.

Records of the National War Labor Board (World War I), Record Group 2, National Archives, Washington, D.C.

Records of the War Department General and Special Staffs, Record Group 165, National Archives, Washington, D.C.

Citizens' Crusade against Poverty Records, Walter P. Reuther Library. Wayne State
   University, Detroit.
Warburton, Amber Arthun, Papers. William R. Perkins Special Collections Library, Duke
   University, Durham, N.C.

Published Primary Sources

American Federation of Labor. *Report of the Proceedings of the Thirty-Seventh Annual
   Convention of the American Federation of Labor.* Washington, D.C.: Law Reporter, 1917.
American Federation of Labor. *Report of the Proceedings of the Thirty-Eighth Annual
   Convention of the American Federation of Labor.* Washington, D.C.: Law Reporter, 1918.
Brawley, Benjamin. "The Profession of the Teacher." *Southern Workman* 57 (December
   1928): 484–86.
Brown, Sterling A. *Sterling A. Brown's A Negro Looks at the South.* Ed. Mark A. Sanders
   and John Edgar Tidwell. New York: Oxford University Press, 2007.
Du Bois, W. E. B. *The Correspondence of W. E. B. Du Bois.* Vol. 3, *Selections, 1944–1963.* Ed.
   Herbert Aptheker. Amherst: University of Massachusetts Press, 1978.
———. *Papers of W. E. B. Du Bois.* Sanford, N.C.: Microfilming Corporation of America,
   1980.
———. *W. E. B. Du Bois: A Reader.* Ed. David Levering Lewis. New York: Holt, 1995.
Fisher, Rudolph. *The City of Refuge: The Collected Stories of Rudolph Fisher.* Columbia:
   University of Missouri Press, 2008.
Fortune, T. Thomas. *T. Thomas Fortune, the Afro-American Agitator: A Collection of Writings,
   1880–1928.* Ed. Shawn Leigh Alexander. Gainesville: University Press of Florida, 2008.
Gompers, Samuel. *The Samuel Gompers Papers.* Vol. 11, *The Postwar Years: 1918–1921.* Ed.
   Peter J. Albert, Grace Palladino, and Marla Hughes. Urbana: University of Illinois Press,
   2007.
Greene, Lorenzo. *Negro Wage Earner.* Washington, D.C.: Association for the Study of
   Negro Life and History, 1930.
Grossman, James. *Black Workers in the Era of the Great Migration, 1916–1925.* Frederick,
   Md.: University Publications of America, 1985.
Hancock, Gordon B. "Thinking in Ultimate Terms." *Southern Workman* 48 (July 1929):
   291–97.
Harrison, Hubert H. *A Hubert Harrison Reader.* Ed. Jeffrey B. Perry. Middletown, Conn.:
   Wesleyan University Press, 2001.
Hill, Robert A., ed. *The Marcus Garvey and Universal Negro Improvement Association
   Papers.* Vols. 1–6. Berkeley: University of California Press, 1983–89.
Larsen, Nella. *Quicksand.* 1928. New York: Penguin Classics, 2002.
McKay, Claude. *The Passion of Claude McKay: Selected Prose and Poetry, 1912–1948.* Ed.
   Wayne F. Cooper. New York: Schocken, 1973.
Mencken, H. L. *Prejudices: A Selection.* Baltimore: Johns Hopkins University Press, 2006.
———. "The South Begins to Mutter." *Smart Set* 65 (August 1921): 138–44.
National Association for the Advancement of Colored People. *Report of the National
   Association for the Advancement of Colored People for the Years 1917 and 1918.* New York:
   NAACP, 1919.
Papers of the National Association for the Advancement of Colored People. Frederick, Md.:
   University Publications of America, 1982–.

Randolph, A. Philip. *Papers of A. Philip Randolph*. Bethesda, Md.: University Publications of America, 1990.Toomer, Jean. *Cane*. 1923. New York: Liveright, 1993.

U.S. Department of Commerce, Bureau of the Census. *Historical Statistics of the United States, 1789–1945*. Washington, D.C.: U.S. Government Printing Office, 1949.

———. *Mortality Rates, 1910–1920, with Population of the Federal Censuses of 1910 and 1920 and Intercensal Estimates of Population*. Washington, D.C.: U.S. Government Printing Office, 1923.

———. *Negroes in the United States, 1920–1932*. Washington, D.C.: U.S. Government Printing Office, 1935.

Work, Monroe N. "Effects of the War on Southern Labor." *Southern Workman* 47 (August 1918): 281–84.

Newspapers and Serials

Baltimore Afro-American

Black Oklahoma City Dispatch

Boston Guardian

Chicago Defender

Crisis

Crusader

Daily Worker

Ebony

Florida Metropolis

Florida Times-Union

Jacksonville Journal

Labor Age

Louisiana Weekly

Messenger

Miami Times

Modern Quarterly

Nashville Banner

Nation

Negro World

New Orleans Picayune

New Student

New York Age

New York Amsterdam News

New York Call

New York Times

Norfolk Journal and Guide

Opportunity

Pittsburgh Courier

Richmond Planet

Richmond Times-Dispatch

Savannah Tribune

Smart Set

Socialist Review

Southern Workman

Spokesman

State

Vindicator

Virginia Pilot

Washington Post

Secondary Sources

Abu-Lughod, Janet L. *Race, Space, and Riots in Chicago, New York, and Los Angeles*. New York: Oxford University Press, 2007.

Alexander, Ann Field. *Race Man: The Rise and Fall of the "Fighting Editor," John Mitchell, Jr.* Charlottesville: University of Virginia Press, 2002.

Anderson, James D. *The Education of Blacks in the South, 1860–1935*. Chapel Hill: University of North Carolina Press, 1988.

Anderson, Paul Allen. *Deep River: Music and Memory in Harlem Renaissance Thought*. Durham, N.C.: Duke University Press, 2001.

Arnesen, Eric. *Black Protest and the Great Migration: A Brief History with Documents*. Boston: Bedford/St. Martin's, 2002.

———. *Brotherhoods of Color: Black Railroad Workers and the Struggle for Equality.* Cambridge: Harvard University Press, 2001.

———. "Following the Color Line of Labor: Black Workers and the Labor Movement before 1930." *Radical History Review* 55 (Winter 1993): 53–87.

———. *Waterfront Workers of New Orleans: Race, Class, and Politics.* Urbana: University of Illinois Press, 1994.

Bair, Barbara. "Renegotiating Liberty: Garveyism, Women, and Grassroots Organizing in Virginia." In *Women of the American South: A Multicultural Reader*, ed. Christie Anne Farnham, 220–40. New York: New York University Press, 1997.

———. "True Women, Real Men: Gender Ideology and Social Roles in the Garvey Movement." In *Gendered Domains: Rethinking Public and Private in Women's History*, ed. Dorothy O. Helly and Susan M. Reverby, 154–66. Ithaca: Cornell University Press, 1992.

Baker, Houston A., Jr. *I Don't Hate the South.* New York: Oxford University Press, 2007.

———. *Modernism and the Harlem Renaissance.* Chicago: University of Chicago Press, 1987.

———. *Turning South Again: Re-Thinking Modernism/Re-Reading Booker T.* Durham, N.C.: Duke University Press, 2001.

Baldwin, Davarian. *Chicago's New Negroes: Modernity, the Great Migration, and Black Urban Life.* Chapel Hill: University of North Carolina Press, 2007.

Baldwin, Davarian, and Minkah Makalani, eds. *Escape from New York: The New Negro Renaissance beyond Harlem.* Minneapolis: University of Minnesota Press, 2013.

Ball, Edward. *The Sweet Hell Inside: The Rise of an Elite Black Family in the Segregated South.* New York: Harper Collins, 2001.

Bandele, Ramla. *Black Star: African American Activism in the Political Economy.* Urbana: University of Illinois Press, 2008.

Barry, John. *Rising Tide: The Great Mississippi Flood of 1927 and How It Changed America.* New York: Simon and Schuster, 1997.

Bates, Beth Tompkins. *Pullman Porters and the Rise of Protest Politics in Black America, 1925–1945.* Chapel Hill: University of North Carolina Press, 2002.

Benson, Melanie. *Disturbing Calculations: The Economics of Identity in Post-Colonial Southern Literature, 1912–2002.* Athens: University of Georgia Press, 2008.

Berg, Manfred. *The Ticket to Freedom: The NAACP and the Struggle for Black Political Integration.* Gainesville: University Press of Florida, 2007.

Best, Wallace. *Passionately Human, No Less Divine: Religion and Black Culture in Chicago.* Princeton: Princeton University Press, 2005.

Bond, Horace Mann. "A Negro Looks at His South." *Harper's Magazine*, June 1931, 98–108.

Boren, Mark Edelman. *Student Resistance: A History of the Unruly Subject.* New York: Routledge, 2001.

Brecher, Jeremy. *Strike!* Boston: South End, 1997.

Brick, Howard. *Transcending Capitalism: Visions of a New Society in Modern American Thought.* Ithaca: Cornell University Press, 2006.

Brophy, Alfred L. *Reconstructing the Dreamland: The Tulsa Race Riot of 1921.* New York: Oxford University Press, 2002.

Brown, Elsa Barkley. "Womanist Consciousness: Maggie Lena Walker and the Independent Order of St. Luke." *Signs* 14 (Spring 1989): 620–53.

Brown, Leslie. *Upbuilding Black Durham: Gender, Class, and Black Community Development in the Jim Crow South.* Chapel Hill: University of North Carolina Press, 2008.

Brown, Nikki. *Private Politics and Public Voices: Black Women's Activism from World War I to the New Deal.* Bloomington: Indiana University Press, 2006.

Brundage, W. Fitzhugh. *Lynching in the New South: Georgia and Virginia, 1880–1930.* Urbana: University of Illinois Press, 1993.

Buni, Andrew. *The Negro in Virginia Politics, 1902–1965.* Charlottesville: University Press of Virginia, 1967.

Burkett, Randall K. *Black Redemption: Churchmen Speak for the Garvey Movement.* Philadelphia: Temple University Press, 1978.

———. *Garveyism as a Religious Movement: The Institutionalization of a Black Civil Religion.* Metuchen, N.J.: Scarecrow, 1978.

Burkett, Randall K., and Richard Newman, eds. *Black Apostles: Afro-American Clergy Confront the Twentieth Century.* Boston: Hall, 1978.

Bush, Rod. *We Are Not What We Seem: Black Nationalism and Class Struggle in the American Century.* New York: New York University Press, 1999.

Bynum, Cornelius. *A. Philip Randolph and the Struggle for Civil Rights.* Urbana: University of Illinois Press, 2010.

Cabell, James Branch. *Jurgen: A Comedy of Justice.* New York: Crown, 1919.

Carmichael, Stokely. *Ready for Revolution: The Life and Struggles of Stokely Carmichael (Kwame Ture).* New York: Scribner, 2003.

Carroll, Anne Elizabeth. *Word, Image, and the New Negro: Representation and Identity in the Harlem Renaissance.* Bloomington: Indiana University Press, 2005.

Chafe, William. *Civilities and Civil Rights: Greensboro, North Carolina, and the Black Struggle for Freedom.* New York: Oxford University Press, 1980.

Chery, Tshepo Masango. "Kingdoms of the Earth: Coloured Identity, African Initiated Churches, and Politics of Black Nationalism in South Africa, 1892 to 1948." PhD diss., University of Pennsylvania, 2012.

Clarke, John Henrik. *Marcus Garvey and the Vision of Africa.* New York: Random House, 1974.

Cobb, James C., and William Stueck, eds. *Globalization and the American South.* Athens: University of Georgia Press, 2005.

Cohen, Lizabeth. *Making a New Deal: Industrial Workers in Chicago, 1919–1939.* Cambridge: Cambridge University Press, 1990.

Dabney, Thomas L. "Class or Race: The Problem before the American Negroes." *Socialist Review,* January 1927, 31–35.

———. "Colored Rural Life Conference of Central Virginia." *Southern Workman* 55 (May 1926): 222–27.

———. "The Conquest of Bread." *Southern Workman* 57 (October 1928): 418–21.

———. "Dominant Forces in Race Relations." *Modern Quarterly* 9 (November 1927–February 1928): 266–71.

———. "Health and Welfare Work in Soviet Russia." *Southern Workman* 55 (December 1926): 541–44.

———. "Negro Workers at the Crossroads." *Labor Age* 16 (February 1927): 8–10.

———. "Organized Labor's Attitude toward Negro Workers." *Southern Workman* 57 (November 1928): 323–30.

———. "Rural Education in Buckingham County, Virginia." *Southern Workman* 55 (February 1926): 79–82.

———. "Southern Labor and the Negro." *Opportunity* 7 (November 1929): 345–46.

———. "Southern Students Study Race Relations." *Southern Workman* 55 (September 1926): 398–400.

———. "The Union Car in the Dining Car." *Locomotive Engineers Journal* 61 (July 1927): 517, 571.

———. "Workers' Education." *Opportunity* 4 (March 1926): 91–92.

Dailey, Jane, Glenda Gilmore, and Bryant Simon, eds. *Jumpin' Jim Crow: Southern Politics from the Civil War to Civil Rights.* Princeton: Princeton University Press, 2006.

Daniel, Pete. *Deep'n as It Comes: The 1927 Mississippi River Flood.* New York: Oxford University Press, 1977.

Davis, Thadious. "Reclaiming the South." In *Bridging Southern Cultures: An Interdisciplinary Approach*, ed. John Lowe, 57–74. Baton Rouge: Louisiana State University Press, 2005.

Dawson, Michael C. *Black Visions: The Roots of Contemporary African-American Political Ideologies.* Chicago: University of Chicago Press, 2001.Devore, Donald E. *Defying Jim Crow: African American Community Development and the Struggle for Racial Equality in New Orleans, 1900–1960.* Baton Rouge: Louisiana State University Press, 2015.

D'Orso, Michael. *Like Judgment Day: The Ruin and Redemption of a Town Called Rosewood.* New York: Putnam, 1996.

Dubofsky, Melvyn. *Hard Work: The Making of Labor History.* Urbana: University of Illinois Press, 2000.

Du Bois, W. E. B. *Black Reconstruction in America, 1860–1880.* 1945. New York: Simon and Schuster, 1999.

———. *The Souls of Black Folk.* 1903. New York: Modern Library, 2003.

Duck, Leigh Anne. *The Nation's Region: Southern Modernism, Segregation, and U.S. Nationalism.* Athens: University of Georgia Press, 2006.

Duncan, Natanya. "The 'Efficient Womanhood' of the Universal Negro Improvement Association, 1919–1930." Ph.D. diss., University of Florida, 2009.

Dunn, Marvin. *Black Miami in the Twentieth Century.* Gainesville: University Press of Florida, 1997.

Eisenberg, Bernard. "Only for the Bourgeois?: James Weldon Johnson and the NAACP, 1916–1930." *Phylon* 43 (Second Quarter 1982): 110–24.

Ewing, Adam. *The Age of Garvey: How a Jamaican Activist Created a Mass Movement and Changed Global Black Politics.* Princeton: Princeton University Press, 2014.

Favor, J. Martin. *Authentic Blackness: The Folk in the Negro Renaissance.* Durham, N.C.: Duke University Press, 1999.

Fisher, Miles Mark. *Virginia Union University and Some of Her Achievements: Twentieth-Fifth Anniversary, 1899–1924.* Richmond: Brown, 1924.

Foley, Barbara. *Spectres of 1919: Class and Nation in the Making of the New Negro.* Urbana: University of Illinois Press, 2003.

Foner, Philip. *History of the Labor Movement in the United States: Labor and World War I, 1914–1918.* New York: International, 1987.

Foner, Philip, and Ronald Lewis, eds. *The Black Worker: A Documentary History from Colonial Times to the Present.* 7 vols. Philadelphia: Temple University Press, 1978–83.

Frank, Dana. *Purchasing Power: Consumer Organizing, Gender, and the Seattle Labor Movement, 1919–1929*. Cambridge: Cambridge University Press, 1994.

Freeman, Jo. *A Room at a Time: How Women Entered Party Politics*. New York: Rowman and Littlefield, 2002.

Gaines, Kevin K. *Uplifting the Race: Black Leadership, Politics, and Culture in the Twentieth Century*. Chapel Hill: University of North Carolina Press, 1996.

Garrett, Gene Andrew. *Readings on Race, Representation, and African American Culture, 1892–1938*. Princeton: Princeton University Press, 2007.

Garvey, Amy Jacques. *Philosophy and Opinions*. 1925. Dover: Majority, 1986.

Gates, Henry Louis. "The Trope of a New Negro and the Reconstruction of the Image of the Black." *Representations* 24 (Fall 1988): 129–56.

Gaughan, Anthony. "Woodrow Wilson and the Rise of Militant Interventionism in the South." *Journal of Southern History* 65 (November 1999): 771–808.

Germany, Kent. *New Orleans after the Promises: Poverty, Citizenship and the Search for the Great Society*. Athens: University of Georgia Press, 2007.

Geschwender, James A. *Class, Race, and Worker Insurgency: The League of Revolutionary Black Workers*. Cambridge: Cambridge University Press, 1977.

Gilmore, Glenda Elizabeth. *Defying Dixie: The Radical Roots of Civil Rights, 1919–1950*. New York: Norton, 2008.

———. "False Friends and Avowed Enemies: Southern African Americans and Party Allegiances in the 1920s." In *Jumpin' Jim Crow*, ed. Dailey, Gilmore, and Simon, 219–38.

———. *Gender and Jim Crow: Women and the Politics of White Supremacy in North Carolina, 1896–1920*. Chapel Hill: University of North Carolina Press, 1996.

Gilpin, Patrick J., and Marybeth Gasman. *Charles S. Johnson: Leadership beyond the Veil in the Age of Jim Crow*. Albany: State University of New York Press, 2003.

Glaude, Eddie S., Jr. *Exodus!: Religion, Race, and Nation in Early Nineteenth-Century Black America*. Chicago: University of Chicago Press, 2000.

Goluboff, Risa L. *The Lost Promise of Civil Rights*. Cambridge: Harvard University Press, 2007.

Gottlieb, Peter. *Making Their Own Way: Southern Blacks' Migration to Pittsburgh, 1916–1930*. Urbana: University of Illinois Press, 1987.

Grant, Colin. *Negro with a Hat: The Rise and Fall of Marcus Garvey and His Dream of Mother Africa*. New York: Oxford University Press, 2008.

Grant, Donald L. *The Way It Was in the South: The Black Experience in Georgia*. Athens: University of Georgia Press, 2001.

Grant, Nathan. *Masculinist Impulses: Toomer, Hurston, Black Writing, and Modernity*. Columbia: University of Missouri Press, 2004.

Greene, Julie. *Pure and Simple Politics: The American Federation of Labor and Political Activism, 1881–1917*. Cambridge: Cambridge University Press, 1998.

Griffin, Farah Jasmine. *"Who Set You Flowin'?": The African-American Migration Narrative*. New York: Oxford University Press, 1995.

Gross, Kali N. *Colored Amazons: Crime, Violence, and Black Women in the City of Brotherly Love, 1880–1910*. Durham, N.C.: Duke University Press, 2006.

Grossman, James. *Land of Hope: Chicago, Black Southerners and the Great Migration*. Chicago: University of Chicago Press, 1989.

Gutman, Herbert. "The Negro and the United Mine Workers of America: The Career and

Letters of Richard L. Davis and Something of Their Meaning, 1890–1900." In *The Negro and the American Labor Movement*, ed. Julius Jacobson, 49–127. New York, Anchor, 1968.

Hahn, Steven. *The Political Worlds of Slavery and Freedom*. Cambridge: Harvard University Press, 2009.

Haiken, Elizabeth. "'The Lord Helps Those Who Help Themselves': Black Laundresses in Little Rock, Arkansas, 1917–1921." *Arkansas Historical Quarterly* 49 (Spring 1990): 20–50.

Harding, Vincent. "Is America Possible?: A Letter to My Young Companions on the Journey of Hope." May 22, 2014. http://www.onbeing.org/program/civility-history -and-hope/feature/is-america-possible/535.

Harlan, Louis. *Booker T. Washington: The Making of a Black Leader, 1865–1901*. New York: Oxford University Press, 1972.

———. *Booker T. Washington: The Wizard of Tuskegee, 1901–1915*. New York: Oxford University Press, 1983.

Harley, Sharon. "Nannie Helen Burroughs: The Black Goddess of Liberty." *Journal of Negro History* 81 (Winter–Autumn 1996): 62–71.

Harold, Claudrena. *The Rise and Fall of the Garvey Movement in the Urban South, 1918–1942*. New York: Routledge, 2007.

Harris, Abram. "A White and Black World in American Labor and Politics." *Social Forces* 4 (February 1925): 376–83.

Harris, William H. *Keeping the Faith: A. Philip Randolph, Milton P. Webster, and the Brotherhood of Sleeping Car Porters, 1925–1937*. Urbana: University of Illinois Press, 1977.

Harrison, Alferdteen, ed. *Black Exodus: The Great Migration from the American South*. Jackson: University Press of Mississippi, 1991.

Henri, Florette. *Black Migration: Movement North, 1900–1920*. New York: Anchor, 1975.

Henry, Charles P. "Abram Harris, E. Franklin Frazier, and Ralph Bunche: The Howard School of Thought on the Problem of Race." In *The Changing Racial Regime*, ed. Matthew Holden Jr., 36–56. New Brunswick, N.J.: Transaction, 1995.

Higginbotham, Evelyn Brooks. *Righteous Discontent: The Women's Movement in the Black Baptist Church, 1880–1920*. Cambridge: Harvard University Press, 1993.

Hirsch, James S. *Riot and Remembrance: The Tulsa Race War and Its Legacy*. Boston: Houghton Mifflin, 2002.

Hobson, Fred. *Serpent in Eden: H. L. Mencken and the South*. Chapel Hill: University of North Carolina Press, 1974.

Holland, Antonio Frederic. *Nathan B. Young and the Struggle for Higher Black Education*. Columbia: University of Missouri Press, 2006.

Holloway, Jonathan Scott. *Confronting the Veil: Abram Harris Jr., E. Franklin Frazier, and Ralph Bunche, 1919–1941*. Chapel Hill: University of North Carolina Press, 2002.

Hornsby-Gutting, Angela. *Black Manhood and Community Building in North Carolina, 1900–1930*. Gainesville: University Press of Florida, 2009.

Horton, Carol. *Race and the Making of American Liberalism*. New York: Oxford University Press, 2005.

Huggins, Nathan Irvin. *Harlem Renaissance*. New York: Oxford University, 1974.

———, ed. *Voices from the Harlem Renaissance*. New York: Oxford University Press, 1976.

Hunter, Tera. *To 'Joy My Freedom: Southern Black Women's Lives and Labors after the Civil War*. Cambridge: Harvard University Press, 1998.

Hutchinson, George. *The Harlem Renaissance in Black and White*. Cambridge: Belknap Press of Harvard University Press, 1995.

Iton, Richard. *Solidarity Blues: Race, Culture, and the American Left*. Chapel Hill: University of North Carolina Press, 2000.

James, Winston. *Holding Aloft the Banner of Ethiopia: Caribbean Radicalism in Early Twentieth-Century America*. 1933. New York: Verso, 1998.

Jarrett, Gene Andrew. *Representing the Race: A New Political History of African American Literature*. New York: New York University Press, 2011.

Johnson, Charles. "The New South and the New Negro." *Opportunity* 4 (June 1926): 175–76.

———. "Our Book Shelf." *Opportunity* 4 (October 1926): 324–25.

Johnson, James Weldon. *Along This Way: The Autobiography of James Weldon Johnson*. 1933. New York: Da Capo, 1990.

Johnson, Karen A. *Uplifting Women and the Race: The Lives, Educational Philosophies, and Social Activism of Anna Julia Cooper and Nannie Helen Burroughs*. New York: Garland, 2000.

Jonas, Gilbert. *Freedom Sword: The NAACP and the Struggle against Racism in America, 1909–1969*. New York: Routledge, 2005.

Jones, Maxine D. "The Rosewood Massacre and the Women Who Survived It." *Florida Historical Quarterly* 76 (Fall 1997): 193–208.

Justesen, Benjamin R. *Broken Brotherhood: The Rise and Fall of the National Afro-American Council*. Carbondale: Southern Illinois University Press, 2008.

Kates, Susan. *Activist Rhetorics and American Higher Education, 1885–1937*. Carbondale: Southern Illinois University Press, 2001.

Kelley, Robin D. G. *Hammer and Hoe: Alabama Communists during the Great Depression*. Chapel Hill: University of North Carolina Press, 1990.

Killens, John Oliver, and Jerry W. Ward Jr., eds. *Black Southern Voices: An Anthology of Fiction, Poetry, Drama, Nonfiction and Essays*. New York: Meridian, 1992.

Kimball, Gregg D., and Elsa Barkley Brown, "Mapping the Terrain of Black Richmond." *Journal of Urban History* 21 (March 1995): 296–346.

Kornweibel, Theodore. *Seeing Red: Federal Campaigns against Black Militancy, 1919–1925*. Bloomington: Indiana University Press, 1998.

Kosef, Joseph Kip. *Acts of Conscience: Christian Nonviolence and Modern American Democracy*. New York: Columbia University Press, 2009.

Kousser, J. Morgan. *The Shaping of Southern Politics: Suffrage Restriction and the Establishment of the One-Party South, 1880–1910*. New Haven: Yale University Press, 1974.

Kreyling, Michael. "Toward 'a New Southern Studies.'" *South Central Review* 22 (Spring 2005): 4–18.

Krugler, David F. *The Year of Racial Violence: How African Americans Fought Back*. Cambridge: Cambridge University Press, 2014.

Kusmer, Kenneth L. *A Ghetto Takes Shape: Black Cleveland, 1870–1930*. Urbana: University of Illinois Press, 1976.

Lamon, Lester. "The Black Community in Nashville and the Fisk University Student Strike of 1924–1925." *Journal of Southern History* 49 (May 1974): 225–44.

Laslett, John H. M. "Samuel Gompers and the Rise of American Business Unionism." In *Labor Leaders in America*, ed. Melvyn Dubofsky and Warren Van Tine, 62–88. Urbana: University of Illinois Press, 1987.

Laurie, Bruce. *Artisans into Workers: Labor in Nineteenth-Century America*. Urbana: University of Illinois Press, 1997.

Law, Peter F. *Democracy Rising: South Carolina and the Fight for Black Equality since 1865.* Lexington: University Press of Kentucky, 2006.

Lebsock, Suzanne. "Woman Suffrage and White Supremacy: A Virginia Case Study." In *Visible Women: New Essays on American Activism,* ed. Nancy A. Hewitt and Suzanne Lebsock, 62–100. Urbana: University of Illinois Press, 1993.

Lentz-Smith, Adriane. *Freedom Struggles: African Americans and World War I.* Cambridge: Harvard University Press, 2009.

Letwin, Daniel. "Interracial Unionism, Gender, and 'Social Equality' in the Alabama Coalfields, 1878–1908." *Journal of Southern History* 61 (August 1995): 519–54.

Lewis, David Levering, ed. *The Portable Harlem Renaissance Reader.* New York: Penguin, 1994.

———. *W. E. B. Du Bois.* Vol. 2, *The Fight for Equality and the American Century, 1919–1963.* New York: Holt, 2000.

———. *When Harlem Was in Vogue.* New York: Knopf, 1981.

Lewis, Earl. *In Their Own Interests: Race, Class, and Power in Twentieth-Century Norfolk, Virginia.* Berkeley: University of California Press, 1991.

Lewis, Hylan. "Pursuing Fieldwork in African American Communities: Some Personal Reflections of Hylan Lewis." In *Against the Odds: Scholars Who Challenged Racism in the Twentieth Century,* ed. Benjamin P. Bowser and Louis Kushnick, 123–46. Amherst: University of Massachusetts Press, 2004.

Lightfoot, Claude. *Chicago Slums to World Politics: Autobiography of Claude M. Lightfoot.* New York: Outlook, 1987.

Litwack, Leon. *Trouble in Mind: Black Southerners in the Age of Jim Crow.* New York: Vintage, 1998.

Locke, Alain. *The New Negro: An Interpretation.* New York: Boni, 1925.

———. "Welcome the New South: A Review." *Opportunity* 4 (December 1926): 374–75.

Long, Richard A. "An Interview with George Schuyler." *Black World* 25 (February 1976): 68–78.

Lynd, Alice, and Staughton Lynd, eds. *Rank and File: Personal Histories by Working-Class Organizers.* Boston: Beacon, 1973.

Madigan, Tim. *The Burning: Massacre, Destruction, and the Tulsa Race Riot of 1921.* New York: St. Martin's Griffin, 2003.

Makalani, Minkah. *In the Cause of Freedom: Black Radical Internationalism from Harlem to London, 1917–1939.* Chapel Hill: University of North Carolina Press, 2011.

Marks, Carole. *Farewell, We're Good and Gone.* Bloomington: Indiana University Press, 1989.

Martin, Tony. *Literary Garveyism: Garvey, Black Arts, and the Harlem Renaissance.* Dover, Mass.: Majority, 1983.

———. *The Pan-African Connection: From Slavery to Garvey and Beyond.* Dover, Mass.: Majority, 1983.

———. *Race First: The Ideological and Organizational Struggles of Marcus Garvey and the Universal Negro Improvement Association.* Westport, Conn.: Greenwood, 1976.

Maxwell, William J. *New Negro, Old Left: African-American Writing and Communism between the Wars.* New York: Columbia University Press, 1999.

McCartin, Joseph A. *Labor's Great War: The Struggle for Industrial Democracy and the Origins of Modern American Labor Relations, 1912–1921.* Chapel Hill: University of North Carolina Press, 1997.

McDuffie, Erik S. *Sojourning for Freedom: Black Women, American Communism, and the Making of Black Left Feminism*. Durham: Duke University Press, 2011.

McGuinn, Henry Jared. "Phylon Profile, V: Joshua Baker Simpson." *Phylon* 6 (Third Quarter 1945): 219–24.

McKee, Kathryn, and Annette Trefzer. "The U.S. South in Global Contexts: A Collection of Position Statements." *American Literature* 78 (December 2006): 691–92.

McPherson, Tara. "On Wal-Mart and Southern Studies." *American Literature* 78 (December 2006): 695–98.

———. *Reconstructing Dixie: Race, Gender, and Nostalgia in the Imagined South*. Durham, N.C.: Duke University Press, 2004.

Meier, August. *Negro Thought in America, 1880–1915*. Ann Arbor: University of Michigan Press, 1963.

Mitchell, Grayson. "Southern Blacks Help Themselves." *Ebony*, January 1975, 78–87.

Mitchell, Michele. *Righteous Propagation: African Americans and the Politics of Racial Destiny after Reconstruction*. Chapel Hill: University of North Carolina Press, 2004.

Mohl, Raymond A. "The Pattern of Race Relations in Miami since the 1920s." In *African American Heritage of Florida*, ed. David R. Colburn and Jane L. Landers, 326–65. Gainesville: University Press of Florida, 1995.

Montgomery, David. *The Fall of the House of Labor: The Workplace, the State, and American Labor Activism, 1865–1925*. Cambridge: Cambridge University Press, 1987.

Moore, Jacqueline M. *Booker T. Washington, W. E. B. Du Bois, and the Struggle for Racial Uplift*. Wilmington, Del.: Scholarly Resources, 2003.

Moses, Wilson J. *Afrotopia: The Roots of African American Popular History*. New York: Cambridge University Press, 1998.

———. *Black Messiahs and Uncle Toms: Social and Literary Interpretations of a Religious Myth*. University Park: Pennsylvania State University Press, 1982.

———. *Classical Black Nationalism: From the American Revolution to Marcus Garvey*. New York: New York University Press, 1996.

———. *Creative Conflict in African American Thought: Frederick Douglass, Alexander Crummell, Booker T. Washington, W. E. B. Du Bois, and Marcus Garvey*. Cambridge: Cambridge University Press, 2004.

———. *The Golden Age of Black Nationalism, 1850–1925*. New York: Oxford University Press, 1978.

Nadell, Martha Jane. *Enter the New Negroes: Images of Race in American Culture*. Cambridge: Harvard University Press, 2004.

Naison, Mark. *Communists in Harlem during the Great Depression*. Urbana: University of Illinois Press, 1983.

Norwood, Stephen H. "Bogalusa Burning: The War against Biracial Unionism in the Deep South, 1919." *Journal of Southern History* 63 (August 1997): 591–628.

Odum, Howard. "Editorial Notes." *Journal of Social Forces* 2 (November 1924): 730–35.

Ortiz, Paul. *Emancipation Betrayed: The Hidden History of Black Organizing and White Violence in Florida from Reconstruction to the Bloody Election of 1920*. Berkeley: University of California Press, 2005.

Painter, Nell Irvin. *Exodusters: Black Migration to Kansas after Reconstruction*. New York: Norton, 1976.

Patterson, Tiffany Ruby. *Zora Neale Hurston and a History of Southern Life*. Philadelphia: Temple University Press, 2005.

Payne, Charles. *I've Got the Light of Freedom: The Black Organizing Tradition and the Mississippi Freedom Struggle*. Berkeley: University of California Press, 1995.

Peacock, James L. *Grounded Globalism: How the U.S. South Embraces the World*. Athens: University of Georgia Press, 2007.

Perman, Michael. *Struggle for Mastery: Disfranchisement in the South, 1888–1908*. Chapel Hill: University of North Carolina Press, 2001.

Perry, Jeffrey B. *Hubert Harrison: The Voice of Harlem Radicalism, 1883–1918*. New York: Columbia University Press, 2008.

Pfeffer, Paula F. *A. Philip Randolph: Pioneer of the Civil Rights Movement*. Baton Rouge: Louisiana State University Press, 1990.

Phillips, Kimberley. *AlabamaNorth: African-American Migrants, Community, and Working-Class Activism in Cleveland, 1915–1945*. Urbana: University of Illinois Press, 1999.

Rachleff, Peter. *Black Labor in the South: Richmond, Virginia*. Philadelphia: Temple University Press, 1984.

Redkey, Edwin S. *Black Exodus: Black Nationalists and Back-to-Africa Movements, 1890–1910*. New Haven: Yale University Press, 1969.

Reed, Adolph, Jr. *Class Notes: Posing as Politics and Other Thoughts on the American Scene*. New York: New Press, 2000.

———. *Stirrings in the Jug: Black Politics in the Post-Segregation Era*. Minneapolis: University of Minnesota Press, 1999.

Reed, Touré F. *Not Alms but Opportunity: The Urban League and the Politics of Racial Uplift*. Chapel Hill: University of North Carolina Press, 2008.

Reich, Steven. "The Great War, Black Workers, and the Rise and Fall of the NAACP in the South." In *The Black Worker: Race, Labor, and Civil Rights since Emancipation*, ed. Eric Arnesen, 147–77. Urbana: University of Illinois Press, 2007.

Reid, Ira De A. *The Negro Immigrant: His Background, Characteristics, and Social Adjustment, 1899–1937*. New York: Columbia University Press, 1939.

Richardson, Riche. *Black Masculinity and the U.S. South*. Athens: University of Georgia Press, 2007.

Robinson, Cedric. *Black Marxism: The Making of the Black Radical Tradition*. 1983. Chapel Hill: University of North Carolina Press, 2000.

Robinson, Dean E. *Black Nationalism in American Politics and Thought*. New York: Cambridge University Press, 2001.

Rodgers, Daniel. *Atlantic Crossing: Social Politics in a Progressive Age*. Cambridge: Harvard University Press, 1998.

Rodgers, Lawrence. *Canaan Bound: The African-American Great Migration Novel*. Urbana: University of Illinois Press, 1997.

Rogers, Kim Lacy. *Righteous Lives: Narratives of the New Orleans Civil Rights Movement*. New York: New York University Press, 1993.

Rolinson, Mary Gambrell. *Grassroots Garveyism: The Universal Negro Improvement Association in the Rural South, 1920–1927*. Chapel Hill: University of North Carolina Press, 2008.

Roll, Jarod. *Spirit of Rebellion: Labor and Religion in the New Cotton South*. Urbana: University of Illinois Press, 2010.

Rosenberg, Daniel. *New Orleans Dockworkers: Race, Labor, and Unionism, 1892–1923*. Albany: State University of New York Press, 1988.

Ross, Marlon B. *Manning the Race: Reforming Black Men in the Jim Crow Era*. New York: New York University Press, 2004.

Russell, Francis. *A City in Terror: Calvin Coolidge and the 1919 Boston Police Strike*. Boston: Beacon. 2005.

Salaam, Kalamu ya. *Revolutionary Love: Poems and Essays*. New Orleans: Ahidiana, 1978.

Savage, Barbara Dianne. *Your Spirits Walk beside Us: The Politics of Black Religion*. Cambridge: Harvard University Press, 2008.

Schneider, Mark Robert. *"We Return Fighting": The Civil Rights Movement in the Jazz Age*. Boston: Northeastern University Press, 2002.

Schneirov, Richard. *Labor and Urban Politics: Class Conflict and the Origins of Modern Liberalism in Chicago, 1864–1897*. Urbana: University of Illinois Press, 1998.

Schuyler, Lorraine Bates. *The Weight of Their Votes: Southern Women and Political Leverage in the 1920s*. Chapel Hill: University of North Carolina Press, 2006.

Sernett, Milton C. *Bound for the Promised Land: African American Religion and the Great Migration*. Durham, N.C.: Duke University Press, 1997.

Sherman, Richard B. "Republicans and Negroes: The Lessons of Normalcy." *Phylon* 27 (First Quarter 1966): 63–79.

Singal, Daniel Joseph. *The War Within: From Victorian to Modernist Thought in the South, 1919–1945*. Chapel Hill: University of North Carolina Press, 1982.

Smethurst, James. *The Black Arts Movement: Literary Nationalism in the 1960s and 1970s*. Chapel Hill: University of North Carolina Press, 2005.

Smith, J. Clay, Jr. *Emancipation: The Making of the Black Lawyer, 1844–1944*. Philadelphia: University of Pennsylvania Press, 1999.

Smith, J. Douglas. *Managing White Supremacy: Race, Politics, and Citizenship in Jim Crow Virginia*. Chapel Hill: University of North Carolina Press, 2002.

Smith, Jon, and Deborah Cohn, eds. *Look Away!: The U.S. South in New World Studies*. Durham, N.C.: Duke University Press, 2004.

Solomon, Mark. *The Cry Was Unity: Communists and African Americans, 1917–1936*. Jackson: University Press of Mississippi, 1998.

Spencer, Jon Michael. *The New Negroes and Their Music: The Success of the Harlem Renaissance*. Knoxville: University of Tennessee Press, 1997.

Spero, Sterling D., and Abram Harris. *The Black Worker: The Negro and the Labor Movement*. New York: Columbia University Press, 1931.

Stansell, Christine. *American Moderns: Bohemian New York and the Creation of a New Century*. New York: Holt, 2000.

Stein, Judith. *The World of Marcus Garvey: Race and Class in Modern Society*. Baton Rouge: Louisiana State University Press, 1986.

Stockley, Grif. *Blood in Their Eyes: The Elaine Race Massacres of 1919*. Fayetteville: University of Arkansas Press, 2001.

Stromquist, Shelton. *"Reinventing the People": The Progressive Movement, the Class Problem, and the Origins of Modern Liberalism*. Urbana: University of Illinois Press, 2006.

Sullivan, Patricia. *Days of Hope: Race and Democracy in the New Deal Era*. Chapel Hill: University of North Carolina Press, 1996.

———. *Lift Every Voice: The NAACP and the Making of the Civil Rights Movement*. New York: New Press, 2009.

Summers, Martin. *Manliness and Its Discontents: The Black Middle Class and the*

Transformation of Masculinity, 1900–1930. Chapel Hill: University of North Carolina Press, 2004.

Sundiata, Ibrahim. *Brothers and Strangers: Black Zion, Black Slavery, 1914–1940.* Durham, N.C.: Duke University Press, 2003.

Taylor, Clyde. "Oscar Micheaux and the Harlem Renaissance." In *Temples for Tomorrow: Looking Back at the Harlem Renaissance*, ed. Genevieve Fabre and Michel Feith, 125–42. Bloomington: Indiana University Press, 2001.

Taylor, Ula Yvette. *The Veiled Garvey: The Life and Times of Amy Jacques Garvey.* Chapel Hill: University of North Carolina Press, 2002.

Terborg-Penn, Rosalyn. *African American Women in the Struggle for the Vote, 1850–1920.* Bloomington: Indiana University Press, 1998.

Trotter, Joe William, Jr., ed. *The Great Migration in Historical Perspective: New Dimensions of Race, Class, and Gender.* Bloomington: Indiana University Press, 1991.

Tuttle, William M. *Race Riot: Chicago in the Red Summer of 1919.* Urbana: University of Illinois Press, 1996.

Vincent, Theodore G. *Voices from a Black Nation: Political Journalism in the Harlem Renaissance.* San Francisco: Ramparts, 1973.

Vinson, Robert. *The Americans Are Coming!: Dreams of African American Liberation in Segregationist South Africa.* Athens: Ohio University Press, 2012.

Voogd, Jan. *Race Riots and Resistance: The Red Summer of 1919.* New York: Lang, 2008.

Vought, Kip. "Racial Stirrings in Colored Town: The UNIA in Miami during the 1920s." *Tequesta* 60 (2000): 56–77.

Walker, Corey, D. B. *A Noble Fight: African American Freemasonry and the Struggle for Democracy in America.* Urbana: University of Illinois Press, 2008.

Whitaker, Robert. *On the Laps of Gods: The Red Summer of 1919 and the Struggle for Justice That Remade a Nation.* New York: Crown, 2008.

White, Walter. *A Man Called White: The Autobiography of Walter White.* Bloomington: Indiana University Press, 1948.

Wilkerson, Isabel. *The Warmth of Other Suns: The Epic Story of America's Great Migration.* New York: Random House, 2010.

Wilkerson-Freeman, Sarah. "Stealth in the Political Arsenal of Southern Women: A Retrospective for the Millennium." In *Southern Women at the Millennium: A Historical Perspective*, ed. Melissa Walker, Jeanette R. Dunn, and Joe P. Dunn (Columbia: University of Missouri Press, 2003), 42–82.

———. "Women and the Transformation of American Politics: North Carolina, 1898–1940." Ph.D. diss., University of North Carolina at Chapel Hill, 1995.

Williams, Chad. *Torchbearers for Democracy: African American Soldiers in the World War I Era.* Chapel Hill: University of North Carolina Press, 2010.

Wilson, Francille Rusan. *The Segregated Scholars: Black Social Scientists and the Creation of Black Labor Studies, 1890–1950.* Charlottesville: University of Virginia Press, 2006.

Wolcott, Victoria W. *Remaking Respectability: African American Women in Interwar Detroit.* Chapel Hill: University of North Carolina Press, 2004.

Wolters, Raymond. *The New Negro on Campus: Black College Rebellions of the 1920s.* Princeton: Princeton University Press, 1975.

Woodard, Komozi. *A Nation within a Nation: Amiri Baraka (LeRoi Jones) and Black Politics.* Chapel Hill: University of North Carolina Press, 1999.

Woodruff, Nan Elizabeth. *American Congo: The African American Freedom Struggle in the Delta*. Cambridge: Harvard University Press, 2003.

———. "The New Negro in the American Congo: World War I and the Elaine Massacre of 1919." In *Time Longer Than Rope: A Century of African American Activism, 1850–1950*, ed. Charles M. Payne and Adam Green, 150–78. New York: New York University Press, 2003.

Woodward, C. Vann. *Origins of the New South, 1877–1913*. Baton Rouge: Louisiana State University Press, 1951.

Wright, George C. *Life behind a Veil: Louisville, Kentucky*. Baton Rouge: Louisiana State University Press, 1985.

Wright, Richard. *Black Boy*. 1945. New York: Harper and Row, 1966.

Ziegler, Robert H. *For Jobs and Freedom: Race and Labor in America since 1865*. Lexington: University Press of Kentucky, 2007.

INDEX

Higgs, Ritchie, 74
Hobbs, Allen, 66–67
Howard University, 108–9, 134
Humbert, Mrs. S. S., 58–59
Hunton, Addie, 49–52

Independent Republican Party (IRP), 56–57
industrial democracy, 17
Intercollegiate Society, 8, 107, 109
International Longshoremen Association (ILA): in Key West, 31–32, 144n13; and NBWA, 44
Ivy, James W.: on black workers, 114–15; and Marxism, 102, 107, 130–31; and Claude McKay, 8, 109, 119–20; teaching career of, 109, 115, 130; at Virginia Union University, 8, 104, 107–9; on white southern liberals, 8, 102–4, 110, 116–18; as a writer for the *Messenger*, 109–11, 115–18

Jacksonville Journal, 93
Jefferson Ward Civic League, 20, 131
Johnson, Adrian, 69–70
Johnson, Charles, 104–5, 115
Johnson, Edward, 54
Johnson, Gerald, 9, 115
Johnson, James Weldon, 12, 16, 32, 106, 115, 121
Johnson, Martha A., 51
Johnson, W. H., 67
Jones, Eugene Kinckle, 24–25
Jones, Thomas Jesse, 24
Joyce, John J., 32, 144n13

Ku Klux Klan, 72–74

Labor Age, 8, 102, 114
Lacey, John, 37–38
Liberia, 71–72, 76–78
Lily-White Republicans, 53–57
living wage, 17, 118
Locke, Alain, 103, 108, 115–18
Lucas, George, 82, 121, 124, 126

Mann, Clara, 59
Marshall, R. H., 48
McAdoo, William, 35

McKay, Claude, 8, 101, 109, 119–20, 136
McKinney, Ernest, 56
McPherson, Charles, 45, 53
Mencken, H. L., 8, 115–17, 154n46
Messenger, 8, 36, 38, 89, 91, 94; and NBWA, 1–2, 36; and Phillips County, Arkansas, massacre, 42; and southern New Negroes, 86–87, 100–102, 107, 109–11, 120; on southern white workers, 43; white southerners' opposition to, 93
Milner, George, 26–28
Mississippi Flood of 1927: and African American relief efforts, 124–27; casualties of, 123; and racial discrimination in relief camps, 123–25
Mitchell, John, 37, 57
Mitchell, W. H., 93
Modern Quarterly, 102, 119
Moore, Fred, 25
Moton, Robert R., 22, 24

National Association for the Advancement of Colored People (NAACP), 16, 23–24; and black labor, 23, 32, 143n31; and congressional reapportionment, 58–59, 148n53; and Mississippi Flood of 1927, 124–25, 128; and southern voter registration, 45, 52–53
National Brotherhood, 44
National Brotherhood Workers of America (NBWA), 1–2, 8, 33–41, 44, 65, 131; and AFL politics, 36–39; decline of, 44; and employment discrimination, 35; and gender politics, 40; and McAdoo's General Order No. 27, 36; and 1919 convention, 39–40
National Republican Committee, 54, 59, 60
National Student Forum, 108
National Urban League, 23–25
Negro Political Union, 83
Negro World, 7, 63, 67–68, 107, 133
New Negroes: and black masculinity, 37–38, 40, 51–52; political formation in the labor arena, 3–5; quest for citizenship rights, 12, 45–47, 50, 83, 139n7; regional differences among, 4, 8–9, 81–82, 103–4, 115–19

voter registration, 6, 46, 134; and black women, 45, 47–50, 51, 52, 53, 59

wages: of African Americans during war, 17–18, 21; pay scales for whites and blacks, 33, 35, 38, 40, 129–30; of railroad workers, 7, 22, 35, 91, 92, 94
Washington, George, 11
Watkins, R. J., 68
Webb, C. W., 48
West Munden Civic League, 83
White, E. W., 47
White, Walter, 82, 123, 124

Williams, G. W., 46
Wilson, Woodrow, 13, 17, 19, 37, 39
Woman Wage Earners Association, 34
Woodland, Thomas, 26–28
Woods, Sylvia, 75–76, 131–33
World War I: black southerners' critique of, 4, 63, 75; and economic changes in South, 15; Marcus Garvey on, 2; and returning soldiers, 10–11, 47, 69, 106–7; work or fight laws, 24, 49

Young, William, 81, 134

Politics and Culture in the Twentieth-Century South

A Common Thread: Labor, Politics, and Capital Mobility in the Textile Industry
by Beth English

"Everybody Was Black Down There": Race and Industrial Change in the Alabama Coalfields
by Robert H. Woodrum

Race, Reason, and Massive Resistance: The Diary of David J. Mays, 1954–1959
edited by James R. Sweeney

The Unemployed People's Movement: Leftists, Liberals, and Labor in Georgia, 1929–1941
by James J. Lorence

Liberalism, Black Power, and the Making of American Politics, 1965–1980
by Devin Fergus

Guten Tag, Y'all: Globalization and the South Carolina Piedmont, 1950–2000
by Marko Maunula

The Culture of Property: Race, Class, and Housing Landscapes in Atlanta, 1880–1950
by LeeAnn Lands

Marching in Step: Masculinity, Citizenship, and The Citadel in Post–World War II America
by Alexander Macaulay

Rabble Rousers: The American Far Right in the Civil Rights Era
by Clive Webb

Who Gets a Childhood: Race and Juvenile Justice in Twentieth-Century Texas
by William S. Bush

Alabama Getaway: The Political Imaginary and the Heart of Dixie
by Allen Tullos

The Problem South: Region, Empire, and the New Liberal State, 1880–1930
by Natalie J. Ring

The Nashville Way: Racial Etiquette and the Struggle for Social Justice in a Southern City
by Benjamin Houston

Cold War Dixie: Militarization and Modernization in the American South
by Kari Frederickson

Faith in Bikinis: Politics and Leisure in the Coastal South since the Civil War
by Anthony J. Stanonis

Womanpower Unlimited and the Black Freedom Struggle in Mississippi
by Tiyi M. Morris

New Negro Politics in the Jim Crow South
by Claudrena N. Harold

Jim Crow Terminals: The Desegregation of American Airports
by Anke Ortlepp

Remaking the Rural South: Interracialism, Christian Socialism, and Cooperative Farming in Jim Crow Mississippi
by Robert Hunt Ferguson

The South of the Mind: American Imaginings of White Southernness, 1960–1980
by Zachary J. Lechner

The Politics of White Rights: Race, Justice, and Integrating Alabama's Schools
by Joseph Bagley